Jewish Pirates

OF THE

Caribbean

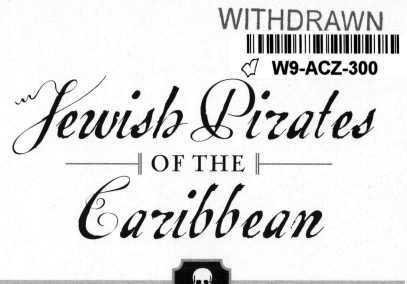

How a Generation of Swashbuckling Jews Carved Out an Empire in the New World in Their Quest for Treasure, Religious Freedom—and Revenge

Edward Kritzler

DOUBLEDAY

New York • London • Toronto • Sydney • Auckland

To my daughter, Eliza

CD

DOUBLEDAY

Copyright © 2008 by Ed Kritzler

All Rights Reserved

Published in the United States by Doubleday, an imprint of The Doubleday Publishing Group, a division of Random House, Inc., New York.
www.doubleday.com

DOUBLEDAY is a registered trademark and the DD colophon is a trademark of Random House, Inc.

Book design by Michael Collica

Library of Congress Cataloging-in-Publication Data
Kritzler, Ed (Edward), 1941–
    Jewish pirates of the Caribbean : how a generation of swashbuckling Jews carved out an empire in the new world in their quest for treasure, religious freedom—and revenge / Ed Kritzler. — 1st ed.
        p. cm.
    Includes bibliographical references and index.
    1. Jews—Caribbean Area—History—17th century. 2. Marranos—Caribbean Area—History—17th century. 3. Buccaneers—Caribbean Area—History—17th century. 4. Pirates—Caribbean Area—History—17th century. 5. Caribbean Area—Ethnic relations—History—17th century. I. Title.
    F2191.J4K75 2008
    972.9'004924—dc22
    2008015790

ISBN 978-0-385-51398-2

PRINTED IN THE UNITED STATES OF AMERICA

1 3 5 7 9 10 8 6 4 2

First Edition

CONTENTS

v

PROLOGUE

A puzzling entry in a pirate's journal jumped out at me. Invading Jamaica in 1643, William Jackson found the island's capital deserted except for "divers Portuguese of the Hebrew nation who came unto us seeking asylum, and promised to show us where the Spaniards hid their gold." I had always learned that early New World adventure was the province of Spanish and Portuguese conquistadors, and that they were all devout Catholics carrying the cross. So what were Portuguese Jews doing on a Spanish island, seeking asylum with an English pirate?

It was 1967. I had moved to Jamaica from New York, and came upon Jackson's journal in the reading room of Jamaica's national library while perusing contemporary accounts of the island's buccaneer beginnings. I was more than intrigued. I wanted an answer.

What I next learned was startling: Before England conquered

Jamaica in 1655, the island belonged to the family of Christopher Columbus, who provided a haven for Jews otherwise outlawed in the New World. The leader of the Jewish community, the late Sir Neville Ashenheim, went even further, telling me that Columbus was a Jew, and that Jamaica's Jews traced their ancestry to the first settlers.

I was so beguiled by these findings that I would spend the next four decades following their lead and unfolding an unknown chapter in Jewish history. Forget the Merchant of Venice—his New World cousins were adventurers after my own heart: Jewish explorers, conquistadors, cowboys, and, yes, pirates.

Forbidden to settle the New World, they came disguised as Christians. They and the other settlers were similar in spirit, but while the others came to conquer, convert the heathen, search for gold, or collect a bevy of Indian women, the Jews came to escape persecution and settle a land beyond the tentacles of the Inquisition.

The story begins with Columbus and the Age of Discovery, when secret Jews sailed with the explorers, marched with the conquistadors, and were among the first settlers in every New World colony. This early history is largely unknown because few then or since realized that these pioneers were Jewish. Forbidden entry in the New World because of their religion, Iberian Jews posed as New Christians from Portugal, the one settler group that was not required to prove their Catholic ancestry. Most Portuguese operating in the Spanish Empire were New Christians, commonly called conversos, and many maintained their allegiance to their ancestral faith.

They were Esperandos, Hopeful Ones, who expected that

the Messiah would soon come, and that He, like them, would appear in the guise of a Christian and so forgive their apostasy. Until then, whatever it would take to get by in the enemy world was not deceit, but strength. As Esperandos, Jews in the New World lived and prospered. Unless exposed by the Inquisition, they went to their graves with their masquerade intact, though even death offered no assurance, as dead heretics were tried in absentia. If found guilty, their bodies were exhumed and burned, and their property confiscated.

Arriving first as explorers and conquistadors, they and the Jewish pioneers who followed soon focused on a field of expertise that had sustained them and made them welcome in the Diaspora. A mercantile people, Jews in the New World went about their business as traders and shipowners, thus becoming the first merchant class in the Spanish Empire. As long as they pretended to be Christian and delivered the goods, no one questioned their religiosity too closely. They set up the first sugar factories, pioneered grain, coffee, and tea cultivation, and traded sugar, tobacco, gold, and silver with covert Jews on the Iberian Peninsula.

First profits to the homeland were the underpinning of the mercantile system. Everything to and from the New World had to go via Seville or Lisbon. For most of the sixteenth century, the parties were content with the trade-off. The king needed the Jews to ensure his cash flow, and they needed him to keep the Inquisition at bay. However, once the trade network was established, Jews became expendable.

At the close of the sixteenth century, Inquisition fires caught up with them. In Mexico and Peru, where Jewish merchants controlled the silver trade, Holy Inquisitors were called in to purify the bottom line: Jewish leaders were burned, their wealth was confiscated, and Christians took over the fabulously rich silver trade. New World Jews got the message. More than profit, their survival in the coming century would require a haven outside the reach of the Grand Inquisitor. Unable to secure a homeland on their own, covert Jews conspired with Holland and England to seize a New World colony.

It was then that a handful of Dutch Jews, inspired by a warrior rabbi, took it upon themselves to change things. Their generation came of age in the early 1600s, when Jews were forbidden in England, France, and most of Europe, and in the Spanish Empire anyone caught "Judaizing" was liable to be burned. Only in Amsterdam could Jews safely call themselves such, and they grew up strong and free in a city that became known in the Diaspora as New Jerusalem. Their mentors were their refugee parents who settled there on the run from the Inquisition, and their rabbi, the pirate Samuel Palache.

Most of the community's fifty or so families were elite merchants from Spain and Portugal whose commercial skills and connections had made them welcome in what was fast becoming Europe's trading capital. Rabbi Palache, a Barbary pirate who was still capturing Spanish ships in his late sixties, held the first religious services in his home. While the aim of their parents was to live freely, grow wealthy on New World trade, and have their portraits painted by Rembrandt, their ultimate goal was nothing less than to bring down the Spanish Empire. Their proxy armies in this struggle were the Dutch, the English, and in the final, successful assault, the buccaneers of the West Indies.

Jewish Pirates of the Caribbean is the history of Sephardic Jews in the early New World, involving intrigue, horror, defeat, survival, and final victory over the hooded Inquisitors of the Holy Terror. It concludes with their last hurrah—their search for the legendary lost gold mine of Columbus. After achieving Jewish rights in Europe and the New World, three Dutch Jews, accompanied by their sons, went into the mountains of Jamaica to find Columbus's mine. They reported that their search was not successful. But I found their map and have reason to believe it was.

INTRODUCTION

On August 1, 1492, when Christopher Columbus set sail for the New World, ethnic cleansing was the order of the day: 100,000 Jews left Spain, expelled as mandated by the Royal Edict of Expulsion of the Jews. Those who remained behind, or crossed the border to Portugal, converted to Catholicism. The more adventurous went on to the New World. It is about this group that our story is told.

Long before Spain was Spain, Jews were living there. King Solomon's trading post (1000 B.C.) developed over the millennium to become Sephard, a strategic outpost of the Roman Empire. It was there, in the first century A.D., that Emperor Titus, after conquering Israel and burning the Temple, exiled thousands of Jews. Although the Jews of Sephard flourished, they were always tenants. The Visigoths who replaced the Romans made it illegal for them to own land, and Spain's subsequent rulers, the Vandals, Moors, and Catholics, found it expedient to continue the ban. Despite this and other restrictions, the tribe of Moses grew and prospered.

In Spain's feudal society, Jews were an educated elite, a merchant class also respected as physicians and financiers. At the end of the fourteenth century, after some 1500 years of residence, the 500,000 Jews of Sephard (half the Jews of Europe) represented the oldest and largest Jewish community outside Palestine. Their leaders boasted lineage to King David and considered themselves the aristocracy of Jewry. These were halcyon days for a people who were unwelcome in most of Europe. But their very prosperity and superior lifestyle were resented by an uneducated mass whose all-consuming religious beliefs could be inflamed by virulent anti-Semitism.

Ferrant Martínez, a friar in Seville, provided the spark. Following a frenzied sermon in which he accused Jews of everything from causing the Black Plague to killing Christian children and drinking their blood, he incited the crowd to rise up and destroy this accursed race. Descending on Seville's Jewish quarter, the rabble slaughtered four thousand men, women, and children. What is known in Jewish history as the Massacre of 1391 had commenced. Pogroms spread from city to city. The mob's admonition "Convert or die" resulted in 100,000 dead Jews, and 100,000 converts for Jesus.

After a bloody year, peace was gradually restored. Spain's 300,000 remaining Jews came forth from hiding places and reconstructed their lives. Those who remained faithful continued to live as Jews but under a host of restrictions. But the 100,000 converted Jews, freed from religious bondage, rose over the next century to positions of power that had been denied them as Jews. Called conversos, or New Christians, to distinguish them from the dominant "Old" Christians, they achieved major positions in government, the army, and universities, and married into the highest nobility. They were prominent at court and in the hierarchy of the Church. However, conversion by coercion rather than conviction had an unforeseen consequence. Forced baptism had brought infidels into the Church, but in doing so, created heretics within.

In the last decades of the fifteenth century, there began what came to be called the Holy Terror. Queen Isabella vowed she would root out all heretics from her kingdom once the Catholic reconquest of Spain from the Moors was complete. Meanwhile, she would begin by ferreting out heretics in Seville, a city known for Jews pretending to be Christians. Her means was the auto-da-fé (act of faith), the church's idea of Judgment Day on earth, with a Grand Inquisitor playing God. In 1482, Isabella gave that role to her confessor, Tomás de Torquemada. In the course of his eighteen-year reign, the former Dominican friar personally condemned nine thousand Jews to the stake at the *quemadero* (burning ground) outside the city walls. He also exhumed the bodies of seven thousand dead heretics and burned their remains. (Whenever Torquemada appeared in public, he was accompanied by fifty agents on horseback and two hundred armed guards.)

Ten years later, on the very day Columbus set sail, Spain's monarchs banished her Jews to purify and thereby unite their nation. Jews settled everywhere they were permitted and, disguised as Portuguese New Christians, where they weren't. Along with other pioneers in the far-off New World, they carved out a niche for themselves, living possibly the most original experience the world has ever known. They thought themselves safe, but the white-hooded Inquisitors soon followed. In the sixteenth and seventeenth centuries, thousands of New World conversos were arrested, tortured, and tried. Found guilty, they saw their wealth confiscated, and they were first flogged, then imprisoned, strangled, burned, or condemned either to work in the salt mines of Venezuela or to row galley ships across the Pacific, a sentence from which none returned.

Inquisitors were thorough in their questioning of heretics, and the trial transcripts offer an intimate look into the condemned Judaizers' secret lives. During the day, they went about as exemplary Catholics, attended Mass, went to confession, and had their children baptized. But on certain nights they met secretly in one another's homes, reverted to Hebrew names, and read from the Torah. History would come to call these secret Jews Marranos, meaning pigs. Though this term has generally lost its pejorative meaning, I prefer to call them what they called themselves in the sanctity of their homes: Jews.

Each New World colony had an underground community of Jews known only to one another and their brethren in other colonies. Together, conversos in the New World dominated commerce. In the sixteenth century, when the known world doubled in size and international trade became big business, they established a trade network that spanned the globe.

- In Lima, Peru, the Inquisition reported: "The city is thick with [Jews]. Everything goes through their hands . . . from brocade to sackcloth, diamonds to cumin seeds . . . to the most precious pearl and the vilest Guinea black."
- In Potosí, Bolivia, with its silver mountain, the Inquisitor reported the silver trade "is almost exclusively in the hands of crypto Jews."
- In Port Royal, Jamaica, English merchants protested,

"Descendants of the Crucifiers of Blessed Jesus eat us and our children out of all trade. [They] purchase the entire cargo of a trading ship, divide it according to paid shares, and distribute the goods through agents in each of the colonies."

In concert with their fellow Jews, scattered worldwide by the Sephardic Diaspora, they formed a global tribe of inside traders, bonded by heritage, language, and a hatred for Spain. New World Jews traded with covert brethren on the Iberian Peninsula, and later sold directly to Jews in Amsterdam and London, often in ships leased from Jewish shipowners in Amsterdam and Antwerp.

Dealing with the People of the Book was very attractive. Their innovative letters of exchange and credit made capital portable. For instance, a shipping merchant trading in pirate waters doubled his risks if he returned with gold. On the other hand, if he could leave the gold and return instead with a draft on a Jewish banking house, he was safe. As a link in a world trade network at the onset of international trade, Jewish merchants were the world's most coveted capitalists. The historian of capitalism Fernand Braudel writes: "It has too quickly been assumed Jews did not invent capitalism; certainly they participated wholeheartedly in its beginnings . . . It is not unrealistic to refer to . . . the 17th century as the 'age' of great Jewish merchants."[1]

Piracy was another lucrative area of commerce in which these Jewish merchants specialized. Questions of morality did not apply. It was the normal business of every nation to license mercenaries to seize and rob enemy ships and share the proceeds. The only difference with the Jews was they did not have to license their freebooters. In coded correspondence with fellow merchants in other colonies, they were able to ascertain what ship was sailing when; its cargo, route, and destination; and what its captain may have secreted in his cabin. Thus informed, Jewish merchants were the brains behind the brawn—financing, advising, and sometimes leading the Caribbean's emerging fighting force: a ragtag crew of misfits of every nation that coalesced as the dreaded pirates of the Spanish Main.

A precedent for this unholy alliance was set by fellow Sephardim in North Africa who had assured their welcome among the Moors by profitably backing and sometimes leading the Barbary pirates. Sinan, Barbarossa's second in command, was referred to in Crown correspondence with England's Henry VII as "the Great Jewish pirate," and the brothers Samuel and Joseph Palache would go from commanding pirates to founding Amsterdam's Jewish community.

In the first decades of the seventeenth century, rival Christian merchants wanting a share of the fabulous wealth being generated by trade in the New World sought to expose the conversos as heretics before the Holy Office of the Inquisition. Thus threatened, covert Jews, beginning in the 1620s, conspired with Holland and England to seize a New World colony. Writing in code to agents in Europe, they proposed to serve as a fifth column in the body of the enemy. "They are good and useful spies," said a confidant of Oliver Cromwell, regarding the Jews who advised Cromwell in the conquest of Jamaica.[2]

Positioned to assist Spain's enemies, they did. Jewish trade links, cultivated since 1492, when Sephardim settled the far corners of the globe, doubled as a worldwide intelligence network. From the time Jews in Portugal got word to Queen Elizabeth that the Armada was sailing, they shared secret intelligence with the enemies of Spain.

Jews had been outlawed from living in France since 1394 and from England since 1290. However, when those two nations and Holland settled a dozen small, uninhabited Caribbean islands between 1624 and 1635, Jews were welcome. Their connections and knowledge of New World trade were indispensable to the success of the new colonies. And they spoke the language. Who else but Sephardic merchants could better pursue illegal trade with the Spanish colonies? How else could these small settlements survive? The islands constituted mere footholds in what was called the New Spanish Sea. Together they totaled less than 1,500 square miles, while the Spanish New World encompassed millions.

The first openly Jewish settlement in the New World was in Brazil. In 1624, the Dutch captured Brazil's capital, Bahia, from Portugal with an invasion force that included "several dozen declared Jews." The invaders were assisted by local conversos who had gotten word that an Inquisition office was to be established in their province, where two hundred of them were living as counterfeit Christians. A year later, King Philip IV of Spain sent a twelve-thousand-man army and temporarily threw the Dutch out. Afterward, the Inquisitor's report charged: "[Secret Jews] had written Holland and asked the Dutch to liberate them . . . had initiated plans for the invasion and agreed to share its costs. [The] Heretics had suckled at the breast of the Mother Church [and when the Dutch came] . . . openly professed the Jewish faith."[3]

In 1630, Holland's forces again invaded. Landing north of Bahia, they conquered Recife and surrounding provinces in northeast Brazil. Under Dutch protection, a Jewish community thrived there for twenty-four years. They called their congregation Zur Israel (Rock of Israel), marketed sugar, and taxed Jewish privateers 3 percent of their booty. Sugar and piracy transformed Recife into the richest trading port in the New World outside of Havana, and Jews, integral participants in both industries, lived a high life. Their favorite pastimes may be glimpsed from what they outlawed: Synagogue leaders banned card playing on Friday afternoon (as too many members missed Sabbath service), and levied whopping fines on members caught taking Christian women into the *mikvah*, the ritual bath.

The situation in Brazil was unique. Elsewhere in the New World, as the midcentury approached, the long-established secret Jewish communities in Peru and Mexico came to a flaming end, with each found guilty of a "great conspiracy." In 1638, hundreds of Peru's Jews were arrested. Their leaders, accused of plotting to blow up Lima's harbor in advance of a Dutch invasion, were burned at the stake. In the 1640s, Mexico's Jews were charged with conspiring to burn down the House of the Inquisition, and by 1650 the methods of the Inquisition—the dungeon, the rack, and the stake—marked a decade-long succession of autos-da-fé that decimated the Mexican community. In both countries, the heretics' wealth was equally divided between the Crown and the Inquisitors, and their property was auctioned off to Old Christians.

In 1654, a similar end threatened the congregants of the Rock of Israel when Portugal reconquered Recife. After twenty-four years, the only legal Jewish community in the New World was no more. Jews were given three months to leave or be turned over to the Inquisition. The destruction of brethren communities in Mexico and Peru convinced the refugees the New World was again off-limits. They departed Recife on sixteen ships: The fifteen that sailed for Holland arrived safely; the ship that went north to New Amsterdam did not.

This ship ran into a storm that, "by the adverse," drove it into Jamaica's enemy waters, where it was seized. The island was home to a secret Jewish community called "Portugals" who had been living as merchants and traders since Columbus's son had settled the island in 1510. The Columbus family owned Jamaica and, in deference to their converso settlers, had kept the island out of bounds to the Inquisition. But when the identity of the Dutch refugees became known, Jamaica's leaders, looking to oust the Columbus family, used the arrival of these "suspect heretics" to invite Inquisitors from Colombia to Jamaica.

Fearing an investigation of the refugees might lead to their own exposure, Jamaica's Portugals sent a note to Cromwell's agent: Jamaica could be conquered with little resistance, and they pledged their assistance. The following year, a Jew from Nevis led thirty-six English ships into the harbor, and two local Jews negotiated and signed the peace treaty surrendering the island to England. The treaty exiled the Spanish, and Cromwell invited Jamaica's Portugals to stay on openly as Jews.

Welcomed by the English, Jews from all over the New World shed their converso cloaks and emigrated to Jamaica. The community soon included shipowners from Mexico and Brazil, traders from Peru and Colombia, and ship captains and pilots from Nevis and Barbados. Together their knowledge of New World trade was unsurpassed. By 1660, Jamaica had become the Jews' principal haven in the New World. Unlike the small, isolated isles in the eastern Caribbean, Jamaica was a major island in the middle of the shipping lanes, an ideal base from which to strike at Spanish shipping, and well positioned to engage in contraband trade with the Spanish Main.

Soon after the English conquest, Jamaica's Jews convinced the island's new leaders that the best way to defend the colony and have it prosper was to invite the pirates of the Caribbean to move there. The Spanish would think twice about attacking Jamaica if its principal port was the home base of the feared buccaneers of the West Indies. In return for a safe harbor, these pirates, the Brethren of the Coast, became Jamaica's defense force and piracy its principal industry.

In the 1660s, Port Royal, with its wealthy Jewish merchants, shipowners, and synagogue, was known as the "Treasure House of the Indies" for all the booty brought there. Catering to a transient pirate population with one bar and brothel for every eight persons, the pirate capital acquired a reputation as the world's "wickedest city." Within fifteen years, pirate raids from Jamaica on the Spanish Main, organized and financed by the merchants of Port Royal, broke the back of the Spanish Empire. In Henry Morgan, the Jews found their Joshua. The buccaneer admiral's six raids on Spanish ports, culminating in the burning of the "Golden City of Panama," brought the Spanish Empire to its knees. In the Treaty of Madrid in 1670, Spain acceded to Europe's right to settle the New World . . . and Jews were finally free to be Jews.

The seventeenth century commenced with Jews outlawed in

most of Europe and the New World; it ended with their freedom. The participants in their liberation struggle are known. They were the children of refugees from the Inquisition who in the early 1600s, after having led underground lives in Spain and Portugal, settled in Amsterdam. Accepted by the Dutch as a valued merchant class, they raised their children in the free air of Holland, where a select group of them, following the example of their warrior rabbi, took it upon themselves to change things. Over the course of a half century of leadership (1623–75), they invaded the New World, battled the Inquisition, and orchestrated their people's freedom.

Chapter One

COLUMBUS AND JAMAICA'S CHOSEN PEOPLE

ay 1504, Santa Gloria, Jamaica: For nearly a year, Columbus had been stranded in Jamaica with a hoard of gold, a mutinous crew, and a few dozen teenage loyalists, some of whom were secret Jews.[1] Alone, melancholy, and confined to his cabin by gout, the great explorer wrote his patron Queen Isabella a despairing letter. He feared that even if he defeated the mutineers, the governor of Santo Domingo, who had promised to send a rescue ship, wanted him dead.

So much had happened since he had been making the rounds of Europe, a would-be explorer going from king to king seeking royal backing for a promised quick passage west across the Ocean Sea to India and the wealth of the East. In 1486, at his first meeting with Spain's royal couple, King Ferdinand, although intrigued by the plan, told Columbus the time was not opportune. They were in the midst of a war and could not seriously consider such an important matter until peace was restored. In parting, Queen Isabella counseled patience and awarded Columbus a retainer, promising they would meet again when the war was over.

On January 12, 1492, Columbus entered the royal quarters. He had been summoned a few days after Spain's final victory over the Moors at Granada, and the queen had sent him money to buy new clothes and a mule to ride. Encouraged by her gift, Columbus was confident. He had honed his proposal into a detailed presentation, with maps and charts from the Jewish astronomer Abraham Zacuto, and quotes from the Bible and Greek sages supporting his view that the world was round, the oceans not large, and Japan lay three thousand miles to the west, across the Ocean Sea. Prepared for questions, he received none.

After an unsettling silence, Ferdinand spoke. Victory over the Moors had emptied the treasury, he said. Moreover, he could not abide Columbus's demand for hereditary rule over lands he might discover. The queen, his admirer, said nothing. The meeting broke up and Columbus left, angry and disgusted. All this time he had waited for the war to end. Now that it had, Ferdinand was pleading poverty. Pausing briefly in the corridor, he informed the king's treasurer that he was leaving for France where Bartholomew, his younger brother, was arranging an audience with the king. If that monarch wasn't interested, he would cross the channel to meet with the English king. He would not be denied his dream, one that, as Cervantes wrote of Don Quixote, "He hugged and would not part with even if barefoot friars had begged him."[2]

Before Columbus rode past the gates of Santa Fe, the royal treasurer, Luis de Santangel, sought and was granted an audience with Queen Isabella. The royal chronicler noted,

"[Santangel] appeared distressed as if a great misfortune had befallen him personally."[3] He had good reason: Santangel was a secret Jew, and as a member of the royal court, he was aware his people were about to be expelled from Spain. There were upward of a half million Jews in the country they had called home since the time of Christ. Where would they go? India? China? Perhaps the explorer Columbus would discover a new land somewhere. Santangel and other secret Jews in the royal service hoped Columbus's voyage would provide an answer.

The Inquisition mandated that Jews, under penalty of death, must either leave or convert to Catholicism. Santangel, like many others, had converted and became a New Christian. If discovered Judaizing, the converts were liable to be burned at the stake. The Santangel family, long established in Spain, was among the first targets of the Inquisition. Luis's cousins had gone up in flames in Saragossa, and only the intervention of Ferdinand had prevented Luis from suffering the same fate.[4]

Santangel addressed the queen. He was astonished, he told her, "to see Her Highness who has always shown such resolute spirit in matters of great consequence, should lack it now for an enterprise of so little risk for so vast a gain." He spoke to the queen of the wealth to be acquired, and the great service she would render to God, "all for the price of a few caravels [ships]." Alluding to Columbus's plan to seek royal backing elsewhere, he cautioned Isabella, "It would be a great damage to Her Crown and a grave reproach to Her Highness if any other prince should undertake what Columbus offered Her Highness." If money was a consideration, Santangel said, he would be glad to finance the fleet himself.

A mounted messenger caught up with Columbus as he was crossing the Bridge of the Pines, seven miles from Santa Fe, and bade him return. Later that day, with all parties again gathered in the royal quarters, the king informed Columbus that the Crown would sponsor his Enterprise of the Indies, and meet his demands. No mention was made of hereditary title. Two months later, it was still a stumbling block in his negotiations when an event occurred that made its inclusion mandatory.

On the morning of March 31, 1492, Columbus was in his room in Santa Fe overlooking the main square when the sound of trumpets brought him to his balcony. Below, the town crier, flanked by mounted guards, read the expulsion order of the Inquisition: Jews had four months to leave. After that, any "caught in Our domains will be punished without trial by death, and seizure of property."[5] The Jews of Spain had been threatened with expulsion before. Rulers since the Visigoths had used this threat to extract more money from them. A period joke compared the Jews to a "money box" that you break open when you need money. But this time it was different: The Church was involved.

To the Jews of the royal court who supported Columbus, the expulsion order made it essential that Columbus hold out for hereditary rule. If no Asian kingdom welcomed Jewish refugees, Columbus, as the ruler of a new land, would be able to provide a haven for Spanish Jews.

It is thought that Columbus himself was a descendant of Spanish Jews, the Colón family, who had converted and moved to Genoa a century before on the heels of the Massacre of 1391. Some even contend he was a Cabalist. Whatever his genealogy, he was in sympathy with the People of the Book, and they with him. In his early years, in Portugal and Spain, he lived in a largely Jewish and New Christian world of navigators, cartographers, astronomers, and mathematicians. While others looked askance at this wandering sailor and laughed at his dream, Iberian Jews and conversos assisted Columbus in developing his Enterprise of the Indies. In their learned circles, they dealt with a round world. Church geography did not apply to them.[6]

On April 17, Columbus agreed to the Capitulations of Santa Fe, which limited his rights to lifetime rule. Two weeks later, this ruling was reversed, and Columbus was granted hereditary rule. No account exists of the final negotiations, but it is likely that court Jews, facing the forced exile of their people, counseled Columbus to hold firm to his demand. One imagines a scene in the royal chambers with Santangel persuading the royals that the explorer's demand should not trouble them. If his voyage were successful, Columbus and his crew of ninety men could not possibly subdue one of the powerful Asian nations. On the other hand, if he took possession of a few islands along the way, the Crown would benefit by having way stations for Spain's trading ships plying the shortcut passage to the wealth of the East.

Whether or not such a scene took place, Ferdinand finally relented: Columbus would sail with his right to rule any new lands he discovered, to be "enjoyed forever by his heirs and successors."[7]

After Columbus returned from his successful first voyage, he made three more trips across the Western Sea. He never reached Asia, and didn't live long enough to fulfill his pledge to Santangel and the court Jews to provide a homeland for converted Jews. But it would be kept by his family in the "new land" the Crown did bequeath to Columbus's descendants, the island of Jamaica. How this came about goes back to a promise he made to the teenage conversos who stood by him when he was marooned there.

Returning from his fourth voyage to the New World, Columbus had been forced to beach his ships in Jamaica after sailing from Panama with a cache of gold objects bartered from the Indians. His two ships were leaking badly. Columbus hoped to reach Santo Domingo to obtain others to return to Spain. But his worm-eaten caravels, described by his son as "more full of holes than a bees' honeycomb," barely made Jamaica. With water rising in their holds, he ran them aground and lashed them together in a shallow, becalmed bay on the island's north coast, "a cross bow's shot from land."[8] Atop his foredeck he fashioned a palm thatch hut to serve as his cabin.

In his first letter to the queen, written soon after he arrived, he bragged that he had discovered the source of Solomon's gold in the mines of Panama, and claimed to have seen more gold in a few days there than in all his previous trips. His fourteen-year-old son Fernando, brought along as cabin boy, later recorded that his father had traded small bells and mirrors for sixty-three gold pendants and other gold objects with the Veragua Indians of Panama.[9]

This was his second trip to Jamaica. When he had discovered the island in 1494, he had named the half-moon bay where he was now stranded Santa Gloria for "the beauty of its glorious landscape."[10] After a year, he thought he might never leave. Was this where his life was to end? Uncertain of his future, he wrote his queen:

We have been confined 10 months, lodged on the decks of our ships. My men have mutinied. My brother, my son, and those that are faithful are sick, starving and dying. Governor Ovando of Santo Domingo has sent to see if I am dead rather than to carry me back alive. I conclude Your officers intend my life should terminate here.[11]

The object of his cynicism was the arrival the previous week of a ship from Ovando. It had anchored outside the reef in the late afternoon, and left before dawn. Before sailing away, its captain ferried over a side of ham, a barrel of wine, and a message from the governor that a rescue ship would soon be sent.

The governor's message did confirm the safe arrival of Columbus's first mate, Diego Méndez, who ten months before had set forth in a dugout canoe to carry news of their plight to Santo Domingo. But, as he wrote the queen, he really believed the ship had been sent "to spy on how I might be totally destroyed."[12]

Made furious by his suspicions, Columbus concluded his letter with an angry vow. Should he die in Jamaica, and his proprietary rights be withdrawn, "ingratitude will bring down the wrath of Heaven, so that the wealth that I have discovered shall be the means of stirring up all mankind to revenge, and the Spanish nation shall suffer hereafter."[13]

Fortunately for Columbus, Isabella never received his threat. Having no way to send this letter, Columbus could only call on "the good angels that succor the oppressed and innocent to bring this paper to my great mistress."[14] Apparently no Heavenly couriers were listening as this little known letter never left the island. His earlier letter, carried by Méndez, had been forwarded to her from Santo Domingo.

The mutiny referred to in his despairing missive had broken out five months earlier, when Francisco Poras, captain of one of the ships, burst in on the admiral in his straw cabin and demanded they leave at once. He and his brother Diego, the fleet's notary, accused Columbus of having deliberately marooned them in Jamaica knowing he was unwelcome in Santo Domingo. The Poras brothers' insurrection was joined by most of the older seamen, who after six months in Santa Gloria wanted out. Columbus declared he would not leave, but rather than battle the mutineers, agreed to let them go.

Crying, "I am for Castile—follow me," the rebel leader seized the dozen canoes Columbus had bartered from the Indians. Forcing the natives to row, the rebels made three attempts to overcome the fierce currents of the 108-mile-wide channel to Hispaniola. On their final try, they gave up, though only after throwing eighteen Indian paddlers overboard, and chopping off the hands of those who clung to the side. Five months later, after a two-week march across the island, marked by rape and pillage, they were encamped in an Indian village a half mile from Santa Gloria, intending to seize the admiral's ships.

Columbus had just finished his troubled letter to the queen when the two men he had sent to parlay with the rebels returned. They had taken an offer of pardon and a promise that they would soon be rescued. But Poras rebuffed them.

When his emissaries reported that Poras's men were preparing for battle, Columbus withdrew to his cabin in despair. But Bartholomew, his fierce younger brother, convinced him to take the fight to the enemy. He armed the fifty young loyalists and set forth to attack the rebel camp. When the mutineers saw Columbus's teenage army approach they laughed. There was no way mere youths, "brought up in a softer mode of life," could defeat such "hardy sailors, rendered robust and vigorous by the roving life."[15] But the rebels' confidence was premature: In a superhuman effort, Bartholomew slew the six mutineers sent to attack him, and had the point of his sword at Poras's breast when the rest surrendered. The Poras brothers were put in irons aboard ship, and the forty-eight rebels were disarmed and kept on shore. With peace restored, a reunited, mistrustful crew nervously awaited their promised rescue.

Even if Ovando did send a ship, Columbus had little faith his gold medallions would be safe in Hispaniola, whose previous governor, he wrote the queen, "robbed me and my brother of our dearly purchased gold."[16] He expected no less from Ovando. During the tense five weeks before two rescue ships arrived (one sent by Méndez, the other by Ovando), he rarely left his cabin. Never again did he set foot on Jamaica.

What happened to the gold of Veragua? The Crown had instructed Columbus that if treasure was found, "you must draw up an account of all this in the presence of Our Notary . . . so that We may know everything that the said Islands and Mainland may contain."[17] Yet the sixty-three medallions from Panama are not mentioned in the notary's account, nor are they listed in the inventory of the ship that brought him home to Spain.[18] Unsure his gold would survive Ovando's rescue, Columbus would not have left the gold in Hispaniola.[19] Columbus also had reason to fear a renewed mutiny on the way back to Spain. It is therefore unlikely that he kept the gold with him.

That leaves Jamaica. Since he never left the ship, and trusted no one but his son and brother and a core group of loyalists, he presumably asked members of this latter group to transfer his gold to safety.

There were two good reasons he could count on these youths, whose unstinting loyalty he vowed to reward.[20] First, they had a fiscal interest in the voyage, as their fathers helped finance it. Second, their families, being wealthy conversos, were targeted by the Inquisition. It is reasonable, therefore, to postulate that to keep their sons safe, Columbus's backers persuaded him to take them along.

While the Jewish youngsters may have looked to Columbus as their Moses (as he himself did), Jamaica was no Promised Land. Still, for teenagers forced to lead underground lives in Spain, a year's idyll on a tropical island was nearly as good. When not swimming around their rotting ships, or diving off a yardarm, they wrestled on the beach and otherwise contested for the favor of the naked Indian girls who daily brought food and lingered to watch the young gods at play.

If Columbus did entrust them with the cache of gold, he would undoubtedly have called the boys to his cabin and instructed them to deliver it to Chief Huero, his Indian ally and the island's most powerful cacique, who had outfitted Méndez on his successful crossing to Hispaniola and remained loyal after a prophetic night when Columbus's God "ate the moon." Columbus had noted in Zacuto's almanac that a full eclipse was due in the early evening of February 29, 1504. The natives, turned off by the rapacious ways of the mutineers, no longer saw their visitors as gods, and, having their fill of Spanish trinkets, had begun withholding food supplies from the Spaniards, who, Fernando wrote, "consumed more in one day than [the Indians] ate in 20."[21]

Columbus saw the celestial event as an opportunity to rectify this "by taking their moon away." On the day of the eclipse, he summoned the chiefs for "a feast and a palaver," and told them: "Attend tonight the rising of the moon: She will rise inflamed with wrath, signifying the punishment God will visit upon you." When the eclipse began shortly after sunset, Columbus retreated to his cabin. "The Indians grew so frightened," wrote Fernando, "that with great howling and lamentation they came running in all directions to the ships, laden with provisions, and praying for the Admiral to intercede with his God that He might not vent His wrath upon them." When the moon was in full shadow, Columbus emerged. He had pleaded with his God, he told them, who agreed to forgive them as long as the Indians kept the Christians supplied. As proof, "they would soon see the moon's anger and inflammation pass away . . . From that time forward," wrote Fernando, "the Indians were diligent in providing us with all we needed and were loud in the praise of the Christian God."

The eclipse vindicated Huero, who afterward presented Columbus with a tribute of small disks of gold from his previously undisclosed mine. Considering Columbus's desperate straits, it is thought he called on Huero to safeguard his gold. If so, he would have had his young allies transport it under the cover of darkness.

Although there is no hard evidence for this account of Columbus's alleged gold mine, it is supported by later developments, including the return to Jamaica of the converso youths after their rescue. Having left the land of the Inquisition, they chose to remain in Hispaniola when the rescue ships landed in Santo Domingo, rather than accompany Columbus and the crew back to Spain.

In November 1504, Columbus had been back only three weeks when his patroness Isabella died. The following May, the king offered him a rich estate and pension if he would relinquish his rights of discovery. Ferdinand regretted allowing Isabella to persuade him to empower Columbus with all sorts of rights and privileges, but although Columbus was in declining health, he was not about to surrender his hard-won titles. A little more than a year later, he made out his will, and died the next day (May 20, 1506) with his loyal mate Diego Méndez and son Fernando by his side.

Three years afterward, Columbus's eldest son, Diego, having inherited his titles, arrived in Hispaniola to replace Ovando as governor. Accompanying him were his younger brother Fernando and his uncle Bartholomew. This was their first trip back to the Indies since their rescue. A contemporary painting shows them seated around a conference table in the governor's mansion.

One issue they hoped to resolve was dealt with right away when Diego recruited "Portugals from Hispaniola"[22] to reconnoiter Jamaica in advance of settling the island. Since Diego's uncle and brother left for Spain right after the "Portugals" returned, it is apparent they had come for the left-behind gold of Columbus. Nothing more is heard of the sixty-three gold pendants, but Chief Huero's mine begat the legend of Columbus's "secret golden mine, which hath not yet been opened by the King of Spain or any other."[23]

To lead the Jamaica expedition, Diego had appointed Juan d'Esquivel, a converso who served under Bartholomew.[24]

Landing on the coast of Huero's domain, Esquivel founded Melilla, which is the name of a Spanish port in Morocco that—coincidentally or not—alone in the empire was exempted from the expulsion order and remained a haven for Jews after the port was captured by Spain in 1497.[25] When Esquivel returned to Hispaniola, and, it is thought, delivered the sixty-three medallions to Bartholomew, Diego appointed him Jamaica's governor and directed the loyal conversos to return to the island. Thus began the settlement of Jamaica, a Caribbean island that, like Melilla in Morocco, would henceforth serve as a haven for Jews.

In 1511, a flotilla of ships, carrying more than a thousand settlers, dropped anchor in Santa Gloria near the beach where Columbus was marooned. Expecting to find gold and create a New World capital rivaling Seville, the settlers laid out a city two miles long and named it Nueva Sevilla del Oro (New Seville of Gold). Unlike the Portugals, the newcomers were of minor Spanish nobility and had come to seek their fortune. A contemporary wrote, "They fancied that gold was to be gathered as easily and readily as fruit from trees."[26] However, when they realized they had to dig for it, and even then with rare success, disillusion quickly set in. The toilsome job of excavating the ore from the bowels of the earth was given over to the Indians.

Within a decade, gold was being mined in Jamaica. But after Diego Columbus and the king had taken their share, the amount from the smelting house was not enough to satisfy the hidalgos, among whom were some former mutineers and their leader, Francisco Poras.[27] That these rebels chose to return to the island they had risked their lives to leave suggests they believed there was more gold in Jamaica than what was being mined.[28] It is therefore not surprising that the Columbus family and their allies, the Portugals, kept Huero's mine a secret.

Despite the paucity of gold, island life was pleasantly rewarding. Jamaica was a fertile land, and the average allotment of 150–200 pacified Indians per settler meant that one could have a successful ranching operation, made all the more comfortable by a modest harem of baptized Indian women. Jamaica was developing nicely as a food depot supplying passing ships and breeding horses for the conquistadors. But then the Indians started dying. Unused to the white man's germs, they expired when they got sick, and a plague of smallpox finished them off. Soon everyone wanted to leave.

In 1513, Esquivel reported that many of New Seville's colonists had left for Cuba, leaving behind their *caiguaes* (Portuguese servants), who had moved to "the south side of the island to carry on the cultivation of foodstuffs."[29] The *caiguaes* had been considered personal baggage, and as such did not have to produce the "clean blood" certificates required of other settlers in the colony. Later developments indicate they were conversos.

While New Seville struggled, the south coast settlement flourished. Though the community was never formally recognized, a cryptic remark by Peter Martyr—from 1511 the "Royal Chronicler of the Indies"—makes an oblique reference to the conversos. After being made abbot of Jamaica in 1514, he wrote the king: "There are two settlements but only one will have my church."[30] The following year, a report from Jamaica's new governor, Francisco Garay, pointedly referred to the community. Having replaced Esquivel, Garay wrote his sovereign on the state of the island, and underlined his intention "to see the country and <u>the site of the town on the other side</u>."[31] Later, he too would desert the island to join in the conquest of Mexico, leaving behind more *caiguaes* to join those who had come before.

From the time that Santangel financed Columbus's Enterprise of the Indies and persuaded the royal couple to grant the explorer's family hereditary rights to any new land he might discover, Columbus sailed with a hidden agenda: Along with his stated goal of gaining the riches of the East, it was hoped he would acquire a new land where Sephardim could live free from the terrors of the Inquisition. The discoverer of the Indies didn't rule long enough to make good his promise to provide a homeland for converted Jews, but for more than a century his heirs kept Jamaica off-limits to the hooded Inquisitors who were empowered to root out heresy in all Spanish territories. As far as Jamaica's proprietors were concerned, as long as their "Portugals" wore a Christian mask, no one might question the sincerity of their religious beliefs. Under the protection of the island's rulers, covert Jews came disguised as conversos from Portugal, their presence there known and approved by the Spanish Crown.

Chapter Two

ADVENTURING IN THE
NEW WORLD

At the dawn of the Age of Discovery, when Spain's monarchs banished the Jews to purify their nation, followers of the Law of Moses sailed with the explorers and marched with the conquistadors. With the discovery and settlement of the New World, they took solace in the hope of finding a safe haven, or at least putting distance between themselves and the Inquisition. Unlike other pioneers, they had no home to return to, and as seen in the preceding chapter, they were among the first foreigners to permanently settle the New World. Going about as bona fide Christians, most carried their secret to the grave. The adventures of some who did not paint an extraordinary tableau of their time. These include a turban-wearing pilot who sailed with three of the early explorers; the first capitalist to own and market New World flora; a suspect Jew who discovered California; a conquistador who was the first Jew burned in the New World; and other Judaizers, men and women, who joined in the conquest of Mexico.

GASPAR, THE JEWISH PILOT

Outlawed in the civilized world and vulnerable in the Diaspora, Jews became skilled in ways to find and explore new lands. They were the era's foremost mapmakers, and also perfected the nautical instruments and astronomical tables the early explorers sailed with. When Jewish expertise was needed, prejudice took a backseat to expediency, and Jewish pilots, adept at reading maps and using navigational instruments, were recruited to interpret those tables. Had they not, many an explorer would have been lost in the vast oceans, and three of the most famous—Vasco da Gama, Pedro Cabral, and Amerigo Vespucci—used the same enigmatic Jew to show them the way.[1]

The story begins in 1494, when the pope, believing (as all did) that Columbus had found the western sea route to Asia, divided the world between the two contending Iberian nations by drawing a line through the middle of the Atlantic Ocean. His ruling, agreed to in the Treaty of Tordesillas, assigned all lands 370 leagues (about 1,175 miles) west of the Cape Verde islands to Spain, and all lands east to Portugal.[2] Three years later, when Columbus was preparing his third voyage across the Western Sea, King Manuel of Portugal commissioned Vasco da Gama to seek the eastern route around Africa. In the event the two explorers should meet, King Ferdinand gave Columbus a letter of greeting for his rival.

———

Da Gama, a learned nobleman, who credited his "Hebrew tutor" for teaching him navigation, mathematics, and astronomy, left Lisbon in July 1497 in command of four ships and 170 men. Two years later (in September 1499), he returned with two ships, fifty men, and a few spices to show for his effort. If not for his fortuitous encounter with the Jewish pilot, he might not have returned at all. But thanks to him, Portugal beat Spain in the race for India's riches, and monopolized the lucrative spice trade.

Approaching the subcontinent, da Gama had stopped at a small island off the coast of Calicut to careen and clean his ships when a small boat approached. In its bow stood a tall, bearded white man, richly dressed in Eastern attire. Calling to them in Spanish, the stranger asked to speak to the captain. Welcomed aboard the flagship, he introduced himself as Moncaide, the harbormaster of Calicut, and explained that his lord, Rajah Samorin, having heard of the "military valor and nautical knowledge of the Portuguese," had sent him to welcome the foreigners.[3]

Da Gama, whose voyage thus far had been marred by attacks along the East African coast, suspected a trap and ordered his men to seize Moncaide's attendants, who immediately confessed their leader's duplicity. Far from being the harbormaster, they said, Moncaide commanded the ruler's navy, and if he perceived the visitors as a threat was to signal four warships, lying in wait, to attack. Da Gama held Moncaide and ordered him to confess or "be boiled in fat and whipped until he died."[4] Admitting his deceit, he agreed to pilot da Gama's ships to port and present him to Samorin. Although Moncaide now claimed to be a New Christian forced to become a Moor, da Gama, writing in his journal, described him as a "renegade Jew" and noted that though his hair and beard were gray, he looked to be about forty.

Samorin was ready to trade with the strangers, but was put off when da Gama offered cheap trinkets in exchange for priceless jewels. Insulted, Samorin sent them away. The two would meet again, but the initial impression persisted and their enmity escalated to hostage-taking on both sides. Eventually da Gama was allowed to depart with a small quantity of spices and jewels bartered from local merchants. Moncaide, meanwhile, having aroused his enemies at court by aiding the foreigners, gladly accepted da Gama's invitation to return with him to Portugal.

Back in Lisbon, Moncaide dropped all pretense. He now claimed to be Alonso Pérez, a Spanish Jew from Castille, and said he wished to be baptized and serve his new host country. With da Gama acting as his godfather, Moncaide took the explorer's name, and was christened Gaspar da Gama. Although he was made a cavalier by King Manuel, who regularly conversed with him about lands he had visited, the king always referred to his new court favorite as "Gaspar, the Jewish pilot."

Manuel, not knowing that Columbus was sailing in circles in a far-off sea, thought Portugal was still in a race with Spain for the riches of Asia and asked the worn-out explorer to go again. But da Gama, newly married and not inclined to set off on such an arduous trip, recommended in his stead Pedro Cabral, a young nobleman and member of the court. Cabral had never been to sea, but he had a commanding presence and was trusted by the king. Given his inexperience, however, the king ordered Cabral to take the Jewish pilot and "follow his counsels in all and every matter." The king also ordered his talented converso physician, Mestre João, expert at calibrating Zacuto's improved astrolabe, to go with the fleet and chart the expedition.[5]

In March 1500, Cabral set off with thirteen ships, loaded this time with better trade goods than those da Gama had tried to palm off. As the fleet sailed past the Cape Verde Islands and approached the Gulf of Guinea, where the continent narrows abruptly to the east, Gaspar had Cabral stay west of the gulf to avoid getting stuck in its becalmed waters. But when it was time for the fleet to sail east to round the horn of Africa, the winds and currents in the South Atlantic drove them further to the west until one morning a lookout shouted *Terra!* Cabral had reached the eastern shore of South America.

Two years before, Columbus, sailing south of Trinidad, had sighted the continent's northern coast, but did not land. Observing the four mouths of the Orinoco River that emptied into the Gulf of Paria, the admiral, with one foot planted firmly in the Bible and the other in Renaissance science, declared them the four rivers flowing out of the Garden of Eden.[6]

Cabral sailed north along the coast to a protected harbor he named Porto Segua (Safe Port). Suppressing his belief that he was trespassing on lands reserved for Spain, he stuck a wooden cross in the earth and carved on it the arms of Portugal. As it was Sunday, he celebrated Mass and handed out little tin crosses to the natives.[7] The following day Mestre João aligned the sun with his astrolabe to determine their latitude. His measurement of 17 degrees south was off by only a half degree. In his report to the king (unpublished for five centuries), the physician included drawings of the Southern Cross and adjacent constellations. Brazil had been discovered.

João shared his observations with Gaspar. Expert in nautical matters, the two conversos judged it a new continent. Cabral was not so sure: "We remained in ignorance," he wrote, "whether it was an island or a mainland, though we are inclined to the latter opinion." In a rush to get back on course, after five days he headed for southern Africa. His intention was to sail in the wake of da Gama, circumvent the continent, and proceed up the coast until he caught the trade winds to India. A simple plan, but owing to heavy storms and the poor skills of his captains, six ships were lost rounding Africa, and Cabral arrived in India with half his original fleet.

This time around, the Hindu Rajah Samorin, pleased by the foreigners' more generous offerings, greeted the Portuguese warmly. For a while all went well—too well, according to competing Muslim merchants. Cabral was given a warehouse to store his trade goods and nearby quarters for his men. But the Muslim merchants gathered a mob to attack the crew's quarters and loot the warehouse, killing many sailors and forcing the rest to retreat to their ships.

When informed of the action, Samorin did nothing. Gaspar, who had commanded Samorin's navy, advised swift retribution. Heeding his pilot's counsel, Cabral

ordered ten Moorish ships in the port to be taken and all the people in the said ships to be killed. Thus we slew 500 and captured 20 or 30 hiding in the holds of the ships . . . One ship had three elephants which we killed and ate; we unloaded and burned the ships; and the following day we bombarded the city, so that we slew an endless number of people and did much damage.[8]

As evident from the notary's account, the temperament of the explorer was little different from that of a conquistador. If peaceful means did not bring the desired result, terror was the alternative. Cabral, having journeyed thousands of miles for spices, silks, and jewels, was not to be put off by recalcitrant rulers or angry locals—and when his men were hungry, elephant meat would do. After Calicut's devastation, Gaspar recommended they head south to Cochin, whose ruler hated Samorin. With the renegade Jew smoothing the way, the rival rajah and Cabral concluded a trade treaty that laid the foundation of Portuguese rule in India. On a palm leaf, inscribed with an iron pen, Cochin's ruler wrote King Manuel: "My country is rich in cinnamon, cloves, ginger and pepper. That which I ask of you in exchange is gold, silver, corals and scarlet cloth."[9] Cabral departed with the holds of his ships loaded with pepper, cinnamon, fine cottons, silks, and perfumes.[10]

Homeward bound, Cabral stopped off at Cape Verde to take on provisions. A chance encounter there with a Portuguese fleet on another voyage of discovery resulted in Gaspar's meeting an Italian explorer whose name would become synonymous with the continent to which Gaspar directed him.

When the crews met and conversed, Gaspar shared his knowledge of the southern continent with the fleet's adviser, Amerigo Vespucci, who had previously explored the continent's northern coast for Spain two years before when he sailed with Alonso de Ojeda, one of Columbus's captains. When Amerigo reported his find to Ferdinand, he expected the king to sponsor a return voyage. But although he was a trusted friend of Columbus, Vespucci was a foreigner, and preference was given to the proposals of Spanish explorers. Shunted aside, Amerigo turned his back on Spain. Having noted that his landfall on the continent might have fallen on Portugal's side of the pope's dividing line, he approached the Portuguese court. King Manuel, intrigued with the idea of a new land and having not yet received news of Cabral's discovery, authorized an expedition to investigate further and sent the Italian along as adviser.

So it was that Amerigo and Gaspar happened to meet in Cape Verde, and as a result the Italian's name would one day be attached to Columbus's discoveries. According to Vespucci's biographer, the Jewish pilot possessed "a storehouse of geographical knowledge and [was] an incomparable source of information for Amerigo who could discuss hundreds of things with him in Italian." Amerigo soon took command of the fleet, and reaching the continent explored nearly a thousand miles of coastline as far south as Río de la Plata.

On his return to Lisbon, he confirmed the continent's massive size and asserted that much of its coastal land was indeed "over the line." Although sailing for Portugal, the loyal Italian wrote his Florentine patron, Lorenzo de' Medici, that he had not reached Asia but had discovered a "New World." He also praised Gaspar as "the best informed man among Cabral's followers . . . a trustworthy man who speaks many languages and knows many towns and provinces from Portugal to the Indian Ocean, from Cairo to the island of Sumatra."[11] The popularity of his account of these discoveries led a young German cartographer named Martin Waldseemüller to label the southern continent "the land of Amerigo," and by 1528 Columbus's Indies were known as the Americas.[12]

Gaspar's own story ends back in India. In 1502, he and his godfather, Vasco da Gama, sailed once more to the subcontinent. On this occasion, he reunited with his wife, who, having escaped from Calicut after the attack, was living in Cochin. Gaspar tried to persuade her to convert so that she could return with him to Portugal, but being a devout Jewess and learned in the Law, she adamantly refused.

After Samorin's demise, Gaspar settled in Calicut in 1505 in service to the Portuguese viceroy. (In 1511, Goa was conquered and became the capital of Portugal's Indian empire.) He often visited his wife, but she never forgave him for turning Christian. Such were the life and adventures of the Jewish pilot who, as Vasco da Gama wrote, "shed his faith with the ease of a reptile."[13]

CAPITALIST PIONEER

A small, fertile island off the northeast coast of South America that Amerigo Vespucci called "a natural wonder" bears the name of Fernando de Noronha, a sixteenth-century converso who headed the first capitalist venture in the New World.

King Manuel, excited by Vespucci's report of coastal forests of brazilwood, which was the source of a valuable red dye in demand throughout Europe, drew up a royal contract with the wealthy shipowning merchant Fernando de Noronha. With the likelihood of also finding valuable spices and other marketable commodities, Noronha recruited other prominent conversos to join his consortium in partnership with the king. Beyond a good business opportunity, however, their interest in the far-off land was to find a refuge to live free from persecution.

In 1503, they set forth on five ships and put in at the offshore island to regroup before proceeding to the mainland. Amerigo, who sailed with them as far as the island, wrote glowingly that its bountiful streams and woodlands attracted all sorts of birds, "so tame they allow themselves to be taken up by hand." Although beguiled, he left to seek out a southern passage to India, which was not found until Magellan rounded the continent in 1519. The conversos he left behind had better luck. Cutting and loading logs of dyewood along the forested coast, they found ready buyers when they returned to Lisbon. Investing their profits, they established logging camps along six hundred miles of coastal land now known by the name of its valuable tree, Brazil.

By 1505, the dyewood business was netting the partners fifty thousand ducats a year. Next to gold, brazilwood was then the most valuable product to come out of the New World. A grateful king gave de Noronha a ten-year monopoly and ceded him the uninhabited island, and gave it his name.

Was de Noronha a secret Jew? He changed the name of his ship the *São Cristóvão* (St. Christopher) to *A Judia* (The Jewess), and a harbor he discovered and named Cananea lies 32 degrees south of the equator, just as Israel's ancient city of that name lies 32 degrees north. Whatever his personal beliefs, it appears Fernando de Noronha did not forsake his heritage.[14]

In 1520, João Rodrigues Cabrilho, "a Portuguese," led thirty men armed with crossbows from Jamaica to Mexico, where they joined Cortés in the conquest.[15] Afterward, Cabrilho set forth to find the legendary Seven Golden Cities. No luck: they never existed. But after this fruitless search, he sailed into San Diego Bay in 1542 and discovered California. Over the next five months, he and his two Portuguese pilots explored the North Pacific coast in hopes of finding a shortcut to Europe via the Northwest Passage, an elusive waterway believed to traverse North America from the Pacific to the Atlantic to Europe. Wounded in a skirmish with the Indians, he died near what is now Santa Barbara.

Like that of other conversos who obscured their past, Cabrilho's ancestry is not known. His written reports and navigation skills show him to be an educated man, apparently from a good family. It is probable that João Cabrilho had Jewish ancestry.[16] Recent scholarship argues he was not Portuguese but Spanish-born, from Cuéllar, a city known for its many Jews, who crossed the border to Portugal at the time of the expulsion.

Forcibly converted in 1497 by the threat of having their children enslaved, the newly baptized Jews referred to themselves in Hebrew as *anusim* (forced ones).[17] Although they made up about 10 percent of Portugal's 1.5 million people, conversos constituted nearly three-quarters of the mercantile community owing to the Portuguese upper class's disdain for commerce.[18] The king, considering his nation's small population and large, talented converso community, viewed his New Christians as indispensable to the success of his expanding empire. Portugal's conversos, who were otherwise forbidden to leave the country, were duly licensed to settle in the Indies.

Prior to the union of Spain and Portugal in 1580, few Portuguese nationals looked to serve the Spanish Empire. Portugal was an independent nation with its own New World empire. Why serve Spain when Portugal's vast empire offered unbridled opportunity? Since Spain forbade their conversos to migrate, a self-proclaimed Portuguese national operating in the Spanish realm was *likely* to be a converso, and in this early period of forced conversion his loyalty to Judaism would probably have been strong. This is particularly true of those originally from Spain who initially chose exile rather than conversion. This supports the theory that Cabrilho, the discoverer of California, whose name appears throughout the state on roads, schools, and even drugstores, was a converted Jew who deliberately hid his origin.

There are, however, notable exceptions that serve as cautionary reminders not to jump to conclusions about the Jewish identity of all the Portuguese serving Spain's empire. The Portuguese explorer Ferdinand Magellan, whose ships sailed around the world for Spain in 1519, was a bona fide pure-blooded Catholic. But even he had a Jewish partner who brokered his contract with the king. Juan de Aranda was a well-known converso, and while the contract he negotiated for Magellan called for the king to receive one twentieth of the profits of his voyage, Aranda himself was to receive an eighth share.[19]

Hernando Alonso had it made. Six short years after serving with Cortés as a carpenter's assistant, "hammering nails into the brigantines used in the recapture of Mexico," he had become the richest farmer in the new Spanish colony. While most soldiers of his rank received nothing more from the conquest than "the cost of a new crossbow," Alonso was awarded a large tract of land north of Mexico City. Turning it into a pig and cattle farm, Alonso became the biggest supplier of meat to the colony.

In September 1528, it was reported that Alonso, now thirty-six and getting as portly as his beef, in emulation of his commander, "swaggered about in a belt of refined gold he had exacted from the natives." He had good reason: In March, his contract had been renewed by Cortés himself and he had taken a new wife, the "very beautiful" Isabel de Aguilar.

This information on Hernando Alonso comes from the trial records of the Spanish Inquisition.[20] On October 17, 1528, Alonso became the first person in the New World to be burned alive at the stake. Alonso was a secret Jew, as was his deceased first wife Beatriz, the sister of Diego Ordaz, one of Cortés's five captains. His undoing came when a Dominican friar charged that, years before in Santo Domingo, he had secretly observed Alonso and Beatriz, following their son's baptismal ceremony, "washing the boy's head with wine to cleanse him of the Holy Water." When threatened with torture on the rack, Alonso confessed that after the wine ran down the child's body and "dripped from his organ," he caught it in a cup and drank it "in mockery of the sacrament of baptism."

Beatriz, having accompanied her husband when he marched

with Cortés's army, died from fever during the conquest of Mexico. The trial recorded testimony of a witness who overheard Alonso telling his new wife not to go to church: "Señora, in your present condition [menstrual period] thou wouldst profane the Church." To which Isabel, his New Christian wife, replied, "These are old ceremonies of the Jews which are not observed now that we have adopted the evangelical grace."

Cortés had no part in the arrest of Alonso. After approving Alonso's contract, he left for Spain to answer trumped-up charges of misrule. In his absence, a rival faction in the colony conspired with the powers of the Inquisition and introduced the Holy Terror to the New World. The holier-than-thou Inquisitors, who considered Aztecs savages for sacrificing prisoners to their gods atop their Great Pyramid, chose the plaza fronting the site, where a lofty edifice of the True Church had replaced the pyramid, to consign the heretic to the flames.

In a time of carefully arranged marriages, Hernando Alonso would not have married his first wife without the blessing of her brother, Diego Ordaz, one of the outstanding figures of the conquest. Alonso's brother-in-law was the first man to climb the volcano Popocatépetl and look upon the Valley of Mexico as an advance scout of the invasion. Mesmerized by what seemed to be a floating city, he compared it to a vision out of the chivalric tale *Amadis of Gaul,* a sword and sorcery book of the time.

Before joining up with Cortés, Alonso and Diego were in Cuba, but on far different rungs of society. Alonso was a blacksmith in town, while Diego and his sisters lived in the governor's mansion, where he served as majordomo. Despite this all-important class difference, Beatriz married the blacksmith. Apparently decisive was the one thing they did share: a common ancestry. Cortés's captain wound up gathering pearls off the Venezuela coast, only to be poisoned by rivals in 1532.[21] Although much is written about him, nowhere is it mentioned that he was a converso, much less a secret Jew. Like most conversos, Diego passed himself off as an Old Christian, and went to his grave with his masquerade intact.

Señoritas were a rarity throughout the New World. With fewer than one Spanish woman for every ten men, to marry one was considered a feather in the cap for the mostly poor, aspiring hidalgos. After Mexico's conquest, some ladies felt the same about them. Most were servant girls who journeyed to New Spain to find themselves a newly rich husband. Exceptions were the four daughters of the royal treasurer Alonso Estrada, the natural son, or so he claimed, of King Ferdinand. Few women were as desirable as the Estrada sisters, who could choose from among many suitors, and it is therefore not surprising that they all married well. What is surprising is that their mother was from a well-known Jewish family and that their husbands would have known of their wives' blemished ancestry. That their progeny would also be stigmatized seems not to have mattered. Despite the aggressiveness of the Holy Fathers, and repeated decrees against conversos, they were able to keep their wives' and children's Jewish heritage secret. The same held true of Beatriz and Diego Ordaz's surviving sister. Only now is their story being told.

FRANCISCA ORDAZ

As Beatriz, the wife of the heretic Jewish conquistador, lay dying during the siege of Mexico, her sister, Francisca, was by her side. The two were among only six Spanish women known to have accompanied the conquistadors during the fighting in Mexico. After the final victory, Francisca was observed enjoy-. ing a wild night of celebration. According to an eyewitness, Francisca and three other "adventurous women went gaily to dance with men still in their quilted armor." It may well have been that night that she danced with her future husband, the son of Ponce de León, one of the legendary figures of the New World.[22]

After Alonso's undoing, Diego Ordaz was not about to fix Francisca up with another Judaizer. Instead he found Juan González Ponce de León, a valiant suitor of noble, unblemished credentials. His father, the conqueror and governor of Puerto Rico and discoverer of Florida, is forever known for his quixotic search for the fountain of youth. His son was distinguished in his own right. Serving as a soldier under Ordaz's command, Juan was the first man to reach the top of the main temple of Tenochtitlán and, despite being badly wounded, led a vanguard force that captured Montezuma. When Cortés asked him why, considering his injury, he had not withdrawn, but instead led the fight up the steps to Montezuma's quarters, Juan answered: "Señor, this is not the time for men to be in bed."[23]

Juan was aware of Francisca's lineage even before Alonso's trial had exposed her sister as a Judaizer. For years he and Alonso were friends, and up until Alonso's flaming death the two men were partners.[24] They shared a royal land grant, an *encomienda,* in Actopan in the modern state of Hidalgo, about sixty miles north of Mexico City, where Alonso had his farm.[25]

ALONSO ESTRADA'S WIFE AND DAUGHTERS

In 1522, King Charles V appointed his alleged uncle Alonso Estrada as Mexico's royal treasurer, perhaps the most important position in the rich territory. In Cortés's absence, Estrada served as acting governor and for a year (1529) was governor. It was a common belief that he was the bastard son of King Ferdinand, the result of a liaison with Doña Luisa de Estrada, the daughter of Don Fernan, Duke of Aragon, when both were teenagers.

Raised in Ferdinand's court, Alonso inherited the title Duke of Aragon and sided with Charles V when he was contending for the throne. While some speculate that Alonso himself had Jewish ancestors, his wife certainly did. It was widely known that Marina Gutiérrez Flores de la Caballeria was from an old Jewish family whose wealth has been compared to the Rothschilds'. Although both sides of her family had converted to Catholicism, for three generations they were condemned as Judaizers by the Inquisition. Some who were already dead before sentencing had their bodies exhumed and burned. Doña Marina, having secured a forged affidavit attesting to her pure blood, followed her husband to Mexico.[26]

Following his death in 1531, Doña Marina cemented her place in colonial society by marrying off her daughters to two of Mexico's prominent conquistadors. The youngest, Beatrice Estrada, married Vásquez de Coronado, who (with his wife's money) set off to find the fabled Seven Golden Cities of Cíbola. Although the object of his search was never found, Coronado was the first to explore America's southwest and discovered the Grand Canyon. Luisa, the oldest, became the wife of Jorge de Alvarado, a conqueror of Mexico and governor of Guatemala. The two other Estrada sisters likewise married nobility.*

What do these marriages portend? Since the Jewish ancestry of those noblemen's wives' mother was known (as was the fact that her Old Christian certification was a sham), it apparently did not overly concern them that their children would no longer be of pure blood.

In the first four decades of the Age of Discovery, known conversos were involved in nearly every venture as explorers, pilots, and conquistadors, or behind the scenes as financiers, shipowners, and administrators. Those mentioned here are but a few of the known Sephardim who participated. How many others there were is unknown. Since all Spanish conversos were forbidden in the New World, it made no difference if one was a true convert, an atheist, or a covert Jew. All were there illegally and therefore subject to prosecution. Today, with the advent of genealogical Web sites, the Jewish roots of other early pioneers are being disclosed in postings by their descendants.[27]

Hernando Cortés, like Columbus, had the support of many conversos. He had grown up across the street from the syna-

---

* A third daughter, Marina, wed the grandson of Columbus's supporter, the Duke of Medina Sidonia; a fourth, Ana, wed her father's successor as treasurer of the colony, Juan de Sosa Cabrera.

gogue in Medellín, home to influential Jews. Some were friends of his family, and that may have been a reason he trusted and favored them. Their sad and sudden exodus in 1492, when he was seven years old, was a major event in his childhood. A leading historian of the conquest of Mexico, Hugh Thomas, puts the number of conversos who served with Cortés at more than a hundred.[28]

As early as 1501, the Crown published an edict that "Moors, Jews, heretics, reconciliados [repentants—those who returned to the church], and New Christians are not to be allowed to go to the Indies." Yet in 1508, the bishop of Cuba reported, "practically every ship [arriving in Havana] is filled with Hebrews and New Christians."[29] Such decrees banning them, followed by letters home complaining of their continued arrival, were a regular occurrence. Conversos with the aptitude and capital to develop colonial trade, comfortable in a Hispanic society, yet seeking to put distance between themselves and the homeland of the Inquisition, made their way to the New World.[30] No licenses were required for the crew of a ship, and as many were owned by conversos, they signed on as sailors and jumped ship. Servants also didn't need a license or exit visa, so that a Jew who obtained one by whatever means could take others along as household staff.[31]

For most of the first century after the discovery, the fanaticism that characterized the Holy Office did not carry over to the New World. By and large, adventurers there—having left the Old World for whatever reason—could identify with the conversos' desire to start anew. In the early New World, despite the edicts barring them, wherever one looks, a suspected Jewish adventurer was carving out a life, often on the run from the Inquisition. We will never know how many there were because even sincere converts hid their Jewish roots behind a mask of hyper-religious piety. As the next chapter demonstrates, as long as their skills were needed, the Crown not only turned a blind eye to their presence, but actively recruited them.

Following a time line, then, we come to 1534, a year when disparate events came together in ways that broke with the past and shifted the century forward to new beginnings. In matters of faith, the Reformation was kick-started when a renegade monk published the Bible in German, and a lustful king became the Supreme Head of the Church of England. In the New World, an illiterate pig herder conquered the gold kingdom of Peru, and in Brazil, a group of exiled Jews from a little island off the Guinea coast introduced an agricultural industry that would prove more valuable than gold and silver. Meanwhile, warring infidels led by one who styled himself "the Magnificent" invaded Hungary. And the Most Catholic Defender of the True Faith, the Holy Roman Emperor Charles V, authorized the first documented Jewish settlement in the New World on the island of Jamaica.

Chapter Three

THE KING'S ESSENTIAL
HERETICS

*W*hen the bad news from Jamaica reached Spain, Charles V, the Lord of Half the World, was not surprised. It seemed that every time he put his crown on in 1534, there was trouble in his kingdom. Even his vaunted title, Holy Roman Emperor, didn't carry the same weight as it had when his grandfather Maximilian wore the crown. So when he read that most of his Jamaican colonists were dead and the rest wanted out, Charles was not unduly grieved. He had seen it coming.

In the nineteen years that he had been ruling the New World, Jamaica had always been more of a problem than the "fairest isle" Columbus thought it to be. New Seville of Gold was now known simply as New Seville. The anticipated flow of the precious metal turned out to be a trickle, and most of the sixty thousand Indians who had greeted Columbus were dead. Aside from a small productive settlement of conversos on the south coast, the colony was going under. Why remain in Jamaica when neighboring Hispaniola and Cuba offered a regal style of life said to rival that of Spain? Why settle Jamaica when the nearby Main offered the promise of Aztec and Inca gold?

The communiqué was desperate: Conditions at New Seville had "turned out so badly that no citizen has prospered nor kept his health for a day." To salvage the colony, his treasurer Pedro de Manzuelo proposed removing the settlement "to the south side of the island where the land is plentiful in bread and beef . . . with very good ports suitable for navigation to the provinces of Santa Marta, Cartagena, and the mainland . . . There is great disposition to settle there because no ship in this trade comes to the north coast but all load on the south."[1]

Manzuelo concluded his report with a seemingly odd request. To pioneer the south coast settlement, he recommended the king send an additional thirty Portuguese families to join with the twenty already there. Together they would be put to work on his sugar estate. Manzuelo's request was couched in such a way as not to arouse suspicion. The king had made growing sugarcane in the Indies a priority and had been subsidizing planters in Hispaniola, Puerto Rico, and Mexico with land grants, duty waivers, and loans. Years earlier, Jamaica's sugar mill in New Seville had shown the island's potential for growing the sweetener, and it made sense to recruit more workers to increase the island's production.[2] But why Portuguese? Portugal was then attracting settlers to its colonies with the promise of riches, so where would the king find Portuguese families in his realm willing to settle a poor Spanish island?

The fact is, he didn't have to. Manzuelo's directive was aimed at enlisting neither sugar workers nor Portuguese natives. In Crown correspondence, reference to Portuguese residing in Spanish lands pertained not to national origin, but rather was a code word for the worst heretics in his kingdom. With the stability of his empire at stake, Charles V took seriously his vows as Chief Knight of the Holy Inquisition to convert the heathen and burn the heretic. Yet when the communiqué specified "Portuguese," Charles read between the lines: Jamaica for the Jews, or the colony goes under.[3]

When Columbus returned from his voyage of discovery, a golden thread had wound its way into the fabric of every Spaniard's imagination. In time it stretched from the New World across the Ocean Sea to a peninsula on the edge of the Old World, where it wove an exotic pattern of desire stirring a man's dreams. Wherever men gathered, the talk was the same—tales of opulent cities with riches beyond belief and beautiful naked maidens aching to please.

Jamaica, thought to have neither, had become a dead end. Only Puerto Rico, where man-eating Indians discouraged settlement, was less popular. Why settle Jamaica when the bounty of the New World was thought to be yours for the taking, if a man be but brave and bold enough? And what Spaniard wasn't? In their own generation, they had defeated the Moors, kicked out the Jews, enslaved the Indians, and conquered more territory than Rome had in five centuries. In forty-two years, their country had swelled from an alliance of Christians fighting over a few thousand square miles to a world empire governing millions. In the process, Spain had become the richest, most powerful nation on earth. Their king and Church told them they had the right, and they had proved they had the might.

Romance novels of chivalry, the pulp fiction of the day,

"fired the imaginations of conquistadors to seek their own adventures in the New World. Their heads filled with fantastic notions . . . their courage spurred by noble examples of the great heroes of chivalry, they were prepared to undergo every kind of hardship and sacrifice as they penetrated through swamps and jungles into the new continent."[4] Fortune seekers from every province of Spain filled the taverns of Santo Domingo, the capital of the New World, plotting, conspiring, and gambling on destinies. Most, like Cortés, were soldiers of fortune, a class of Spaniard that had evolved during the Reconquista—the seven centuries of warfare against the Moors. In a grasp at nobility, they called themselves hidalgos, meaning sons of somebody, but the true somebodies, the grandees, would wait another fifty years before sending their sons to the New World. Provided you wore the cross of Jesus, your origin didn't matter: an acrobat and a musician had looted Colombia for gold; a former scribe got the pearls of Venezuela; a soldier of fortune ruling New Spain, a nation bigger than Europe, was said to be richer than the king himself. And in the summer of 1534, word spread through Spain that a pig farmer turned conquistador had plundered an Indian nation of limitless gold.

While Charles was mulling the Jamaican communiqué in the royal palace, the pig farmer's brother, Hernando Pizarro, was thrilling court attendees with the tale of how his illiterate brother Francisco, taking a cue from Cortés, had passed himself off as a god, kidnapped the Inca chief, and after accumulating a ransom of nineteen tons of gold and silver, had strangled and then burned the heretic. Even as Hernando spoke of this maleficent deed, a rumor spread in the court: A fleet of seventy ships from the New World had arrived at the Spanish port of Laredo with ten thousand Amazon women on board, hungry for Spanish men to father their children. Given the lure of Inca gold and the lust for Amazon women, Charles knew that would-be settlers would line up for Peru.[5] But none would be interested in settling Jamaica, except the Jews. Along with an empire, Charles had inherited the Inquisition, and soon found the threat of being burned alive a handy means to control false conversos.

While tons of New World gold poured into Charles's treasury each year, it leaked out just as fast, and in the summer of 1534 he would need every ounce to defend his borders.[6] His empire was under attack. Jacob Fugger, the German banker who had loaned him a half million ducats to bribe the electors to name him Holy Roman Emperor, had died, and the Fuggers refused to advance him any more coin.[7] It was one thing for a pig herder to capture a New World empire and gather its riches; it was quite another to ensure their safe transfer to the Crown to fund his extravagances, fill his nobles' pockets, and pay for soldiers to fight his enemies.

The New World was his golden goose. If Jews were best suited to care for the golden egg, then he would send them to the New World and get on with more pressing matters of state. France's King Francis I and the Ottoman emperor, Suleiman the Magnificent, his two challengers for world dominance, were allied against him. Francis was backing border raids into Italy; Suleiman's cavalry of 100,000 horsemen was camped on the eastern shore of the Danube rattling their sabers, while in the Mediterranean the sultan's naval commander, Barbarossa, was on his way to attack Tunis, Charles's last stronghold in North Africa.

There was also the enemy within, walking around in a monk's habit spreading heresy. That summer three German princes rejected the True Faith and declared for Martin Luther, who was turning all of northern Europe into heretics. Charles hated Luther and would have smiled to see him roasted by the Inquisition, but he needed the princes' help to defend his empire from the hordes of Suleiman. So he swallowed his anger, abided their heresy, and received their support.

The survival of Jamaica, in the midst of the Caribbean trading lanes, was essential to the security of the treasure ships that passed offshore, carrying the New World's riches back to Spain. If it meant dealing with converted Jews to ensure their safety and prevent the strategic colony from becoming a pirate base, so be it. In 1522, three treasure-laden ships dispatched to him from Mexico by Cortés had been captured and diverted to France by an Italian pirate better known today for the bridge bearing his name as the discoverer of New York harbor—Verrazano. The Aztec plunder the Italian delivered to the royal court in Paris included a half ton of gold, 682 pounds of pearls, jewel boxes encrusted with topaz, mirrors of polished obsidian, an emerald as large as a man's fist, three live jaguars—and of even greater value, the sea charts of the captured Spanish pilots.[8]

When Charles demanded that Francis return the loot, the French king spoke for Europe's other rulers when he mockingly told him: "The sun shines on me just the same as on you, and I would like to see the clause in Adam's will that bars me from my share of the riches of the New World!" With these words, state-licensed piracy, known as privateering, commenced in the Caribbean and became the clarion call of sea rovers.[9]

Given the threats to his empire, Charles was "quick to temper" when June 1534 passed and his treasure ships, due in May, hadn't arrived. Finally, in early July, the galleons landed at Cádiz and off-loaded 21 million pesos' worth of silver. When informed, Charles "danced a wild jig around with his son Philip and dwarf jester Perico." When Perico said to the eight-year-old prince, "Your father is Lord of Half the World; soon you will be Lord of All," it was said that Charles, who rarely let loose, "laff with no end."[10]

It was then that Charles, having received the communiqué that his Jamaica colony was foundering, agreed to send the "Portugals." Although he may have suspected the converted Jews of heresy, Charles knew that he could count on them to conduct the necessary business of managing his empire.

The conversos of 1492 were initially welcomed into a society desperate to fill those positions in which the Jews of Spain had specialized. As New Christians, they quickly became an elite bourgeoisie of merchants, physicians, tax collectors, mapmakers, financiers, and advisers to the crown. But the rapidity of their success stirred emotions that only the flames of the Inquisition would calm. In 1534, even as their baptized children filled important commercial positions in an expanding empire and in the councils of her church, the Limpieza de Sangre (Pure Blood) law introduced to Santo Domingo in 1525 decreed the New World off-limits to all but Old Christians able to trace their ancestry back four generations.[11] Whether one was a recent converso or a New Christian from 1391, a drop of Jewish blood rendered one unfit to forward God's glory in Spain's empire. The law barred New Christians from a growing list of professions, and even parts of Spain. To discourage escape, conversos were not permitted to sell their land or exchange promissory notes or bills of exchange.

Like his grandfather Ferdinand, Charles adhered to the principle that the end justifies the means. He therefore had no qualms about using conversos to salvage his Jamaican colony. Although he saw himself as a soldier for God, he did not let religious posturing stand in the way of self-interest. He financed wars in Europe by borrowing from anyone he could, sold futures in the gold ships to foreign bankers, pawned the Molucca islands to the king of Portugal, leased Venezuela and Chile to German bankers who hoped to discover El Dorado, and the following year (1535), courted Doña Gracia Méndez Nasi, a famous Jewess, for a sizeable loan from her Portuguese bank.

In Charles's lifetime, his subjects explored and settled a world three times as big as the one into which he had been born, and he needed help, even if it meant dealing with suspect heretics. They would help him maintain his empire in ways no one else could. Throughout his reign, Charles needed, but never trusted, them. He was used to dealing with nobles and clergy, but the Jews were something else. The People of the Book had the arrogance of royalty and valued themselves not by physical prowess or even riches, but by knowledge, wisdom, and business acumen. They were his essential heretics, efficient pawns in his global chess game, to be moved about and sacrificed at will.

Included in the Royal Fifth Pizarro brought the king was

a small gold box belonging to Atahualpa, the Inca chieftain, for the cocoa leaves that he and his subjects chewed for energy. Charles kept it for his snuff and may have been toying with it as he took time out from conquering the New World to ponder the problems of administering it. The king was known for his silent reflections—he often stared into the air, his clear blue eyes focused on some unknown object, while his mouth lay open (due to the protruding lower jaw characteristic of the Hapsburg line)—and one imagines him turning to Francisco Cobos, his hovering counselor, and saying in his constrained and measured way of talking: "Send for Acosta [the court Jew]; we require new settlers bound for Jamaica."

Arriving at Port Esquivel in October, the new settlers were welcomed by the twenty "Portuguese" families already there. Today, these fifty Jewish families are credited with founding Villa de la Vega (Town by the Fertile Plain), Jamaica's capital for more than three centuries. Now called Spanish Town, La Vega, founded in 1534, represents the earliest documented settlement of converted Jews in the New World.[12]

Charles turned his attention next to the heathens at his door: Sultan Suleiman's army, having overrun Persia and occupied Hungary, was on the move, and in the Mediterranean, Barbarossa's armada of eighty-four ships had embarked from Constantinople to sweep Spanish power from the sea.[13]

The sultan's naval commander, Khair-ed-Din, known to Christians as Barbarossa for his flaming red beard, was a terror in the Mediterranean even before he joined with Suleiman. The son of an unknown Greek father and a renegade Christian mother, he earned his infamy for his treatment of Christian prisoners: He tortured the men, while keeping the most comely women for his harem.

The sultan, having no navy, had left the sea's defense to Barbarossa and ex-Iberian Moors who had crossed over to North Africa after their defeat at Granada, and were joined by a second wave in 1525 when Charles ordered all who remained to convert to Christianity. Made furious by their forced exile, they made up the bulk of Barbarossa's crew. Barbarossa himself claimed to have ferried over seventy thousand Mudejares (Spanish Moors who stayed faithful to Islam). Returning to a region whence their ancestors came, they were welcomed by the region's Turkish overlords, who also followed the ways of Mohammed.

The North Africa shore, known as the Barbary Coast, was likewise familiar to Iberian Jews, whose forebears had settled there in the first century after Rome's legions conquered Jerusalem and dispersed upward of fifty thousand Jews to Spain and ports around the Mediterranean. The displaced citizens of Judea took to the sea, becoming the region's major shipowners, merchants, and traders. Fifteen hundred years later, when the Sephardic exiles arrived in North Africa, they were consigned special quarters by their Muslim hosts. Together, the two exiled immigrant groups forged a formidable force.

Positioned to wreak vengeance on those who labeled them infidels and heretics, they partnered in the region's most profitable industry—piracy. Sephardic merchants financed the Moors' devastating raids on the coastal towns of Spain and Italy and shared the booty—spices from the East and Christian slaves from Europe. Setting forth in swift, multi-oared galleys from Algiers and other seaside bases, the Barbary pirates (known as corsairs) sacked and burned villages and carried off men, women, and children.[14] If not ransomed, the males were stripped, chained naked to the oars, and forced to row until they died of fatigue; the women were sent to harems; and the children were raised as Muslims.

That July, Pope Clement, a Florentine Medici more concerned with his family's interests than supporting Charles's religious bent, delivered a blow against the Defender of the True Faith when, on his deathbed, he pardoned conversos for past offenses. This did not sit well with Charles. He and the pope had gotten along only when mutual self-interest demanded.[15] Now that it did not, Clement's decision to free up those masters of commerce threatened to turn the Mediterranean in matters of trade into a Jewish sea. If they were unchecked, Charles would be forced to deal with that deceitful race. Under the sultan's suzerainty, the Jews had turned Turkey's Constantinople and Greece's Salonika into the sea's richest ports, and via links with their brethren around the Mediterranean had developed new, lucrative trade routes to the East.

Although incensed by the prospect, Charles withheld action—figuring that, with Clement dying, he could throw his support to a new pope who would reverse the pardon. But a month later, he received devastating news he could not abide: a Jewish pirate had conquered Tunis, his last stronghold in North Africa.

SINAN, "THE FAMOUS JEWISH PIRATE"

While Barbarossa's name was feared throughout Christendom, he was not really a naval commander or even much of a sailor. Instead he occupied himself with building his navy and plotting its moves, and left most of the sea battles to his favored captain, Sinan, a Jewish refugee from Spain via Turkey.[16]

On August 20, 1534, Sinan, commonly known as "the Great Jew" or "the Famous Jewish Pirate,"[17] led a hundred ships into the harbor and occupied the North African city of Tunis—hitherto a possession of Spain—on behalf of Suleiman. The strategic port was situated across from Sicily astride a narrow strait linking the eastern and western Mediterranean basins. Suleiman, who ruled the Black Sea, the Red Sea, and the eastern Mediterranean, had established a presence in the western basin when Barbarossa conquered Algiers in 1529. Now, with the crescent flag flying over Tunis, he held dominion over the entire Mediterranean. No longer could Charles's ships venture safely beyond home waters; instead the Mediterranean had become an alien sea dominated by Muslim corsairs and Jewish merchants.

Charles's first reaction showed that his religious fealty took a backseat to realpolitik. Not without some holy guilt, he dispatched an agent to Tunis to offer Barbarossa "the lordship of North Africa" to come over to his side. Failing that, he instructed that the agent was to poison or cut the pirate's throat in the evening, when he was known to be in his cups. But evening never came. Punctuating his rejection of Charles's offer with a swing of his curved scimitar, Barbarossa decapitated the agent.

Charles saw the mission's failure as divinely ordained. Over the next year, obsessed with the idea of a crusade to reconquer Tunis, he secretly assembled an armada of four hundred ships and an army of thirty thousand from all parts of his empire.* He himself would lead the hosts of Christendom to strike a decisive blow against the infidel. Tunis would be his holy crusade to show the world he was its righteous ruler.[18]

---

* Approximately 10,000 from Spain, 6,000 Italians, 7,000 Germans, 5,000 Genoese, and 1,000 Knights of Malta.

On June 10, 1535, as the imperial fleet was about to embark, Charles addressed the assembled nobles. Unfurling a banner of the crucified Christ, he pointed to the savior, exclaiming: "He is your captain-general! I am but his standard-bearer."[19] Five days later, the fleet anchored at the entrance to the captured port.

Having known of Charles's intentions, Barbarossa likewise preached a holy war, and recruited several thousand mujahideen (Muslim warriors) to battle the crusaders. With spies keeping him current, Barbarossa fortified the fort at the entrance to the port, named La Goletta (the throat) because "it held Tunis by the throat." Barbarossa had assigned its defense to Sinan and five thousand of his best men.

On June 15, 1535, the cannons of seventy ships bombarded the fort's twin towers. For twenty-four days, Sinan and the defenders held out. Three times Sinan sallied forth to engage the attackers, but the odds were overwhelming and his sorties were repulsed. Finally, the fortress walls were breached by the relentless pounding of forty-pound iron balls fired from the Knights of Malta's eight-decked galleon, the largest fighting vessel then in existence. Spanish, German, and Italian forces poured into the fort. Sinan, forced to evacuate, crossed the bay to the city with the remnant of his men. With the fort's capture, Charles had seized control of the bay and with it Barbarossa's eighty-seven galleys.

Barbarossa knew he was beaten, but was still determined to give the Christians a blow they would not soon forget. The next day, as Charles gathered his army for a final assault, an enraged Barbarossa told Sinan he had decided to slaughter the twenty thousand Christian slaves packed in the city's underground dungeons. Sinan dissuaded him: "To stain ourselves with so awful a massacre," he told his commander, "would place us outside the pale of humanity forever."[20] Human compassion aside, it made no sense to destroy one's property before the battle was joined. Besides, he added, slaughtering so many prisoners would take too much time. His logic was persuasive, but as things turned out, sparing their lives proved the defenders' undoing. Defecting Moors, looking to curry favor if the Spanish assault succeeded, freed the prisoners. Once released, the slaves raided the city arsenal, overpowered the guards, and threw open the gates.

Charles's forces stormed in. For a day the battle raged. Charles, on a gallop around the city, had his horse shot from under him. Charles, known for his courage and cool composure, smiled when his men entreated him to take shelter from the barrage of bullets, and said: "An Emperor was never yet known to be shot."[21] So it was with Barbarossa, who reportedly killed dozens of men "with the keen blade of his scimitar." But the issue was never in doubt. Sensing that all was lost, Sinan and Barbarossa mounted their camels and, with four thousand men, escaped to the desert to fight another day.

On July 21, Charles's victorious army swept through the city. For three days, his righteous crusaders looted Tunis and massacred its citizens. An estimated seventy thousand people were killed and forty thousand taken captive. The carnage was called the worst of the century by Catholic chroniclers who wrote of the shameful affair, for the victims were not Barbarossa's men but the innocent people of Tunis who a year before had been the Christians' allies. Only when the crusaders and freed Christian slaves began killing one another in a fight over the spoils did the assault end. Jews were not exempted from this bloodshed of murder and looting. As one noted, "The Jews had no savior on the day of the Lord's wrath." Those not "smitten with the edge of the sword when the uncircumcised came to the city" were taken captive and held for ransom, while those who escaped into the desert were left destitute when the Muslims "plundered everything they brought with them."[22]

To memorialize his victory, Charles had brought along a poet and historian to record his victory, and a court painter whose mural of Sinan's force unsuccessfully counterattacking was made into a tapestry that hangs today in a Vienna museum.

On their return home, the twenty thousand rescued Christians sang their emperor's praise, hailing him as the knight-errant who had vanquished the scourge of Christendom. His reputation as defender of the faith was enhanced when the new pope approved his demand that an Inquisition commence in Portugal. Charles had been pushing for this, though not for any sanctimonious religious reason. Rather, the conversos in Portugal had accumulated wealth that Spanish conversos had transferred to them for safekeeping, thereby bleeding Spain's riches. To rein in the conversos' power, he called on Portugal's King John to threaten them with the holy fire. The concerted action of the two monarchs brought about a further exodus of conversos from both nations.

King John went along with Charles, but did so reluctantly. Though the two were close—John's sister Isabella was happily wed to Charles—Portugal's king could ill afford to bar these talented people from his empire. He sought their advice for most endeavors he undertook; moreover, he was heavily in debt. Conversos had loaned him 500,000 ducats and he knew they were good for more. Just as Spain's New Christians rose to influential positions denied them as Jews, so too had Portugal's Jews. From the time they were forcibly converted in 1497, as New Christians they had married into the best families and filled the highest offices of state. Portugal's nearly 100,000 conversos represented 10 percent of King John's citizenry. Despite their elevated status, the general populace did not trust them. Having rejected conversion in Spain, it was not likely that a forced baptism had truly altered their beliefs. From infidels outside the church they were now seen as heretics within.

By the mid-1530s, Charles had come around to the view that while many Spanish conversos only pretended to be Christian, they were neither numerous nor powerful enough to threaten him. He appreciated their ability to stimulate commerce and thereby increase the cash flow to his treasury, which by March 1536 was nearly empty. His adviser Corbos cautioned him that he was "on the verge of bankruptcy."[23] Thus, in line with his laissez-faire attitude to their presence both in Jamaica and elsewhere in the New World, he directed the magistrates of Antwerp, northern Europe's trading capital, to grant Spanish conversos full settlement rights, and solved the problem of Jamaica by giving the island away.

Although little is known about the Portugals Charles sent to Jamaica, apparently there was trouble right away, because at the same time Charles was recruiting his crusading army, he hurriedly dispatched an abbot to the island to keep an eye on religious matters. In March 1535, Father Amador de Samano arrived in Jamaica. He had gone ahead on the king's orders before being accredited by the pope. Unable to produce papers from Rome, he was not recognized by Jamaica's governor, who "used many disrespectful words unto him and other things worthy of censure and punishment." When Charles was notified that his governor had acted "in disservice of God and in disrespect of our royal decrees," he ordered him to "purge his offence before the Royal Audiencia* in Santo Domingo."[24]

For Charles, Jamaica's rejection of his abbot was a final straw. Years before, he had allocated money for a Jamaican church that was still being built and a hospital that never was. He received samples of gold ore, but not much more. His two haciendas and their livestock were valued at five thousand pesos, and though he also had two sugar mills, the only profit he made was selling produce to the starving settlers. Even then he had to loan them money to buy the goods, and if they didn't pay, threaten to sell the produce to his other colonies.

Jamaica was a losing proposition, and the governors he sent there were no better. Each accused his predecessor of diverting funds and selling off the king's acreage "as their own private property." It had been ten years since a plague of smallpox wiped out most of Jamaica's Indians and the island's more ambitious settlers left to seek their fortunes elsewhere. The allure to leave in 1536 was even more compelling as word spread that the search for El Dorado was on, with three conquistadors climbing over mountains in a competitive race to find the haunt of "the Golden One," the Indian king bathed in gold dust. Between the island's Portuguese, whom he needed but didn't trust, and the lazy Spaniards who remained, Charles was convinced that he wasn't going to realize much of a profit from Jamaica. The island, he concluded, would be good only as a trading post, a way station for ships en route to and from the New World.

---

* A court of judges with jurisdiction over Spain's New World colonies.

The answer he settled on was to deed Jamaica to the Columbus kin. Since the summer of 1536, Charles had been negotiating with Diego Colón's widow, María de Toledo, to settle a lawsuit she brought to recover Columbus's rights of discovery on behalf of his grandson, her eight-year-old son, Luis Colón. In January 1537, she agreed to drop the suit in return for Jamaica. Charles did not question why Doña María wanted Jamaica; he was glad to get rid of it. But when he drafted the agreement to relinquish the troubled colony, she rejected it because it did not include power over the Church.

After a month's stalemate he reluctantly gave in.[25] This provision—subordinating the Jamaican church to the Columbus family—was unprecedented. For the next century, the family kept Jamaica, alone in the Spanish Empire, out of bounds to the Inquisition. Doña Maria's decision was critical to the Portugals with whom she worked closely to develop the island's trade. Like the court Jews who counseled Columbus on the issue of hereditary rights, Jamaica's Portugals would have encouraged her to hold firm to this demand.

Unfortunately, the absence of an Inquisition in Jamaica also means there is almost a complete absence of information about these Portugals who opted for New World adventure over Old World connections. While most conversos fled east or settled around the Mediterranean, these Portugals chose Jamaica, an island in a new sea. Rather than reside in restrictive exile communities under the watchful eye of another ruler, they opted for the unknown. In these peak years of discovery and conquest, they looked to a New World where each man could be his own ruler and had the same hot blood for adventure that surged through all who came.

In February 1537, Charles formally ceded Jamaica to the

Columbus family.[26] It would still be a part of the Spanish realm and the family could not erect forts without Crown permission or pursue an independent foreign policy. Except for these stipulations, Jamaica, and "all the mines of gold" therein, were now the personal estate of the Columbus family whose heirs would bear the title Marquis de la Vega.* After the matter was settled, Pedro de Manzuelo, royal treasurer of Jamaica, wrote the king. He had "heard that His majesty had bestowed the island of Jamaica on the Admiral" and cautioned:

> This will be a loss to the Crown because Jamaica is another Sicily in Italy, for it provides all the neighboring countries as well as the Main and New Spain and is the centre of them all. If times should change . . . whoever is Lord of Jamaica will be Lord of these places on account of its situation . . . His Majesty should on no account part with it.[27]

Over time, the remaining Spanish colonists in New Seville joined the Portugals in La Vega. However, with ownership vested in the discoverer's family, few Spaniards were interested in settling what came to be called Columbus's island. Those already there were mostly ranchers, raising horses, cattle, and pigs. By midcentury, their power was at a low point, while the Portugals, who were mostly engaged in trade, prospered, in part by supplying passing conquistadors with horses and provisions.

Although the hidalgos were often in conflict with the Portugals, a century would pass before accusations of Judaizing

---

* The wording of the title perhaps signifies the guardian role of the Columbus heirs over the Portugals and their founding of Villa de la Vega in 1534.

surfaced. Apparently they maintained a Christian façade, attended church, and had their children baptized. Probably they adhered to some of the same practices as the secret Jews in Mexico and other Spanish colonies, who gathered in secret on certain nights to read from the Torah. They fasted twice a week for their apostasy, adored Purim's Queen Esther as a covert Jew like themselves, and viewed Haman as the Grand Inquisitor.

Meanwhile, back in the Mediterranean, Charles's nemesis Sinan, who never hid behind a Christian mask, continued the marauding that would seal Suleiman's power in the eastern Mediterranean. In 1538, the Jewish corsair destroyed most of Spain's naval fleet off the port of Preveza in Greece, and the following year he blockaded the Gulf of Cattaro on the Dalmatian coast and forced the surrender of the last Spanish garrison. These defeats for Charles, coupled with the death in childbirth in 1539 of his beloved wife, Isabella, plunged the emperor into a despair that was only dispelled by aggressive action against false conversos and planning a renewed war against the infidel.

Charles's motive when he allowed Spain's conversos to settle in Antwerp in 1536 was purely mercenary. What they believed didn't concern him. But this attitude changed when King John followed suit, and soon Portugal's conversos were outperforming those from Spain in the burgeoning East Indian spice trade, netting Portugal's king nearly a million ducats a year.[28] Accordingly, Charles reversed the policy. Knowing that Portugal's Jews, having been forcibly converted, were more likely to Judaize, in 1540 he ordered Antwerp's bailiff "to proceed with utmost severity" against suspect conversos.[29]

Charles next turned his attention to capturing Algiers, the Ottoman outpost closest to Spain. As he had taken Tunis, so he would conquer the sultan's primary stronghold in his sector of the Mediterranean. In the fall of 1541, Charles advanced on Algiers with a force of fifty warships, two hundred support vessels, and an army of nearly twenty thousand. As the port was lightly defended by a garrison of four thousand men, he had good reason to be confident.

But on the night of October 23, as his army was disembarking on a beach near Algiers, thunderous black clouds out of the northeast darkened the landing site and burst upon them. For three days, an unceasing storm and gale-force winds wracked the invaders. Fourteen warships were dashed against the rocks and a hundred transport vessels destroyed, with the loss of eight thousand men. Those who made it ashore were stuck in a muddy quagmire. At the end of the tempest, Moorish horsemen charged down from the hills, their swords flaying the imperial troops. Charles, soaked to the skin, with sword in hand, tried to rally his men, but considering the situation, ordered his army to re-embark. When the fleet regrouped fifteen miles down the coast, the conqueror of Mexico, Hernando Cortés, whom Charles had invited along, advised a counterattack. But the emperor, his troops dispirited, exhausted, and ill-equipped, reluctantly ended the expedition, blaming its failure on the weather. During the invasion, the two thousand Jews of Algiers, knowing the fate that had befallen their brethren in Tunis, lived in great fear. Afterward, in commemoration of the three days when the heavens opened up in their defense, they instituted a special holiday with three days of fasting and celebration.[30]

In 1544, a year after his Algiers disaster, Charles left Spain for Flanders and did not return until 1556. As Charles departed in sadness, Sinan rejoiced. The Jewish corsair was at the Red Sea port of Suez that year, building a fleet to support an Indian prince's effort to evict the Portuguese, when he got word that Barbarossa had rescued Sinan's kidnapped son. Five years before, the boy had been taken by imperial forces on his way to rejoin his father after Sinan's latest victory. He was eventually delivered to the Lord of Elba, who baptized the child and raised him at court. Several times Barbarossa tried to ransom the boy without success. Finally in 1544, when sailing near Elba, he sent an envoy to bargain for the youth's return, only to be told that the ruler's "religious scruples forbade him to surrender a baptized Christian to an infidel." A furious Barbarossa landed his men, sacked the town of Piombino, and blew up the fort. At this point the Lord of Elba agreed to surrender his "boy-favorite."[31]

In 1551, after a stint as governor of Algiers, Sinan, now Kaptan Pasha, commander of the Turkish navy, captured Tripoli. Occupying the port, he imprisoned the Knights of Malta, who had moved there from their island. After first hauling them back to Constantinople and parading them in chains before the sultan, Sinan—gracious in victory in contrast to Charles's crusaders at Tunis—set the humbled knights free.

In May 1553, in his final recorded action, Sinan sailed down the Dardanelles from Gallipoli with 150 ships, including twenty French galleys, and ravaged the coastal districts of southern Italy and Sicily. Before returning to Constantinople, he landed on Corsica at the behest of the king of France and expelled the Genoese. That is the last we hear of "the famous Jewish pirate," noted for his humane treatment of prisoners and his magical powers. His untutored crew bragged that he needed no more than a crossbow to find the height of the stars to determine their position at sea. (In truth, his crossbow was a "Jacob's staff," an early form of sextant.)

Charles's final years were not as fortunate. In 1556, the pressures of the job drove him to abdicate in favor of his son Philip II, give half his empire to his brother Ferdinand, and retire to a monastery.[32] The Venetian ambassador wrote that he was "not greedy of territory, but most greedy of peace and quiet."[33] Yet war was his constant affair and he was utterly worn out by it. In the company of monks, the emperor spent the last two years of his life fishing for trout from a tower window over a rushing stream and trying to synchronize his sizeable collection of 159 clocks. He is said to have exclaimed after giving up in vain: "How foolish I have been to think I could make all men believe alike about religion or unite all my dominions when I cannot even make these clocks strike the hour together?"[34]

In September 1558, after a long illness and tormented by the gout that left him an invalid, Charles cried, "Oh Lord, I go," and died. Sinan, who had always been a thorn in his side, also died that year. His tombstone at Istanbul's Scutari cemetery reads in part:

> Towards his friends, Sinan was another Joseph; his enemies dreaded him like a dart. Let us pray to Heaven for Sinan; may God cause his soul to rejoice . . . The Kaptan Pasha has entered the realm of Divine Mercy.[35]

An assessment of Charles's reign has to conclude that he overreached and overspent. The empire was too big, his enemies and the forces against him too powerful. The tides of history were not in his favor. Spain had stopped producing. Relying on gold and silver from the New World to import most everything doubled the prices of goods. Europe thereby profited, while Spain's treasury by the time he abdicated was 20 million ducats in debt.

Moreover, Luther's translation of the Bible into German in 1534 proved a capstone to Protestants. Although they would be fiercely opposed by the Society of Jesus, founded that same year, whose members saw themselves as soldiers of God and whose Counter-Reformation was supported by Charles, there was no stopping the heretical sect that spread like plague through his empire. Even Charles's vaunted prestige as conqueror of Tunis dissipated when the son of his vassal there dethroned (and blinded) his father and thereafter favored the Turks; at La Goletta as well, his Spanish commander wound up renouncing his faith and became a Muslim.

Charles could not hold back the winds of change. He resented that his enemies made a point of aiding and abetting Sephardim, whom he saw as *his* heretics. By midcentury, France's new king, Henry II, allowed "Portuguese merchants" known as "New Christians" to settle at Bordeaux and Bayonne, two ports on the Atlantic just north of Spain enriched by peninsula trade, while in Constantinople an estimated fifty thousand Sephardim contributed their talents to his rival empire. In 1551, a Spanish visitor to Turkey cursed the Portuguese Jews' rearming of the military:

Would that it had pleased God that they had drowned in the sea in coming hither! For they taught our enemies the villainies of war such as how to make harquebusiers, gunpowder, cannonballs, brass ordnance and firelocks.[36]

As they had in the Mediterranean during Charles's reign, Sephardim would come to dominate Caribbean commerce and the flow of wealth. The discovery of the Americas and the establishment of new sea routes to the East placed world trade within the ambit of Sephardim resettled throughout the known world. By midcentury, the land routes of the Middle Ages had given way to ocean highways. In Jamaica, before her death in 1549, Doña María worked with converso merchants to transform a nonperforming colony into a major transshipment port, a natural development (albeit illegal) for an island astride Spain's trade routes to and from the New World.

Although Charles eventually expelled all New Christians from Antwerp, he continued to abide their presence in the New World. His son Philip II likewise found it in his fiscal interest to turn a blind eye to converso merchants and administrators and knowingly licensed New Christians to serve there as crown treasurers, notaries, and judges. As long as they genuflected to Jesus, no one questioned their faith. However, once they had established the lucrative commercial routes that directed all trade through Seville and Lisbon, they were expendable. When their presence was no longer needed, Old Catholic "purebloods" wanted in. Their means was the Inquisition.

The union of Spain and Portugal in 1580 brought with it a resurgence of Inquisition activity. In the last decade of the sixteenth century, as the Holy Terror descended on the New World, covert Jews began to look to Europe's other powers to provide a haven outside the reach of the Grand Inquisitor. They would find one in the Low Countries on Europe's northeast coast, in a corner of the empire battling for liberty, in revolt from Spain.

Chapter Four

SAMUEL PALACHE,
THE PIRATE RABBI

In Morocco, ancestral home of the Moors, a youth named Samuel Palache came of age around the time that Sinan was ending his life. Although the boy was raised in the *mellah,* the Jewish ghetto of Fez, and never met "the famous Jewish pirate," he knew of his exploits and emulated his deeds—with one defining difference: Samuel's swashbuckling career was supplemented by a religious one as a rabbi. Samuel thus followed his father and uncle in carrying on a centuries-old family tradition.[1]

Jews lived in Morocco centuries before the Arabs conquered the native Berber tribes in the seventh century and introduced Islam. When Fez was founded as the Arab capital in the ninth century, the city's Jews prospered as moneylenders and dealers in precious metals, professions the followers of Mohammed avoided. In 1428, in light of Muslim riots over allegations that Jews had placed wine in the mosques, the sultan confined them to the *mellah,* a gated area near the palace.

When Samuel was growing up, the walled ghetto, swelled by new arrivals from Spain, rivaled Constantinople as a Jewish haven. An estimated fifty thousand Jews crowded the narrow streets lined with shops, stalls, and tall buildings with apartment-like quarters. The wealthy lived apart, in luxurious homes of Moorish design bordering the palace gardens. The *mellah* became a renowned center of Jewish life. Its many synagogues and religious schools were a magnet for Talmudic scholars who came from all over the Mediterranean to discuss and debate the commentaries of Rashi and North Africa's celebrated seer Maimonides.

Within the confines of the *mellah,* Israelites lived free, but outside, in the city proper and in the grand bazaar where they sold their wares, they faced a familiar hostility. A Spanish visitor noted this dichotomy:

> [Inside the *mellah*] Jews have a sort of governor who administers justice and delivers their tributes to the king. They pay taxes on everything and are left undisturbed . . . Outside they are greatly despised and made to wear a black cloth on their heads and a piece of colored cloth on their clothing [to make] them known to the Moors . . . Wherever they go, Moors spit in their faces and beat them . . . If any becomes wealthy and the king manages to find out he takes their riches away. But they are so hard-working and know so much about business they commonly administer the estates of Moorish gentlemen [who] do not hold trading in much esteem, nor understand as do the Jews the little details and

subtleties, so each one endeavors to have a Jew as his majordomo to govern his estate. In this way the Jews enrich themselves greatly.[2]

Like the Catholic clergy, the mullahs castigated financiers as parasitic usurers and forbade their followers from engaging in such matters. The vagaries of finance were thus left to the Jews, who minted coins, collected taxes, loaned capital, and backed proven ventures like the marauding voyages of the corsairs.

Samuel and his younger brother Joseph, from the time they were four, attended religious school with other boys in the *mellah*. Their father was the school rabbi, and his watchful presence weighed heavily on the brothers as they studied Torah and Talmud. The boys were fluent in many languages. They spoke Spanish at home, were conversant in Arabic and Portuguese, and learned Hebrew and Chaldean at school. Because their family's rabbinical lineage stretched back six centuries, Judaism in all its aspects was inculcated in them and permeated nearly everything they did. The sporadic visits of a roving uncle, an itinerant preacher who roamed the Mediterranean exhorting the faithful, sparked in them a desire to venture beyond the *mellah*.[3]

Judaism and piracy were dominant influences that shaped the brothers' lives after they left the cloistered ghetto behind. For derring-do and profit they turned to piracy, especially targeting enemies of their people, and parlayed that success with other activities that would one day gain Jews a haven in Amsterdam, which would become known in the Diaspora as New Jerusalem.[4]

In the last decades of the sixteenth century, Morocco's sultan, although officially at peace with Spain, did not rein in his corsairs. The Palache brothers were then living in the *mellah* of Tetuán, a pirate port astride the Strait of Gibraltar. Although the gates of the Jewish quarter were locked at night, the brothers' reputation as merchant pirates allowed them to go and come at will. It was said by their compatriots that after a successful cruise the brothers would brazenly enter Spanish ports pretending to be innocent traders and boldly seek out buyers for their repackaged booty.[5]

In 1602, their audacious conduct reached the ear of the sultan. Sensing they had the requisite skills to deal with his traditional enemy Spain, he sent them to Lisbon as his trade representatives to broker a deal for jewels in exchange for the beeswax needed to make candles and seals. To enter the forbidden peninsula, the brothers required an entry permit from the Duke of Medina Sidonia, the ruler of Melilla, the Spanish outpost in Morocco.

Conferring with him, the brothers intimated that they had more to offer than a few tons of beeswax. In approving their passage, the duke wrote his sovereign, Philip III, that they had intelligence concerning Morocco and recommended that he meet with them. However, when the brothers arrived in Madrid in January 1603, Philip, having been warned by a counselor that they were *maestros dogmatizadores* (dogmatizing tutors) out to win back conversos, declined to meet with them: "They will do much harm among those of their nation," he wrote the duke, "as experience has taught us."[6]

Their sponsoring duke thought otherwise. That was not their intention, he wrote. Had he known what Samuel, the older brother, intended when he left Spain in 1603 and journeyed to the Netherlands, he would not have been so quick to dismiss the king's suspicions.

In the fall of 1605, the brothers were back in Spain, seeking Philip's permission to settle there. In exchange, they promised to divulge a secret plan to halt the Ottoman advance along the North Africa coast, which, if unchecked, would soon have the Turks at Spain's doorstep across the narrow divide of Gibraltar. The brother's scheme entailed the capture of Larache, Morocco's strategic port southwest of Tangiers. Its possession had become important the previous year when the sultan had died and his son, Muley Sidan, assumed the throne. However, the Duke of Medina Sidonia now suspected Samuel was a double agent. When the king asked him if Palache was to be trusted in "finding things out about Barbary," the duke was blunt in his reply: "His business is all trickery."[7] Philip's adviser seconded the duke's judgment, saying: "It would be good to stop the Jew from deluding himself," and recommended he "be given something to get rid of him."[8]

But Samuel was not easily dissuaded. Persuasively loquacious, over the next two years he won over other influential Spaniards to endorse his petition for domicile. In March 1607, his persistence got him again invited to the palace for an audience with Philip. Again he promised to divulge intelligence on the Barbary States and spoke of his family's deep desire to convert to the True Faith so as to better serve "Our Lord and Your Majesty."[9] Whatever doubts the king had were swept aside by Samuel's effusive spiel, and he gave the pandering Jew a royal *cédula* (license) to go to Morocco to collect his family.

How this might have turned out is not known because agents of the dreaded Inquisition were suddenly on the brothers' trail. Had their bravado and haughty disdain for Spanish authority let out that their intended conversion was a sham? Did a rival Jew seeking royal patronage alert the Holy Fathers? No answer was forthcoming, but when the brothers learned that the Inquisitors were after them, they took refuge in the Madrid home of the French ambassador, Count de Barrault. The count knew their professed loyalty to Spain was feigned because they had earlier approached him with an offer to share (for a price) Spanish intelligence with his monarch, Henry IV.

Over the summer and into the fall of 1607, while the brothers were safely ensconced in the diplomat's home, in the nearby Plaza Mayor, dozens of suspected Judaizers were paraded half-naked to be tried and sentenced in successive autos-da-fé. In September, when the opportunity arose to flee Spain, Samuel wrote Philip a farewell letter denying any wrongdoing and vowing continued fealty: "Wherever we may happen to be, we are and shall be servants of Your Majesty. May God increase your life and estate."[10]

That said, he turned his back on Spain and the following spring (April 1608) was in Amsterdam conferring with Prince Maurice of Nassau on a grand scheme to combat Spain. Samuel shared with him an idea he had meditated upon during his confinement, namely that Holland and Morocco should form an alliance. Since both peoples, Calvinists and Muslims, were viewed as heretics by Spain, it was natural that these nations should ally against their common enemy. Sultan Sidan and his father had fought Spain most of their lives, as had Holland's Prince Maurice and his father, William of Orange. As Dutch privateers, known as Sea Beggars, defeated Spanish attempts to crush their rebellion and funded the war with plunder, so too had Morocco's corsairs crippled Spanish shipping.

Maurice was receptive to the proposal, and Samuel left for

Morocco to present it to Sidan. The treaty came about as Samuel proposed. But for a clearer understanding of what follows, a digression is necessary to account for the prince's trust in Samuel and what lay behind the Jew's mendacious dealings with Spain. Before he went to Spain with the beeswax, Samuel was a familiar figure in Dutch ports, and it was his actions then that made the Statholder credit his intent in this new venture.

In 1579, when the rest of Europe was still a dangerous place for Jews, Prince Maurice's father lit a lamp of political and religious liberty when he unilaterally declared his nation's independence from Spain. Assembling the six other leaders of the northern provinces, they agreed in the Union of Utrecht to support his war effort and affirm "freedom of conscience" as a founding principle of the United Netherlands.[11]

The following year, Spain annexed Portugal, thereby uniting the lands of the Inquisition, and suspect New Christians became the object of a renewed purge. Tribunals of the Inquisition, operating in Portugal's three major cities, convicted thousands of Judaizers.

In 1591, Samuel decided to test the Netherlands' promise of religious freedom. He established residence in Middleburg, the prosperous capital of Zeeland, and petitioned the city fathers to allow further Sephardic settlement. In return, he promised they would "develop the city into a flourishing commercial center by means of their wealth." The magistrates initially favored his petition but the intolerant attitude of the Calvinist clergy prevented them from granting it.[12] Seven years later in Amsterdam, a similar situation occurred. The burgomasters of the City Council, who had power "next to God and the Prince,"[13] agreed to grant conversos admittance, but when the local clergy objected, they backed off, adding the proviso, "confiding they are sincere Christians."[14]

So it was that the first conversos who followed Samuel to Holland found that it was one thing for a nation to declare religious toleration and another for that nation to practice it. Although the newcomers no longer had to fear the Inquisition, any public display of their faith was deemed illegal and, as on the peninsula, they had to Judaize in secret. It was because of that clandestine need that their observance of the Day of Atonement in 1603 has been preserved in police record books as the first Jewish service in Holland.

As we have seen, this was the year the Palache brothers and their beeswax were turned back from Spain. Samuel thereupon proceeded to Amsterdam, having moved there after his failure in Middleburg. What happened next lends credence to the charges of chicanery made by their Spanish foes. With Passover approaching, Samuel invited the covert community to hold services in his home. The holiday that year began on Sunday evening, a time when Roman Catholics attended their devotions. Samuel's Calvinist neighbors were thus suspicious when they noticed Spanish-speaking men entering his home. Believing they were a group of Catholics holding secret Easter services, they alerted the authorities.

Without warning, the police burst in on the frightened assembly, who surmised that the Inquisition had somehow uncovered them. Their attempt to flee only made their guilt more certain in the eyes of the police. Sixteen men and a number of women were arrested. Samuel tried to explain to the authorities in all the languages he knew but he was not understood. However, the congregants' leader, Jacob Triado, who knew a little Latin, was able to convince the officers that while they all had Spanish names, they were not idolatrous papists. Rather, they were Jews who had fled the lands of the Inquisition, where their people were persecuted even more than Calvinists. Thus the incident was peacefully resolved. Henceforth the authorities looked the other way as Jews congregated in one another's homes for services. As long as they did not parade their religion in public, their presence was tolerated.

The early community, numbering about fifty merchant families, represented the elite of Iberian Jewry, whose forebears, rather than leave their ancestral home, had converted but continued to follow the Laws of Moses. When the émigrés left the peninsula, they took with them investment capital from conversos who stayed behind. Each community served as the other's agent. Thus the riches of the New World, via Lisbon and Seville, followed them to Amsterdam.

So the matter stood six years later in 1609, when Prince Maurice, who was undoubtedly familiar with the machinations of Samuel, approved the proposed alliance with Morocco. Samuel then engaged in shuttle diplomacy between the two countries, first to Morocco to deliver the prince's endorsement of the proposal, then back to Holland with the sultan's letter confirming Palache as "our servant and agent" and authorizing him to negotiate the treaty.[15] He then returned to Morocco, this time leading three warships loaded with munitions that the prince had agreed to loan the sultan for his ongoing fight against his brother who, backed by Spain, was trying to usurp him. When Samuel reached Morocco, a Spanish agent in the sultan's court sent a hurriedly worded dispatch to King Philip, noting that along with the ships

> [Palache] brought 1000 lances, 1000 *alfanjas* [short, curved sabers] 600 guns and a gift of weapons from Count Maurice [whereupon] Sidan ordered them to go with the ships to the coast of Spain to make a fine capture of Spanish ships. Sidan fancied that in a short time he would be the lord and master of many ships and that the world would become too small for his conquests, for they (Samuel and the Dutch ambassador who had accompanied him) had filled his head with airy notions.[16]

Sidan's "airy notions" were quickly deflated. The borrowed ships had barely left Moroccan waters when, according to the agent, "the galleons of Spain came and sank them." Samuel and the Dutch ambassador escaped, but among documents found in Samuel's cabin was one that stipulated the expedition was to attack Spanish shipping.[17] Spain and the Netherlands were then at peace, having agreed in 1609 to a twelve-year truce. In righteous anger, Philip wrote Prince Maurice protesting this blatant violation. The prince, pleading ignorance, wrote back that he had loaned the ships to Morocco and should not be held accountable for their misuse. Philip was not mollified by this flimsy excuse and issued a stern warning that Spain would not tolerate the buildup of a Moroccan navy of Dutch origin.

In January 1611, Samuel's proposed treaty between Calvinist Holland and Muslim Morocco was signed by Prince Maurice, with Samuel signing for Sultan Sidan. Holland's governing body, the States General, thereupon awarded Samuel a gold chain, a gold medal, and six hundred florins, and his nephew Moses (Joseph's eldest son) was honored with a gold medal for serving as interpreter. When Samuel delivered the signed treaty to Sidan, a grateful sultan awarded him "the monopoly of trade with the Netherlands."[18]

In the spring, Samuel returned to Amsterdam with diamonds and rubies to exchange for Dutch arms, and an ambitious proposal from Sidan to test the new pact. According to the Spanish ambassador's letter to his king, Samuel asked for eight ships and two thousand harquebusiers (riflemen) to join a "company of *moriscos* banished from Spain." Together they would sail under Samuel's command and raid "the coast of Malaga where they are bound to make off with many captives and much wealth."[19]

Maurice was to supply the ships for a percentage of the booty. However, mindful of Philip's previous warning, he did not want to jeopardize the truce with Spain that had virtually established the independence of the Netherlands. Unwilling to get involved in what he considered Sidan's personal vendetta, but not wanting to offend his new ally, the prince granted Samuel permission to organize a pirate fleet to carry out the mission. Samuel thereupon recruited Dutch Sea Beggars to join his Barbary Corsairs and placed his younger brother Joseph in command.

So it was that in the summer of 1611, a Dutch flotilla, flying the flag of Morocco and led by a Jew, sailed for the Mediterranean. The result of this expedition is not reported. But in the wake left by Sinan, once more the sea became the arena for a Jewish pirate to assail Spanish ships.[20]

As a fillip to the Holland-Morocco treaty, Jacob Triado's group, known for its leader as Beth Jacob (the House of Jacob), no longer hid their observance, and in 1612 Holland's first synagogue, called Neveh Shalom (the Abode of Peace), opened in Amsterdam. Samuel, now addressed as "Rabbi," was elected its president.[21]

Unfortunately, there is no known portrait of Samuel Palache. If his looks bore any relation to his character, he was a giant—merchant, pirate, conspirator, rabbi, ambassador, and founder of Amsterdam's Jewish community. While his Christian neighbors addressed him as "Don Samuel," and his wife, Malica, as "Reina" (Queen), within the Jewish community he was called "Rabbi." Though often absent from Neveh Shalom, he bore his title proudly and it is inscribed on his tombstone.[22] Sailing to and fro between Holland and Morocco, a fifty-day sail each way, he engaged in a brisk arms trade, selling gunpowder, muskets, and other munitions to the corsairs in return for sugar, spices, diamonds, and Spanish booty.

Age neither lessened Samuel's ardor nor slowed him down. In the fall of 1613, Rabbi Palache was in his seventh decade when he informed synagogue elders that he was again taking leave to lead a pirate crew to seize Spanish ships. In October, at the urging of Prince Maurice, the States General granted him a commission and a loan of five thousand florins to equip "a voyage to Barbary."[23] The onset of winter delayed his departure until the following spring. In March, "by strike of drum," he recruited his crew, and appointing himself "general," selected two Dutchmen to captain his ships—an English warship and a locally built *jaght* (yacht). In deference to the Spanish truce, the States General identified Palache as Sidan's agent, averring that his expedition was to combat pirates off the coast of Morocco. However, given that his crew, as one later testified, was "mainly made up of former pirates, as the general knew full well," it is not likely that anyone believed he intended to fight other pirates.[24]

From Amsterdam, Samuel sailed to Morocco to consult with Sidan, now finally secure on his throne and thirsty for vengeance. The murder of his rebellious brother (by a former supporter) had ended Spain's support for his overthrow, and enabled Sidan to redeploy his army to defeat an uprising of radical Islamists who wanted to rid the nation of Jews and otherwise "restore the pristine purity of Islam."[25] With an eye to exacting payment from King Philip for having backed his brother, Sidan issued Samuel a privateer's license with specific instructions to "harm the Spaniards and make war on them."[26]

Samuel, having had the foresight to obtain a safe-conduct pass from England, sallied forth on a mission that united the three foes of Spain—the Dutch, the Moors, and the Jews. Carved on the bow of his ship was a phoenix, a mythical bird that lives a thousand years, is consumed by fire, and rises afresh from the ashes. It was his way of saying that Inquisition flames might burn individual Jews, but could not destroy their ancestral faith.[27] It is interesting to note that Samuel's allegiance to the strictures of his faith included his diet, and he brought along a Jewish chef to prepare kosher meals.

The pirate rabbi captured a Portuguese caravel and a Spanish galleon returning from Santo Domingo with sugar and animal hides and sent them on to Holland. When their owners protested, the States General replied that Palache was sailing for Morocco and they were not responsible for the actions of a foreign privateer.[28]

In the fall of 1614, Palache was sailing back to Holland when he ran into a squall and had to land at Plymouth, England. When that nation's Spanish ambassador, Count Gondomar, was alerted to his presence, he immediately petitioned the Privy Council to bring an action against him for piracy. Palache, he argued, was a Christian and a Spanish subject who converted to Judaism and became a pirate: "[He] is guilty of piracy, spoil and outrage at sea upon vassals of the king, my lord, who has apostatized from the faith of Christ our Redeemer to become a Jew, then became a corsair as an ally of the Moors, and has captured two ships of the realm."[29]

On November 20, 1614, Samuel was arrested and so charged. Gondomar called for him to be hanged. When Prince Maurice received news of his arrest, he immediately wrote King James deriding the "sinister accusations made by the ambassador of the king of Spain. [Rather] the said Palache has done no more than follow the orders of the king of Barbary his lord, with whom the States General have a treaty of peace and alliance."[30]

Maurice's letter asked James to release Palache. James demurred, but rather than send Palache to the Tower of London, the king treated him as a quasi-royal visitor. Palache was placed under house arrest in the home of the Lord Mayor of London, Sir William Craven, and the two regularly supped together. Sir William even stood his bail and allowed him to travel freely about the city.[31]

Samuel's popularity with Londoners was matched by their

dislike of Count Gondomar. When Samuel's carriage actually collided with Gondomar's, leaving the fuming Spaniard stranded in the road, London's broadsheets reported that the "passersby considerably enjoyed themselves at the Ambassador's expense." Another time, as Gondomar was being carried in a litter near Convent Garden, a passerby shouted, "There goeth the Devil in a dung cart!" When Gondomar's servant confronted the Londoner, the man gave him "a box on the ear that struck up his heels."[32]

In defending himself before the Privy Council, Palache maintained that Morocco was at war with Spain and that he held a legitimate privateer's license, as well as a safe-conduct from England. The Dutch ambassador, Noel de Caron, testified in a long, roundabout speech that while it was well known that Palache was "a Jew and a Barbarian" (i.e., from Barbary), and did not warrant better treatment than "a dog," there was an overriding need to respect international law. As a licensed pirate, in service to a recognized sovereign, his action was legal and for reasons of state he should be released. A delegation of prominent English barristers also called for the charges to be dropped, citing the safe-conduct Palache had wisely obtained. The Privy Council agreed and dismissed the case. When Gondomar complained that it seemed the English favored Jews over fellow Christians, Caron replied there was a reason for this, as the Spaniards did not differentiate between Englishmen and Jews but burned both equally.[33]

On March 20, 1615, the pirate rabbi returned to a hero's welcome in Amsterdam. Palache would live only another ten months, but not one to rest on his laurels, his final year was the stuff of high drama. In August, the man of many coats donned another when he put into play a convoluted scheme that has historians today questioning his loyalty and faith. That month, Gondomar heard from the Spanish ambassador in Flanders that Palache had contacted him, promising to divulge intelligence that would serve Spain's interest. So skilled was Palache in the art of subterfuge that Gondomar, despite his stated abhorrence of "that damn Jew," recommended his recruitment. Negotiations followed. In November 1615, Samuel agreed to spy for Spain for two hundred escudos a month. Beyond conveying intelligence on Holland and Morocco's dealings with England, France, and Turkey, he promised to get Sidan to stop trading with those countries. King Philip himself signed the agreement, but obviously did so with reservation. Over the years, Palache had periodically briefed him on enemy plans, but as the king once confided to the Duke of Medina Sidonia, he always suspected Palache was "a double agent."[34]

In the agreement, there is a clause about "captive books" that may offer a clue to Samuel's apparent betrayal. The reference is to a library of four thousand books and manuscripts that Sidan inherited from his father, but never received. Instead they were captured en route by a Spanish pirate and taken to Spain. Sidan's offer of 100,000 ducats for their return was rejected by Spain's Council of State. Instead they demanded that he free all Spanish captives before they would even discuss the issue. This was untenable. King Philip then upped the stakes by donating the books to El Escorial monastery. After viewing the collection, Turkey's ambassador, when asked their worth, replied "infinite ducats."[35] The so-called captive books had become a major sore point dividing the two nations, and it is thought Samuel was in league with Sidan when, feigning disloyalty, he offered to spy for Spain, seeking the books as his reward. Nothing came of the spy pact, however. Shortly afterward, Samuel fell ill and spent the winter months bedridden in his Amsterdam home.

On February 6, 1616, the pirate rabbi died. Six mounted horses draped in black pulled the hearse. Prince Maurice and the city magistrates marched behind the bier, honoring the man and the community he led.[36] Next came the Jewish elders, heads covered and cloaked in black. Each and every one of the 1,200 men, women, and children of the nascent Jewish community also turned out. Among the marchers were Samuel's brother Joseph, who would succeed him as the sultan's agent, and Joseph's five sons, who continued their uncle's work in cementing relations between Morocco and Holland, and regularly used intrigue and double-dealing to further their aims. The new French ambassador in Madrid, Monsieur Descartes, concluded that the Palaches were always "cheating one side and the other for their own benefit."[37] One cannot fault his observation. But what Samuel and his family did "for their own benefit" likewise benefited their people.[38]

The funeral procession wound through the wealthy Jewish quarter to a bridge over the Amstel River, where the coffin was transferred to a flat-bottomed skiff and rowed with muffled oars to the new cemetery at Ouderkerk, five miles north. The community's youngsters ran along the riverbank following the barges that carried the mourners to the cemetery. It was the most impressive thing they had ever witnessed. To them, the rabbi was a hero who went out and captured enemy ships when he might have been home studying the Talmud. It is true that Samuel was often absent and his relationship with the boys can only be conjectured. But their later lives are indicative of his influence and the high esteem they held for him. Following his example, they never stopped fighting those who would persecute Jews. Before the century was out, they would succeed in winning their people's rights in a hostile world.

Chapter Five

AMSTERDAM, THE NEW
JERUSALEM

The date was January 16, 1605. Freezing winds blowing off the Atlantic did not deter the citizens of Lisbon from crowding the roadside to jeer the prisoners on their way to the plaza to be tried at the auto-da-fé. The victims, barefoot and naked to the waist, were whipped along the icy cobblestone streets by white-hooded guards of the Holy Brotherhood. On horseback, heading the procession, were the *familiars* (officials) of the Holy Office, wearing black tunics silhouetted with a white cross. Behind them, the 155 half-naked penitents stumbled along, six abreast, their backs lashed raw by the guards' studded whips. The Judaizers carried unlit candles to signify that the light of the True Faith had not yet illuminated their souls. Their punishment, known as *verguenza* (shame), was dealt them for having confessed and declared their desire to join the Church in earnest. Prisoners not admitting their guilt were tortured until they did, and those who remained unrepentant were liable to be burned. Age made no difference: Ten-year-old sisters were tortured, and a ninety-six-year-old woman burned at the stake.

For six successive Fridays, the 155 penitents were subjected to such a parade before being allowed to rejoin the Church. Then, having "seen the light," they could light their candles and "donate" a fifth of their possessions to the Church. Even then, they could not hold any honorable office or wear jewels or fine clothes. On this, their sixth and final Friday, the penitents were herded to the central plaza opposite the church, where two stages had been erected, one to hold the prisoners, the other for the Grand Inquisitor. One by one, they were called before him to receive their sentence. Only when led off the stage were they told that on this particular day their *verguenza* would end. The week before, King John had agreed to a bribe of two million ducats to forgive their offenses. On the day of the auto-da-fé, a "General Pardon for Crimes of Judaism" was to take effect. Portugal's other two tribunals in Oporto and Coimbra freed their 255 prisoners at first light, but Lisbon's Inquisitor, incensed at the pardon, held off until his Judaizers had experienced the parade of shame and been sentenced before setting them free. He then waited another month to inform and release those who had not confessed.[1]

Two penitents that day were Joseph Diaz Soeiro, who had been "thrice tortured by the Inquisition," and Antonio Vaez Henriques, one of Lisbon's principal merchants. It is not known if the two knew each other. The next we hear of them is in Amsterdam, where they fled during the pardon's one-year grace period. Finally free to live as Jews, they underwent circumcision* and dropped their baptismal names to signify their return to Judaism. Joseph Diaz Soeiro now called himself Joseph ben Israel, and Manuel, his two-year-old son, was renamed Menasseh (Menasseh was the biblical Joseph's first son). The merchant Antonio Vaez Henriques replaced Vaez with "Cohen" and, to celebrate his family's escape from bondage, changed four-year-old Antonio Jr.'s name to Moses. When his wife gave birth, soon after they arrived, he named his new son, born in freedom, Abraham.

Changing one's name was a common practice among conversos, both men and women, when they came out as Jews. The émigrés had taken upon themselves the burden of Jewish survival and adopted the names of biblical heroes and patriarchs. They called themselves Moses, Abraham, Jacob, Isaac, Joseph, Benjamin; their ships bore such names as *Prophet Samuel, Beautiful Sarah, Prophet Daniel, Queen Esther,* and *King Solomon.*[2]

Menasseh, Moses, Abraham, and the community's other young boys attended Neveh Shalom's religious school. Mornings were devoted to Torah studies and, from two until dusk, the Talmud. Their teacher explained the portion being studied and the boys repeated the lesson in singsong voice. They learned Hebrew at school and spoke Spanish and Portuguese at home, where they were also tutored in Dutch.

Menasseh, a gifted student, was the pride of the congregation. He was quoting Scripture and commentary at the age of seven, and was fluent in six languages by the time of his bar mitzvah. Some of his scholarly focus may have been due to squalid

---

* To avoid detection, many covert Jews were not circumcised until they arrived in Holland. Once there, if one died before being circumcised, it had to be done to his corpse if he was to be buried in the Jewish cemetery.

circumstances at home. His family lived in New Timber Market, a poor, marshy land, far from Houtgracht Canal Street, where the wealthier émigrés resided. The community paid for Menasseh's education and supported his indigent family, as the Inquisition had confiscated their possessions, and the tortures his father suffered left him disabled and unable to work.

In contrast to Menasseh's devotion, Moses Henriques and his friends were more interested in Rabbi Palache's spellbinding tales and the adventures of their elders. All the boys had to memorize the Talmud's 613 daily rules of living, but did not have to abide by them. On the Iberian Peninsula, their families had been cut off from Jewish writings, and their clandestine lives limited their observance to the basics they remembered. For generations, they had been Catholics without belief; now they were Jews without knowledge. The religion they were eager to embrace was foreign to them. As one writer observed, they were no longer Christians, but not yet Jews.[3]

Born and reared in the True Faith, the émigrés had learned that sin was forgiven by going to confession. This was not a part of Judaism. Rabbis, unlike priests, could not grant absolution, but it was comforting to believe they could. Many therefore found it convenient to believe that they might "yield to the impulses of their passions without endangering the salvation of their souls."[4] Polygamy, forbidden under Judaic law, was common, particularly among the North African Jews of Neveh Shalom, who made concubines out of their house servants. The legal status of a "natural child," born of such a union, was considered equal with the children of the first wife.

Initially, the Amsterdam community connived at this looseness, but after Samuel Palache's death, his sister's husband, Isaac Uziel, assumed the rabbinate and condemned what he saw as the evil habits of the community. From the Neveh Shalom pulpit, the new leader of the congregation, whose father had been the grand rabbi of Fez, raged against polygamy and preached that no one could buy indulgence for sins and vices by "mere observance." Lashing out at the most prominent members of the community, he incurred their hatred and soon fractured the congregation.[5]

By 1620, the two hundred or so Jewish families in Amsterdam had split into three synagogues of varying orthodoxy—Neveh Shalom, Beth Jacob, and Beth Israel. Finally free to be as orthodox as the Old Catholics they left behind, some were, while others couldn't be bothered. Many, having rejected the metaphysics of Catholicism, were content with a minimal observance; others were turned off by all religion. The same degree of adherence held true for their children.[6]

Despite religious differences, the entire community worked together in charitable organizations to support the poor and rescue brethren from the lands of idolatry (as Spain and Portugal were known). Decades later (in 1639), Samuel's nephew Jacob Palache persuaded the three factions to worship together in a building he bought and named Talmud Torah (Study of Law). In homage to Samuel Palache, the united congregation adopted his emblem, the phoenix, to represent Talmud Torah.[7]

"Michelangelo's Moses had horns; Rembrandt's does not" is how one historian described the artist's naturalist sketches of his Jewish neighbors and the Dutch everyday acceptance of the Jew in his midst.[8] The Dutch tolerated no bigotry when it came to making money. Calvinism was a businessman's religion—work defined who they were, profit was seen as a part of the scheme of salvation, and prosperity was a sure sign of God's favor. Unlike Hispanic nobility, which considered the mercantile profession beneath them, Calvinists saw work as a calling; they believed that "to work was to pray."[9] A motto of the Sea Beggars was "Help thyself and God will help thee."[10]

Dutch freedom had an economic quotient, and her citizenry welcomed Jews as merchant adventurers who would advance their interests in high-risk areas of the economy. Linked by language, heritage, and trust with others in the Sephardic Diaspora, the newcomers formed the first trade network to span the globe. Palache had opened up North African trade as a gateway to the Ottoman Empire, and early émigrés had capital and access to trading partners in the New World, the Levant, and the Iberian Peninsula, all areas the Dutch had not penetrated.[11]

While the Sephardim were not as wealthy as the Dutch tycoons, who controlled the trade in herring, grain, and other staples, their economic contribution was considerable. One researcher noted: "Jewish trade, especially the sugar trade, was the engine of the Dutch Golden Age . . . comparable in scope with that of the Dutch East and West India Companies."[12] By 1636, Amsterdam's Jews, who numbered no more than 1 percent of the population, controlled 10 percent of the city's trade and, dealing mostly in luxury items, accrued nearly 20 percent of the profits. Their overall contribution was even more impressive, as these figures do not include their profits from joint ventures with native Dutchmen, nor the commissions they received for transit trade.[13]

For centuries, Iberia's Jews had been the peninsula's merchant class. Forced out at the dawn of the Age of Discovery, they settled everywhere they were permitted and many places they weren't. Those in Amsterdam, in consort with those on the peninsula, were from the early days of settlement the chief marketers of the Spanish Empire's colonial goods.[14] This was especially true in Portugal, where their partners controlled most of the trade. A prominent converso merchant from Lisbon noted their commanding position in Portugal. Appealing to the Crown for relief from persecution by the Holy Office, he wrote:

> The Kings of Portugal are lords of the sea . . . and the
> life blood of all this is commerce which is only sustained
> by merchants of Hebrew descent by whose industry it
> flourishes and without them all the trade would be lost
> because the Old Christian gentry do not esteem mer-
> chants and do not have the industry of those of Hebrew
> descent.[15]

While the trading prowess of Amsterdam's Jews was an important element in the emerging nation's financial growth, it is important to note that the Dutch Golden Age was advancing before the Jews came. When Samuel Palache was first meeting with Prince Maurice, Holland was already a flourishing mercantile state: Amsterdam had a commodities market; the Dutch East India Company was pushing the Portuguese out of the Asia market; the Dutch dominated the slave trade; and their builders owned most of Europe's trading ships.[16] Most trade, however, was in bulky products of relatively low value—grain, timber, iron, and salt. This changed with the influx to Amsterdam of Jewish merchants, who specialized in the far more lucrative commodities of sugar, spices, specie, and tobacco. As primary dealers of Iberia's colonial imports, Amsterdam's Jews, connecting with converso traders throughout the known world, helped turn what was a grain and herring port into Europe's richest trade mart, a supermarket to the world.

Amsterdam's harbor, filled with hundreds of foreign ships, looked like a floating forest of masts and riggings. While each waited to deliver its cargo and carry off the valuable merchandise from the huge brick warehouses lining the canals, their sailors, representing a carnival of nations, filled the dockside bars and brothels. In contrast to the Dutchmen in their sober black and white outfits, turbaned sailors, with rings in their ears and dirks in their belts, were a familiar sight, along with bewigged Frenchmen, flamboyant Italians, and other foreigners in colorful native dress.

The Dutch Republic was an anomaly. In an age of kings and emperors claiming divine rule, the fledging nation was seen as "an island of bourgeois tolerance in an ocean of theocratic absolutism."[17] Sephardim, reflecting the ways of Spanish nobility, possessed the requisite social graces to stand on an equal footing with the city's leading citizens. Men of considerable secular culture, they were courtly, courteous, and accustomed to moving in the best Christian circles.

From the outset, Sephardim were at home in this cosmopolitan setting, and displayed a worldly lifestyle marked by opulent self-confidence. They lived in palatial mansions, held musicals, staged theatricals and poetry competitions, and entertained sumptuously. They formed literary and philosophical academies and a score of social organizations covering every aspect of community life. They also frequented gambling houses run by Samuel Pereira and Abraham Mendes Vasques, and a popular brothel that featured Jewish prostitutes from Germany.[18]

Along with other religious dissidents who gained sanctuary here, the émigrés found they could be loyal both to their religion and to Holland. Outwardly, they didn't appear far different from their Dutch neighbors, but their long ancestry on the peninsula left them loyal to its language and culture. Whether they came directly from Iberia or elsewhere in the Diaspora, all referred to themselves as members of La Nação, the Portuguese Nation. On the banks of the Amstel River, the Jodenbreestraat (Jewish Broad Street) came to resemble a miniature Lisbon or Madrid:

> No caballero could outdo them in dignity; no grandee could bear himself with more *grandezza* than they. The Jewish caballeros of Amsterdam strutted about in jeweled garments of golden threads adorned with pearls and precious stones, and rode about in fancy coaches emblazoned with their coat of arms. Even the cases of their prayer shawls were decorated with coats of arms. Their spice boxes were of ivory, their wives' bonnets of Brabant lace . . .[19]

There were still restrictions: Jews could not join craft guilds, engage in retail business, or hold political office. Neither could they marry Christians, employ them as servants, or have sexual relations with "the daughters of the land," even prostitutes.[20] Despite such legal restraints, they had more freedom and security in Holland than anywhere in Europe and are thought of as "the first modern Jews."[21] Proud of their heritage and accomplishments, they may have felt, in the words of one period historian, that "if the Jews were God's chosen people, then they were God's chosen Jews."[22] It is little wonder that their children blossomed unafraid and determined to live free.

Rembrandt, who lived in the Jewish quarter at 2 Jodenbreestraat, drew his neighbors as they appeared, an assimilated group, for once no longer caricatured as mistrustful aliens. An example is his painting of the biblical scholar Menasseh ben Israel, who, dressed in a familiar broad-brim hat and white-collared coat and sporting a Vandyke beard, looks no different from other Dutch burghers.[23] Rembrandt also used his neighbors in his biblical paintings, seeing in their countenance the patriarchs and prophets, including Jesus and Matthew.

While the economic impact of this first generation is impressive, a simple recounting of facts and statistics does not convey the emboldened character of the men who created it. As much as their livelihoods, it was their remarkable lives their Dutch-born children emulated when, still in their teens and early twenties, they invaded the New World and, in an unremitting struggle lasting decades, took on and defeated those who would deny Jewish rights. Two adventurous role models who strutted along the Jodenbreestraat, and whose deeds were bandied about with awe, were a cardsharp and a slave trader.

Samuel Palache was the second man interred at the Jewish cemetery, having been preceded by his friend Don Manuel Pimental, who had purchased the cemetery two years before. Like Palache, his friend exemplified the diverse character and bravado of Amsterdam's Jewish pioneers. Pimental (alias Isaac Ibn Jakar) was the wealthiest member of the Neveh Shalom congregation, and owed his fortune to his skill in the era's favorite pastime—playing cards. He had honed his skills at the French court during the reign of King Henry IV. The king's nightly passion, when not dallying with one of his sixty-four mistresses, was gaming at cards. One night, after losing heavily to Pimental, the lustful and humorous monarch told him: "I am the king of France, but you are king of gamblers."[24]

Jews were then outlawed from France, and while Pimental had converted, he freely admitted being a Judaizer. His honorific title "Don" is evidence that he was comfortable with the court etiquette that required regal dress and appropriate manners. Henry, known for tolerance, defended his Jewish friend: "Those who honestly follow their conscience are of my religion, and mine is that of all brave and good men."[25] Pimental's presence in France was cut short in 1610, when his royal protector was assassinated by a fanatical Catholic schoolmaster who, fearing Henry intended to destroy the Catholic Church, leaped onto the king's passing carriage and stabbed him to death. After Henry's demise, the gambler moved to Venice, and three years later settled in Amsterdam. He joined Neveh Shalom, and in 1615, one year after purchasing the Ouderkerk cemetery, was buried there. In his honor, Palache's congregation passed a resolution to recite a yearly Sabbath prayer in memory of the king's favorite cardsharp.[26]

In 1611, Spain's Grand Inquisitor, in his annual *aviso* to the Madrid Council, reported that the Dutch Jew Diego Diaz Querido

> employs several Negro slaves, natives of the coast, who had received instruction in the Portuguese and Dutch languages so that they could serve as interpreters in Africa to assist him in his Africa dealings . . . [Furthermore] in his house, the Negroes are

given instruction in the Mosaic Law and converted to Judaism.[27]

If true, Querido, a religious man, would have first freed his slaves, as Jewish law forbade their conversion unless previously set free.[28] Querido was born in Portugal and lived many years in Bahia, Brazil's capital, until he was denounced as a Judaizer in 1595. He then left for Amsterdam, where he joined the Beth Jacob group, and in 1612 was one of the twelve founders of Neveh Shalom. He may have been among those arrested at Palache's home on Yom Kippur the night the Dutch police raided.

In the Inquisitor's denunciation, he accused Querido of "large scale transactions damaging to the royal treasury." Reportedly, his ten ships were illegally engaged in triangular trade between Amsterdam, Africa, and Brazil. Their holds filled with manufactured goods, his ships left the Dutch port for the Guinea coast to barter for slaves for Brazil, where they were exchanged for sugar.

In 1609, the slave trader was one of the twenty-five Jewish merchants who established bank accounts at the opening of Amsterdam's Exchange Bank. The Inquisitor, however, wasn't so much troubled by Querido's lucrative trade as by the fact that he was a proselytizer for Judaism. Evidence of this was disclosed at a 1595 Inquisition hearing in Brazil, when an informer testified that a friend had told him that when he first arrived in Bahia, Querido had said to him: "I am glad you came here to save your soul," and urged him to marry his sister. The friend, a candy manufacturer, told the informer he declined "because she was a Jewess."[29] Querido, in doing business on four continents (he also traded with India), was a man on the move. In an age when ocean voyages were perilous and took months, Jews like him and Palache strode over continents and oceans. They braved new worlds, negotiated with kings, and robbed them as well. Querido's story does not end here.

"Cursed by day and cursed by night; cursed when he goes forth and cursed when he comes in."[30] So reads the condemnation of Uriel da Costa, excommunicated by holier-than-thou Jews who felt compelled to outdo the Christians in orthodoxy. Jews might have been freer in Amsterdam, but they still had to abide by the strictures their religious leaders demanded of the community. Before da Costa wound up killing himself, he wrote an account of his life and of the early community's severity and religious dogmatism.

So stringent were these constraints that they drove away many young Jews, including members of da Costa's family, who, seeking personal freedom, settled in the New World and led the fight for Jewish rights. Their parents, having been raised with the strictures of Christianity and being newly returned to Judaism, felt compelled to adhere—or pay lip service—to the numerous tenets of their religion. As if doing penance for all their years pretending to be Catholic, few of the older émigrés looked to confront those rabbis who (like Palache's brother-in-law) were zealous in their litany of do's and don'ts, and quick to excommunicate those who didn't toe the line.

Uriel da Costa was one of those who refused. His autobiography, excerpted below, illuminates this early period as few other sources can.[31] Born in Oporto, Portugal, in 1585 to a wealthy converso family, he studied for the priesthood and served in the local church before moving to Amsterdam in 1615 with his mother and four brothers. What prompted his return to Judaism is best described in his own words:

> I grew up in the Roman Catholic religion, and since I was terribly afraid of eternal damnation I occupied myself with reading the New Testament and other spiritual books . . . I became completely confused . . . It seemed to me impossible to confess my sins in accordance with Roman Catholic custom to obtain absolute absolution . . . I began to doubt if it was really true what I was taught of the life to come and tried to reconcile faith with reason, for it was reason which whispered into my ear something utterly irreconcilable with faith . . .
>
> Longing to find some satisfaction in any religion, I began to read the Books of Moses and the Prophets, knowing full well there was great competition between Jew and Christian. I found in the Old Testament many things that contradicted the New Testament completely. In addition, the old covenant is accepted by Jews as well as Christians, and the new one only by Christians. Finally I began to believe in Moses and decided to live according to his law because he received it from God, or so he maintained, and he simply considered himself an intermediary.
>
> Considering all this and the fact that in my country there was no freedom of religion, I decided to leave my beautiful house built by my father, and did not think twice about giving up my ecclesiastical office. So we

embarked on a ship under the greatest danger, for it is known that those descended from Jews were not permitted to leave the country without a permit by the king. My mother was with me, as well as my brothers whom I had won over to my newly won convictions . . . It was a daring enterprise and could have failed, so dangerous was it in this country to even discuss matters of religion. It was a long voyage and finally we arrived in Amsterdam where we felt Jews could live in freedom and fulfill the commandments. And since I was imbued with it, my brothers and I immediately submitted to circumcision.

Uriel's concept of Judaism was based on the Old Testament. He had expected to find a biblical Judaism that no longer existed. Like many conversos, his knowledge was based solely on the Old Testament as transcribed in the Christian Bible. Instead, he encountered the Judaism of the Diaspora, an evolving faith built on interpretations and the commentaries of learned Jews found in the Talmud rather than the Torah. Wishing to live in accordance with the Commandments, da Costa rejected any new rendering of divine law not intoned in the Five Books of Moses.

When a converso moved to Amsterdam, he was immediately embraced by the rabbis. No matter how idolatrous he had been while in "Babylonian exile," he was absolved. But now that he had returned to the bosom of Judaism, the rabbis smothered him with their laws:

After the first few days I began to understand that the customs and institutions of the Jews in Amsterdam were not at all in accordance with what Moses had written. If Moses' commandments were observed strictly as written, then the Jews here were wrong to have invented so many things which deviated from them. It was not right for a man who had exchanged security at home for freedom abroad, and had sacrificed every possible advantage to permit himself to be so threatened . . .

Not reticent about his views, Uriel accused members of the Mahamad, the synagogue's executive committee, of inventing a new Torah: "They call themselves the sages of the Jewish people, inventing a host of laws which are totally opposed to it [and] do all these things in order to sit in the first row of the Temple and to be greeted in the marketplace with particular respect."[32]

In 1623, two incidents occurred that led to his excommunication. His nephew, "who lives with me, went to the community leaders and accused me of eating food which was not in accordance with Jewish law, and said that I could not possibly be a Jew." Soon after, da Costa met two new arrivals, who "I advised against joining the Jewish community, telling them they did not know what kind of yoke they were about to be burdened with."

I asked them not to mention our conversation to the Jews. But these scoundrels betrayed me . . . As soon as the elders of the synagogue learned of my conversation, they met with the rabbis, who were hot with anger. A public war ensued. The rabbis and the people began to persecute me with a new hatred and did so many things against me that I could only react with utter and justified contempt.

Expelled from the synagogue, he was shunned. "Even my brothers, whose teacher I was, passed me by. So afraid were they of the authorities that they did not even greet me on the street." When his wife, Sarah, died, his only close companion was a faithful housekeeper. After seven years, he could take it no longer. He asked to be reconciled, and agreed to the humiliating subjugation demanded by the Mahamad for reinstatement. On the appointed day:

I entered the synagogue, which was crowded with men and women who had come to observe this spectacle. When the time came, I went to the pulpit . . . and read in a loud voice the list of my confessions, concluding "I merit to die a thousand deaths for what I have committed." . . . After, the sexton told me to go to a corner of the synagogue and strip off my clothes. I disrobed to my waist, wrapped a scarf around my head, took off my shoes, and the sexton tied my arms to one of the columns of the synagogue. The cantor came, and with leather whip beat me 39 times according to the law which provides for 40 lashes. But these people are so conscientious, they are afraid they might give me more than the law states. While he whipped me I recited the psalm.

When this was over . . . I dressed and lay down over the threshold of the synagogue while the sexton held my head, [and] all the men, women and children passed over me into the street, stepping with one foot on the lower part of my legs. No monkey could have invented a more despicable, tasteless and ridiculous action. Afterward when everybody left, I rose and someone helped me get the dust off my clothes, so that no one should say that I was not treated honorable. Although they had whipped me just a short time ago, they expressed their pity for me and patted my head, and I went home.

Sometime later, in 1640, Uriel da Costa bought a pistol, went home, put the gun barrel to his temple, and pulled the trigger. No one in his family had openly supported him, but after his death, one brother left for the New World to live free from a Jewish version of the Holy Inquisition, and other relations, exhibiting a similar combative spirit, directed their energies to gaining civil rights elsewhere in Europe and the New World. Indeed, in the latter half of the seventeenth century, everywhere that Jews struggled for rights, the da Costa name is prominent.[33]

The trials and tribulations of Uriel da Costa paint a rabbinical portrait of Jewish Amsterdam at its most extreme. Samuel Palache would have been aghast at the treatment accorded da Costa, and certainly many of the congregation who went along did so reluctantly. Although not fanatical about their own beliefs, they deferred to those who were. It is one of history's anomalies that their religious leaders, themselves survivors of religious fanaticism, should have formed their own Inquisitional tribunal, rather than show tolerance to the new Jews. Granted, no dissidents were held in dark dungeons, stripped naked, and subjected to the rack, or suffered the Holy Terror's other specified tortures.[34] Even so, the lives of those expelled were ruined just the same.

The most notable figure banished from the community was nine years old when he stepped over da Costa's body in the synagogue entrance. The celebrated philosopher Baruch Spinoza would publicly question every religious tenet of Judaism and deny that the Bible was God's word. Like Uriel, he was condemned to be "cursed by day and cursed by night; cursed when he goes forth and cursed when he comes in." However, unlike him, Spinoza is embraced today as a champion of the Enlightenment and considered one of the great men in Jewish history.

Only a handful of Jews were drummed out of the congregation. However, when one considers the oppressive religious atmosphere that permeated the small community, it is little wonder that a younger generation, raised in freedom, wanted out. Among the Jewish youth who quit Amsterdam for the New World were the Cohen Henriques brothers. Moses was fourteen and Abraham eleven when Rabbi Palache was buried, and a decade later they were in Brazil. Little is known of their parents, but the lasting influence of the pirate rabbi is apparent when, after the death of his first wife, Abraham married Samuel Palache's grandniece, Rebekah, and the couple's two children also married into the Palache family.[35]

Moses left Amsterdam as a soldier and spy and embarked on a spectacular piracy career that would span a half century. Abraham soon followed him to the New World, where he became a powerful international merchant and used his economic muscle to orchestrate Jewish settlement. He never used Henriques, his Spanish "oppressor" name. Indeed, his fealty to his ancestry was such that, whenever possible, he signed his patronymic name, Abraham Cohen, in Hebrew.[36]

———

During Holland's armistice with Spain, from 1609 to 1621, Brazilian sugar found its way to foreign countries, transported by Dutch Jews to Portugal and then to Holland, France, Germany, and points east. This traffic, combined with Holland's own consumption of the granulated product, boosted Brazil's output by more than 50 percent. Likewise, the number of sugar refineries in Amsterdam increased from four to twenty-five.[37] Once a confection only the very rich could afford, the sweetener was fast becoming an affordable treat for everyman.

This traffic came to an abrupt halt in 1621, and the Dutch resumed their fight for independence. The desirability of regaining the sugar market was a major factor in the creation of the Dutch West India Company (hereafter called the Company), a trading combine with privately held shares modeled after the earlier Dutch East India Company. In April 1623, Prince Maurice presided over a conference at The Hague, where it was decided to fight Spain by targeting her colonies, the source of her wealth. To accomplish this, the States General approved the formation of a militant Company with the right and means to wage war against any that stood in its way.[38]

No private corporation would ever again be granted such power—a monopoly on foreign trade, governorship of settlements, and the right to raise an army, wage war, and negotiate peace. The Company's mandate was not simply to bypass Portugal and deal directly with Brazil. Rather, its initial mission was to conquer the sugar colony and then seize the silver mountain of Potosí, which for a half a century had financed Spain's armies and funded her empire. To penetrate the interior of the southern continent where the silver mountain was located (today's Bolivia), the Company's plan called for a pincer movement to close in from both coasts—from Brazil on the Atlantic side and Peru on the Pacific.

Jews were not involved in the formation of the Company but were wholly in favor of it and quick to enlist. While the Company's motives were wholly mercenary and political, the Jews had another, more pressing agenda. In Portugal in 1618, the Inquisition arrested more than a hundred wealthy converso traders who had agents in Amsterdam and seized their cargos from Brazil in transit to the Dutch port. Amsterdam's Jews, who were related to many of those arrested, and were holding their money, protested to the States General. A formal complaint was duly sent to King Philip, but it had no effect.[39] The arrests in Portugal coincided with an Inquisition hearing in Brazil, where ninety conversos were denounced.[40]

For a century, Brazil's New Christians had been living in relative peace while developing the colony into the world's richest sugar producer. Owing to its vastness and Portugal's small population, conversos (along with petty criminals) had been encouraged to emigrate there. By 1623, an estimated 15 percent of the colony's fifty thousand settlers were conversos. The authorities knew this included a clandestine community of nearly a thousand Judaizers, but as long as its members didn't flaunt their beliefs, no one at first was particularly concerned.[41]

This laissez-faire policy changed after the union of Portugal and Spain in 1580. Inquisition proceedings were initiated throughout the consolidated empire, and over the next decades, hearings by Inquisitors from Lisbon regularly targeted the colony's Judaizers. The fourth hearing in 1618, in which the ninety conversos were accused, coupled with the arrests in Portugal, was a clear warning to those who were not the Christians they pretended to be.

Although many of the colony's conversos were sincere Christians, and a small percentage remained loyal to Judaism, by the 1600s most former Jews had become indifferent to religion. Having to choose between a faith that was forced on their ancestors and remaining true to outlawed beliefs, the majority chose mammon. A leading authority on Brazil's New Christians, Anita Novinsky, opines that it was not so much a question of religiosity as it was "the economic prosperity of the colony [that] awoke the greed of the Inquisitors."[42] Conversos constituted most of the wealthy class. The hearings revealed that they dominated the sugar trade and in 1618 owned twenty of the thirty-four largest sugar mills.

The production of sugar, fueled by African slaves, was the main business of Brazil, and the specialty of conversos. To appreciate the role the sweetener played in their New World welcome, we must digress into history to account for this connection.

The association of Brazil's conversos with this most valuable and contentious industry can be traced to 1503, three years after the Portuguese explorer Pedro Alvares Cabral, accompanied by his Jewish pilot Gaspar da Gama, discovered Brazil. As previously related, Portugal's King John had leased the colony to the enterprising converso merchant Fernando de Noronha to export brazilwood, a red dyewood that grew there in abundance, and for which the colony was named. From the sale of this timber, prized by Europe's textile industry, Noronha's consortium derived an annual profit of fifty thousand ducats. However, his hold on the colony ended when he had the bright idea of transplanting the cane root from the islands of São Tomé and Madeira. The success of his crop, and its potential profits, convinced the king to void Noronha's contract and reclaim the colony. In 1516, Brazil's first sugar mill began operating. To encourage the industry, new settlers were supplied with necessary tools and other equipment for the production of sugar.

In 1534, the king appointed Duarte Coelho as feudal lord of Brazil, and directed him to recruit sugar experts from Madeira and São Tomé to establish large plantations. Sugar had been grown in the New World since Columbus brought the first roots from the Canary Islands, but not on the vast scale on which it was then being produced by a particular group of conversos in São Tomé, a small island off Africa's west coast. What they did in São Tomé, the king would have them do on the vast savannahs of northeast Brazil. So it was that in 1534, the same year Charles V sent Portuguese conversos to salvage Jamaica, Coelho brought over Portuguese conversos—foremen, mechanics, and skilled workmen, principally from São Tomé—to Brazil. In São Tomé, they had transformed the cultivation of sugar into an agro-industry fueled by slave labor, and would do the same in Brazil, a land of three million square miles, larger than Europe and all the other colonies in the New World together.

From the time of the Crusades, when the cane root was transplanted from Asia to the Mediterranean basin, "the making and selling of sugar was dominated by Jews."[43] In the 1400s, Morocco was the primary producer of sugar, a commodity so dear only royalty could afford it. But the Mediterranean climate—too cool in winter and too dry year-round—was not optimum for sugar growth. Late in the fifteenth century, the grape growers of Madeira, Portugal's Atlantic island known for its namesake wine, overtook Morocco in sugar production.

Madeira's vintners, mostly conversos, had obtained the cane root from their Moroccan brethren and were soon outproducing them.

Madeira's success inspired the king to introduce the crop to São Tomé, an uninhabited island off the coast of Africa his sailors had discovered in 1470 in the Gulf of Guinea. The island's lush tropicality was suitable for sugar. Moreover, its location ensured an unlimited supply of slave labor. Enslaving Africans was nothing new. Portugal had been engaged in the slave trade from the time her ships first reached tropical Africa a half-century before. What was introduced in São Tomé for the first time was using slaves in a major agricultural enterprise.

But first the king had to settle his uninhabited island. This proved difficult. None of his countrymen had any interest in migrating to an isolated isle, far from home, populated mostly by snakes and mosquitoes. Soon, however, the king hit upon an answer when his nation was overrun by displaced persons whose sugar-growing skills had already been proven.

In August 1492, tens of thousands of Jewish refugees from Spain were halted at the border to Portugal. King John, forewarned of his neighbor's expulsion order, had ordered his guards to permit their entrance with the proviso that they pay eight crusados and agree to depart in six months. On March 31, 1493, when the six-month period elapsed, the king ordered his soldiers to seize seven hundred Jewish children and declare them Crown slaves as an example to all who overstayed. As noted by King John's chronicler:

> Torn from their parent's arms, the children were forcibly converted and shipped to São Tomé. All youths were taken captive from among the Castilian Jews who did

not betake themselves away at the appointed time according to the conditions of their entrance . . . that, being separated, they would be better Christians; as a result of this the island came to be more densely populated, and to thrive exceedingly.[44]

If their average age at capture was eight to ten years old, they would have been in their midforties in 1534 when Coelho sent his recruiters. Most were probably too settled to accept his offer, but some of their children would certainly have welcomed the chance to carve their niche in the New World. In the ensuing decades, when Brazil sugar entered the market, the plantation model Coelho's workers established became the New World standard. Portugal dominated the trade and Coelho is credited as the first man to engage in the "systematic and intensive development of the sugar industry."[45]

The Inquisition hearings in Brazil began with the posting on a church door of an "Edict of Faith," listing the heretical rites and ceremonies of Judaizers and offering a thirty-day grace period with the promise of confidentiality and merciful treatment for those who came forward. Many conversos did so, either to acknowledge their guilt or, as was usually the case, to accuse others of Judaizing. Although few of those charged were sent to Lisbon for trial, the entire converso community, sincere New Christians and secret Jews alike, was alarmed and saw the hearings as a prelude to the establishment of a permanent seat of the Inquisition.[46]

Such fears were further aroused in the summer of 1623, when

Bishop Marcos Teixeira arrived from Lisbon with authority to imprison accused Judaizers and confiscate their holdings. No longer was a trial required; an anonymous charge was enough to destroy one's life. An unknown number of covert Jews left for the safer climate of neighboring countries, including Columbus's island, Jamaica. Some who remained took more drastic action: In a coded message to their brethren in Holland, they pledged to serve as a fifth column in support of a Dutch invasion to liberate the colony.[47]

The dissidents' likely courier was the rabbi pirate's friend, the slave merchant from Amsterdam, Diego Diaz Querido. Five years before, in 1618, King Philip IV had warned Brazil's governor that Querido was a known smuggler of contraband and to keep a close watch on his ships. The governor took no action. As it happened, Querido had earlier loaned him thirty thousand crusados "from the stores of his ships."[48] It was not an outright bribe—the loan was repaid—but it served the same purpose: Querido continued his triangular trade, carrying manufactured goods to Africa, slaves to Brazil, and sugar to Amsterdam . . . and on one of his trips may have secreted in his cabin a pouch containing the rebel Jews' invasion promise.

If, as alleged, Querido was the courier, he would have delivered the message to the Brotherhood of the Jews of Holland, a clandestine group dedicated to fighting the Inquisition. The secret organization was founded in the decade after Rabbi Palache's death to carry on his struggle for Jewish rights and against Spain. Its existence was revealed in the tortured confessions of four convicted Judaizers.[49] In separate Inquisition trials in Cartagena and Lima, they described La Cofradia de los Judios de Holanda as an underground organization headquartered in Amsterdam, with cells of three to five men each in various colonies in the New World that forwarded intelligence and funds to Holland to buy arms to aid the war effort against Spain. They testified that the cells also sent money from local conversos looking to move to Holland, which the Brotherhood invested and remitted to the owner when he settled in Amsterdam.[50]

Bento Osorio, the Amsterdam community's richest trader, is thought to have been the Brotherhood's leader.[51] He imported olive oil from Turkey, nutmeg and pepper from India, and sugar from Brazil. In a city that taxed the merchants' dazzling homes (described by visitors as "palaces"), Osorio's palatial mansion was the most heavily taxed on the Jodenbreestraat.[52] Although the Dutch West India Company was founded without Jewish participation, an Inquisition document accuses Osorio of being in league with the Company: "[By] maintaining spies in many cities in Castile, Portugal, Brazil & elsewhere [Osorio] gives the orders and plans for plundering . . . thinking by this means to destroy Christianity."[53]

Despite Brazil's enormous area, the Company reckoned it would suffice to conquer the coastal province of Bahia to secure the colony. Assured by the Brotherhood of fifth-column support, Prince Maurice agreed to a policy of religious freedom in the conquered territory, and that Jewish soldiers could form their own company.[54] On May 8, 1624, an invasion force of 3,300 men that included "several dozen" Jews arrived at Bahia on twenty-six ships.[55] In the initial assault, Vice Admiral Piet Heyn easily captured the two main forts guarding the port. His quick victory panicked the defenders, who soon deserted.

The next night, Bishop Teixeira, the conversos' nemesis, gathered his cassock and beat a hasty retreat. Described as "the most alarmed person in the city," he fled with his priests into the forest.[56] As the prince had promised, with victory a policy of religious tolerance was declared, and the Dutch invaders pledged to respect Portuguese property rights. The following day, two hundred conversos came forward to proclaim their adherence to their ancestral faith, and welcomed the Dutch Jews who participated in the invasion.[57]

While Bahia was under attack, a flotilla of Dutch ships sailed around Cape Horn and up the Pacific coast to Peru's Port Callao and laid siege to Lima. When the news reached Portugal that Bahia had fallen and Lima was blockaded, the governing council was understandably alarmed. Their quickly composed message to Philip noted that the Dutch invaders had been aided by the *"Hebrea da Nação . . .* not so much to make themselves masters of the sugar of Brazil as of the silver of Peru."[58]

Spain's king, convinced the Dutch were bent on further conquest, assembled a massive force to break the siege. He need not have bothered. The Dutch effort was already spent. After blockading the port for three months, they ran out of supplies and withdrew. Meanwhile, back in Brazil, Bishop Teixeira, having regained his courage, organized a guerrilla force that surrounded the city and prevented the Dutch from advancing. On March 29, 1625, a combined armada of fifty-two Spanish and Portuguese warships landed 12,566 men on the coast of Bahia and cordoned off the port. Defeat was inevitable, but for two weeks the Dutch held out, their resistance encouraged by the Jews. As a Spanish soldier noted in his diary:

A Dutch prisoner reported the enemy was very strong and that many Jews and Jewesses who had come with them from Holland, encouraged them to defend themselves and supported them with large sums of money.[59]

On May 1, the Dutch surrendered. To secure favorable terms for his Jewish contingent, Vice Admiral Heyn, in a communiqué to the enemy commander, requested that "Portuguese of the Hebrew nation who remained in Bahia during the occupation not be molested."[60] The Spanish leader refused, and demanded that the vice admiral hand over their names; but Heyn held firm. After a standoff, the matter was dropped. Although the surrender terms stipulated that only Hollanders could depart, most Jewish soldiers and their collaborators left with them. The few who remained behind shouldn't have. In the aftermath of the reconquest, the Spanish commander hanged four of them as traitors. The Inquisitor's report on the invasion blamed Bahia's defeat on the Jews:

Secret Jews had written Holland and asked the Dutch to liberate them . . . had initiated plans for the invasion and agreed to share its costs. [The] Heretics had suckled at the breast of the Mother Church [and when the Dutch came] allowed themselves to be circumcised and openly professed the Jewish faith.[61]

Later, an informer identified two of the collaborators who had gotten away:

Bahia was taken by order and plan of one Nuno Alvarez Franco, a Jew of Holland and resident of Bahia for more than 12 years and by order of one Manuel Fernandez Drago. Both lived in the said Bahia. Their fathers lived in Amsterdam and received from the States 200 pounds each year for their support.[62]

The Dutch occupied Bahia for a year and never took Lima. The ambitious pincer plan to capture Brazil and the silver mountain had failed. Disheartened, the army limped home to a near bankrupt country, made poor by the cost of the invasion and occupation.

Two years later, the nation's spirits and fortunes were suddenly revived when Vice Admiral Piet Heyn and his young adviser Moses Cohen Henriques sailed into Amsterdam Harbor leading Spanish galleons, their holds filled with silver and gold. It was the biggest haul in history. For the first time since the discovery of the New World, the Spanish silver fleet had been captured and the Dutch were again on the offensive.

In the vanguard would be Moses and other young warrior Jews. Influenced by the likes of the pirate rabbi, the first generation born in freedom dominated Amsterdam's nascent community. Their numbers tell the tale: In the 1620s, when there were fewer than two hundred Jewish families in the city, "several dozen" of them took part in the Brazil invasion, and the following decade, an Inquisition spy accused a hundred Dutch Jews of planning to invade Portugal and burn down the Inquisition prison.[63] There is no record of this happening, but the informer's charge gives an indication of the mind-set of these rebel youths—they had a Maccabean picture of themselves as militant Jewish deliverers, derived from their parents, their community, and Rabbi Palache. With the Holy Terror raging about them, these youths were called and encouraged to become a generation of warriors for Zion.

Chapter Six

ZION WARRIORS IN
THE NEW WORLD

*Antonio Vaez Henriques alias Moses Cohen is nothing but
a spy to learn when the fleet comes and goes and when an
assault can be made . . . as he did at the capture of the fleet by
Piet Heyn in whose company was said Antonio Vaez.[1]*

Sunrise, September 8, 1628: On board the admiral's flagship, the *Amsterdam*, a few miles west of Havana, Moses
Cohen Henriques, with his reputation on the line, was looking
westward, scanning the sea. Unexpectedly, over the northern ho-
rizon, the topsails of the Spanish silver fleet, the *flota*, appeared:
twelve ships loaded with ninety-two tons of silver, and treasure
chests filled with pearls, rubies, and gold worth 16 million guilders, or in today's currency, nearly one billion dollars.

Closing in on the unsuspecting fleet, the twenty-five ships
of the Dutch armada cut off and captured nine ships without

incident; but the three leading galleons, including the grand admiral's, fled down the coast to the nearby port of Matanzas. The Dutch, in hot pursuit, boldly entered the harbor and drew abreast of two of the ships. Their soldiers, armed with cutlass, pistol, and musket, quickly clambered up the sides.

> As quickly as we boarded, the Spaniards went over the side, swimming and paddling toward shore. Within minutes the flag of the United Provinces flew where the lions & castles had been. We then came to the admiral's ship. We attacked with a musket charge and boarded her, calling to them "Buena Guerra."[2]

Writing in his cabin on his victorious voyage home, Vice Admiral Piet Heyn noted that this sardonic greeting ("Good War") so demoralized the defenders that "upon hearing [it] they put down their muskets and went below deck."

One lone sailor who jumped overboard, hoping to swim ashore, was hauled up from the sea and brought before the vice admiral.

> I asked him how many Spaniards were aboard. He said about 150 . . . I told him to go back and tell them I promised them quarter and would put them ashore. He asked me what kind of person I was. I said I was the fleet general, at which he asked me to let one of our men go with him so that he would not be killed by our people on board to which I consented.*

---

* Moses was the likely designate, since he spoke Spanish and was trusted by Heyn.

The next day:

We unloaded the silver as fast as possible and divided
it among all our ships. We figured there were about 46
lasts of silver, consisting of minted reals of eight, and
bars of silver and silverware, altogether 2,851 pieces.

The plate fleet had been captured in a little more than three
hours without the loss of one Dutchman's life. A fast yacht carried the news to Holland. In early January, Heyn returned
home, leading his fleet into the port of Amsterdam with the
grand admiral's galleon bringing up the rear. It took five days
to unload the bounty on a thousand mule carts, which were
then paraded in triumphal procession through the streets of
Amsterdam behind the vice admiral's coach. "Heyn was received as a visiting prince might have been."[3] The country
blazed with bonfires. Since the defeat at Bahia, the nation's
finances had been in dire straits. The government had exhausted its credit. Public debts were unpaid. Now suddenly
Holland was rich again. The Company declared a dividend of
50 percent and, with its new wealth, prepared the fleet to again
invade Brazil.

Moses Cohen Henriques, who had celebrated his bar mitzvah in 1616, sometime after the death of his mentor, had learned
from Rabbi Palache to live as he dreamed. Moses wasn't royal,
but his ambitions were as grand as any aspiring noble's. An
early and valued member of the Brotherhood, he was sent undercover to Seville, where he soon acquired information that
convinced the Company it made more sense to attack at sea
the Spanish fleet that carried the ore to Seville rather than
to mount a land invasion to capture the silver mountain. At

twenty-five, Moses was half the admiral's age, but he had proven himself in the Bahia invasion four years before, and so was invited by Heyn to sail with him.

Spain's treasure fleet consisted of two heavily guarded armadas of twenty to thirty ships. The *Tierra Firme* group gathered the wealth of the Spanish Main; the *flota* picked up silver from Mexico at the port of Vera Cruz, along with the riches of Asia brought by the Manila galleons. After securing their bounty, the two fleets rendezvoused in Havana for a joint return to Spain. In 1628, when the *Tierra Firme* sailed north to Havana to meet up with the *flota,* it arrived too late. Except for the grand admiral's galleon, all the ships were there, but their holds were empty; the plundered cargo was on its way to Holland.

The treasure fleet's departure from Spain was a ceremonious occasion, but for security reasons the sailing date shifted radically from one year to the next, and was a closely guarded secret—one that young Moses Cohen Henriques somehow became privy to. How he acquired this vital intelligence is not known. Possibly he learned it from Bento Osorio's agent there, who was fronting the Brotherhood leader's illegal trade.[4] In any event, Moses was able to alert the Company of the *flota*'s intended sailing date. This allowed sufficient time to man and outfit twenty-five ships under the vice admiral's command to sail to Cuba and await the fleet's arrival.

To avoid the hurricane season, the *flota* had left Spain a month after the *Tierra Firme.* As always, its arrival in July 1628 transformed the marshy port of Vera Cruz into a carnival town swelled by merchants, gamblers, hustlers, and revelers. Traders from all over descended on the port, desiring not so much the *flota*'s cargo of European goods as the treasures of the Orient, the silks, jade, rugs, ivory, porcelain, and spices that had been carried by the Manila galleons to Acapulco, then by mule to Vera Cruz. The town rollicked until early August, when the *flota* sailed for Cuba, its holds filled with silver from Mexico's mines and the bounty of Asia.[5] Havana was only a few hundred miles to the west, but that year contrary winds, the northers, forced the *flota* to follow the currents to the Florida Keys and approach Cuba from the north. Piet Heyn and his anxious young associate were waiting, having arrived two weeks earlier. In the course of two centuries, fifty attempts were made to capture the treasure galleons. Only theirs succeeded.

When the victorious fleet returned to Amsterdam, the young Jewish adventurers, who a few years before had joyfully participated in the Bahia invasion only to be depressingly dislodged, greeted Moses's triumph with an enthusiasm that reflected their resurgent morale as much as his extraordinary deed. His victory, on the heels of their bitter defeat, had shown them that failure and success are best measured over time. It was a lesson they might have learned from their parents, who overcame Inquisition trials before gaining the free air of Amsterdam, or from Rabbi Palache, who first fled in retreat to the French diplomat's home before renewing his fight.

Moses didn't remain long in Amsterdam. The next year found him in Recife, the capital of Brazil's Pernambuco province, plotting with the local underground to prepare for a renewed Dutch invasion. Moses then returned to Amsterdam to join the fleet. This was revealed four years later at a Madrid tribunal investigating the invasion. A turncoat who sailed with the Dutch testified:

The Jews of Amsterdam were responsible for the capture of Pernambuco & the principal one was Moses Cohen Henriques who went with the Hollanders & instructed them & gave them plans showing how to take the place, for he had spent many days in Pernambuco & was well acquainted with the entrances & the exits. The Hollanders did this by his secret counsel.[6]

Historians have overlooked the audacious role of this dauntless young man who (1) participated in the first invasion of Bahia; (2) plotted and took part in the *flota*'s capture; (3) infiltrated Recife as an advance spy to coordinate fifth-column support; and (4) returned to Amsterdam to accompany the fleet for the second invasion. Scholars note only that in 1630 Moses was invited to go as a "guest of the Company," but do not explain why he was so honored.[7] If not for the traitor's account, quoted above, Moses's role in Holland's military adventures would be unknown. It was, however, no more than an opening salvo of an action-packed life, in which he would reign over his own pirate island, and later advise Jamaica's famed buccaneer Henry Morgan.

On February 14, 1630, the Dutch fleet landed seven thousand soldiers at Recife. The next day, Moses, identified only as the Company's "guest," led three thousand more men ashore at a beach north of the port. Meeting him there was Antonio Dias Paparrobalos, the local underground leader who brought "two native mulattoes" to guide the invaders.[8] Encountering little resistance, inside of two weeks the Dutch were masters of northeast Brazil, an area embracing Pernambuco Province, the port of Recife, and outlying districts.

For the second time in a decade, Brazil's conversos came out of the closet. This was noted by a Portuguese priest, Father Manuel Calado, who lived in Dutch Brazil from 1630 to 1646, and hated the Calvinists as much as the Jews: "[The conversos] welcomed the Dutch, greatly relieved that their double lives had come to an end, and they could cease feigning loyalty to Catholicism." In his clerical report, Father Calado described the initial rush of freedom:

> The Jews who had come from Holland had many relatives in Pernambuco who had lived in conformity with the law of Christ. However, after the Dutch had conquered the country, they lifted the mask which had disguised them and circumcised themselves, and declared themselves publicly as Jews . . . I heard it said many a time by the Jews that there was no man of their nation [i.e., conversos] in Pernambuco who was not a Jew, and if they did not declare themselves as Jews it was because of the fear that the world might turn and Brazil might return to Portugal, otherwise all of them would have already publicly declared themselves Jews.[9]

One converso had cause to regret his unbridled enthusiasm. As Dutch officers, haughty in victory, strutted past his shop, the wine merchant Simon Drago threw open the doors of his cellar and welcomed them inside. Proudly, he declared himself a Jew, and in celebration of their victory and his personal freedom, he offered the officers a case of his finest wine. Quaffing that, they wanted more. Claiming they were entitled for having liberated his "kind," they departed with eighty barrels of wine. This incident was revealed years later when Drago filed suit in Amsterdam, charging the officers had emptied his warehouse.[10]

After the conquest, Moses settled in Recife and pursued a successful career as a licensed pirate, a privateer. With his share of the booty, estimated at one ton of silver, he bought ships, munitions, and an empty island off Recife to serve as his base. As a jab against his country of origin, he named the island, which today forms the heart of Recife, Antonio Vaz, cynically christening the redoubt with his old converso name.[11] Joining him, as officers and crew, were other recusant Jews who, having rejected the stifling embrace of Amsterdam, shared his quest for unbridled adventure at the expense of the evil empire. It is not known how many enemy ships Moses seized, but Dutch privateers in the New World were very successful. For the period 1623 to 1636 (the year that Moses sold his island to Governor Maunce), Dutch privateers captured 547 Iberian ships, an average of nearly one a week.[12]

Unlike Moses, who was a firstborn son, most Jewish settlers were younger sons. As such, they had not acquired a stake in the family business. It was reported they usually arrived with "only the ragged clothes they wore upon landing,"[13] to find their status quickly changed for the better. Fluent in Dutch and Portuguese, they bridged the language barrier between the newly arrived Dutch and the established Portuguese. Soon many occupied a profitable niche in Holland's colony as middlemen in commercial dealings between the two groups. Prominent among them was Moses's younger brother Abraham, who rose to become the colony's buying agent, and was so widely respected that, in times of trouble, all sides turned to him to mediate their squabbles.

New Holland was the Company's name for the captured colony. Despite this conceit, the new owners were not so provincial as to expel the people responsible for the region's wealth. Portuguese sugar growers may have been despised as papist idolaters, but as with the Jews, they were urged to remain and grow rich. Again Prince Maurice issued an edict of religious toleration, pledging that "the liberty of Spaniards, Portuguese and natives, whether they be Roman Catholics or Jews [will] be respected, [and no one] permitted to subject them to inquiries in matters of conscience."[14]

By his decree, New Holland was officially a land of freedom: Catholics, New Christians, Jews, Calvinists, and Indians lived and worked side by side. Most Jews lived in Recife, where they formed the first legal settlement of Jews in the New World and ran their community as a self-contained government. The Portuguese Catholics accepted the newcomers, but considered traitors the native conversos who, with the coming of the Dutch Jews, had shed their Christian robes to embrace their ancestral faith. Still, compared to the religious intolerance elsewhere, there was relative harmony in the colony. Each group had a share of the wealth and contributed to transforming Dutch Brazil into the world's richest sugar-producing area.

Much of New Holland's success was due to its governor, Johan Maurice van Nassau, who arrived in January 1637 with an entourage of scholars, artists, and scientists and ruled for seven years. The Prince of Nassau (as he liked to be addressed) was a cultured man at home with the arts and sciences, and an extraordinary diplomat who related well to all factions. The Portuguese felt him simpatico to their situation; the Calvinists knew him as one of their own, and the Jews called him "wise," their ultimate compliment.[15]

Within weeks of his arrival, the governor received a complaint from a delegation of Calvinist merchants that there were too many Jews in New Holland: "The country is flooded with Jews. Every boat is filled with them."[16] The petitioners requested that Christians, rather than Jews, be encouraged to come, bringing up all the historic reasons that "Christ killers" should be suppressed. The governor interrupted. Brandishing a copy of the colony's charter, he told the Calvinist complainers there would be no favoritism: "Article 32 guarantees protection for persons of Jewish and Catholic faith."[17]

While the governor rejected the petitioners, it wasn't the whole truth. As in Amsterdam, there were restrictions: Jews were not allowed to hold government office, hold religious services in public, or take a Christian lover.[18] But, again, these restrictions were relatively minor in the seventeenth-century Diaspora world. The People of the Book might be despised, but those in Brazil had fundamental rights. More important, they were needed. They called their congregation Zur Israel, Rock of Israel—a pun on Recife, which means "rock of Brazil." But it also imparted a messianic message from the book of Isaiah (30:19–29): "For the people shall dwell in Zion at Jerusalem . . . when they come to the Rock of Israel."[19]

For security reasons, the governor wished to establish his residence on Antonio Vaz Island, as it commanded the harbor entrance. Moses agreed to sell. Living in the Diaspora as strangers in a strange land, the Hebrew nation had long ago learned the importance of being on good terms, especially fiscal ones, with the ruling class. Moses had no need of the governor's money, but welcomed the opportunity to ingratiate himself with the self-styled Prince of Nassau. Coincidentally or not, the governor then hired Moses's brother Abraham and nephew Jacob as buying agents for the colony.

When the governor acquired the island, it was a barren place. Moses had built a dock and some shacks, referred to as "smugglers' cabins," and there were the crumbling remains of a deserted convent.[20] Immediately the governor brought in work crews to develop the island, which he now named Maurica in line with his princely tastes. A magnificent castle of brazilwood timber was built, as was an aviary, a zoo, and a fishpond ("He brought thither every kind of bird and animal."). He also created parks with bandstands and planted thousands of coconut palms and orchards of fruit trees. A new town, Mauritania, was raised, and two bridges connected it to the mainland. "Hither came the ladies and friends to pass the summer holidays, enjoy picnics, drinking parties, concerts and gambling . . . The Prince liked everyone to come and see his rarities and delighted in showing and explaining them."[21]

When the Dutch first arrived, Recife was a rural village of 150 houses; when they left two decades later, it was a bustling port of two thousand homes.[22] During the colony's peak years, it was a rare family in Amsterdam who did not have a relative or friend living in Recife. Brazilian Jewry numbered about 1,500; Amsterdam Jewry, 1,200. Working together as financiers, brokers, shippers, importers, and insurers, they dominated commerce between the two nations.[23]

In the 1640s, the Jews had a hundred ships plying the sugar

trade and the Periera family in Amsterdam owned the refineries that turned the brown sweetener into the white crystal grains everyone desired. Recife became known as "the port of the Jews," and its main thoroughfare was Rua dos Judios, the Street of the Jews.[24]

Although their number in Recife was only somewhat greater than in Amsterdam, relative to the latter's Christian population the difference was huge. In 1640, Amsterdam's Jews numbered less than 2 percent of the populace, while those in Recife constituted 30–40 percent of the white population. Given their merchandising bent, "Christian merchants soon found themselves reduced to the role of spectators of the Israelite business."[25] However, once they learned Portuguese and no longer needed the Jews as intermediaries, their leaders objected: "Almost the entire sugar trade is dominated by Jews [who] lie, use false weights, and practice usury."[26]

Competing merchants called on the colony's governing body, the Supreme Council, to force the Jews, if they couldn't be exiled, to at least wear red hats or a yellow insignia: "Everywhere else in the world this cheating and dishonest race is compelled to wear distinguishing signs on their clothing to identify them and show their inferiority."[27]

Against the envy and hostility of the Calvinists, and the grudging acceptance of the Portuguese planters, La Nação was defended by the ruling authorities, the Prince of Nassau, the Company, and Holland's States General, all of whom recognized and valued their indispensable role in transforming Recife into the richest port in the New World outside of Havana. Also, they were cognizant that, threatened by the Inquisition, the Jews more than any other group could be counted on to defend the colony.[28]

While the Company held a monopoly on the slave trade, and made a 240 percent profit per slave, Jewish merchants, as middlemen, also had a lucrative share, buying slaves at the Company auction and selling them to the planters on an installment plan—no money down, three years to pay at an interest rate of 40–50 percent. As debts were usually paid in sugar, Jews became the major sugar brokers. With their large profits—slaves were marked up 300 percent and dry goods 700 percent—they built stately homes in Recife, and owned ten of the 166 sugar plantations, including "some of the best plantations in the river valley of Pernambuco."[29]

Given their commanding position, and the time-honored prejudice against them, it is not surprising that competing merchants grumbled. "[The Jews] have become masters of the entire business of trade," and, sugar growers lamented, they "could not prosper because Negroes were too dear and interest too high."[30] These complaints were noted by a Dutch traveler to Brazil in the 1640s, who observed: "For the most part the Jews [are] concerned with business which would have been advantageous had their trade been confined to the ordinary rules of business and not reached such excesses."[31]

While their profits and interest rates appear excessive, in their defense, one must take into account that New Holland was a frontier society, a New World outpost surrounded by enemies. In spite of the colony's apparent wealth, capital was scarce and investments high risk. Jews, numbering approximately one-third of the population, were entitled to a third of the broker licenses. To offset this restriction, they sold shares in their licenses to other Jews. This aroused the ire of their competitors, who objected to the governor that "[the Jews] purchase the entire cargo of a trading ship, and divide it according to paid shares." Dismissing their complaint, he reminded them, "in the early days, Dutch brokers and merchants had lost the people's confidence through speculation and carelessness, which resulted in advantages for the Jews."[32]

During New Holland's existence, the Company transported 26,000 slaves to Brazil.[33] Over the course of the next two centuries, this number increased a thousandfold, and the slave trade spread to every New World colony and involved every European nation that had an oceangoing ship. Along the West African coast, men from Sweden, France, Denmark, Portugal, Germany, Holland, England, and Spain sailed slave ships and manned the slave forts.

While the Arabs controlled the East African slave trade, the West African trade was essentially a European-African enterprise—Africans sold Africans to Europeans to serve other Europeans. The Jews' role in the commercial process shows them to be neither better nor worse than others in an era when the morality of slavery was a nonissue. Color was not a criterion: Whites also bought and sold other whites, and Africans enslaved Africans. Slaves were coin in every realm, and Europe's seagoing nations bid for and zealously guarded the right to sell Africans to a Christian New World. As the historian Eli Faber documents in *Jews and the Slave Trade*, after the demise of New Holland, Jewish involvement in the trade was negligible.[34]

Brazil's Jews were more liberal in their observance than those in Holland. Whereas in Amsterdam, synagogue officers might rule for decades with an iron hand, those in Recife served only a year and could not stand for reelection. Disputes in the colony were settled by a majority vote of the Mahamad, and any member of the congregation could request an alternate judge if he felt the presiding one was biased. In Holland, Jews had to wait three years after being circumcised to join the congregation; in Recife the wait was one year. Ashkenazic Jews could not join Amsterdam's Sephardic synagogue, nor marry a member; in Recife, all Jews were treated equally. Their *hazan* (spiritual leader) was Isaac Aboab, a Cabala-practicing rabbi who later returned to Amsterdam, voted to excommunicate Spinoza, and subsequently followed the false messiah Sabbatai Zvei to Salonika.

Zur Israel funded a number of charitable programs: a ransom committee for captured brethren; dowries for poor unmarried women in Holland desiring a mate in Brazil; a fund that sent money to Israel; and another that served as a bank of last resort for debts to Christians. To finance these initiatives, members remitted a portion of every commercial transaction to the Mahamad and could be excommunicated if they failed to do so. Moses and other privateers were not exempt from the ruling, which specified a payment of 3 percent of the net proceeds of their booty.[35]

These payments comprise most of the entries in Zur Israel's minutes book. Others deal with laws and rulings made by the Mahamad to govern the community. Two that forbade social indulgences are of particular interest as they illuminate what must have been all too common vices: gambling and philandering. The Mahamad outlawed gambling on Friday afternoons, as too many members arrived late for Sabbath dinner, and in an effort to cool excessive libidos, imposed a whopping fifty-florin fine on any member caught bathing with a Christian woman in the *mikvah* (the ritual bath).[36]

Most members were from Holland, but Zur Israel's congregation also included Sephardim from Turkey, Spain, Portugal, and North Africa, as well as Ashkenazim from Germany, Poland, and Hungary.[37] If they philandered and gambled too much, well, this was the New World. Few settlers were overly concerned with morality. Indian and African concubines were common, but Christian women, however tempting, were out of bounds. Not all Jewish settlers were merchants, but whatever their vocation, their Judaism was always up front. Once during the holiday Simat Torah, they loudly paraded in the streets carrying the Torah. So enthusiastic was their celebration that the Calvinists accused them of "shameless boldness" and slandering the Christian religion. In response, Prince Maurice ordered them to hold their ceremonies in private, "so secretly that they should not be heard."[38]

An insight into the character of these pioneers is found in the further testimony of the informer who disclosed the role of Moses Cohen Henriques.

The spy, Captain Esteban de Fonseca, was a renegade Jew who left Amsterdam to return to Spain. In Madrid in April 1634, he appeared before the Inquisition. Testifying on "the damage done to His Majesty by the Jews of Holland,"[39] he alleged that eighteen ships were then being readied in Amsterdam to transport a hundred Jews to Brazil. But first they intended to go ashore near Coimbra, Portugal, the seat of the Inquisition, where two hundred Judaizers had recently been burned: "The men are to go to Coimbra . . . to sack the Inquisition and set its prisoners at liberty, and to plunder the convent of Santa Cruz."

Fonseca claimed that funds for the expedition had been "raised by subscription among all the Jews of Holland," and that the armada was "governed by a Jew who takes in his company 100 Jews . . . I shall name only the principal ones, for I should never get through if I named them all." Fonseca then named ten Jews—a minyan—including Moses's close friend Abraham Israel, whom he identified as the fleet's adjutant (administrative officer). Beyond elaborating on Moses's piracy and spying, Fonseca also accused him of concocting a particularly bold plan to capture Havana with African warriors disguised as slaves: "The landing is to be made under a flag of truce, pretending they escaped from the Hollanders, and [once inside the city] under cover of night, they would arm themselves and slaughter the soldiers."

Neither event occurred: There is no record of a Brazil-bound fleet stopping off in Portugal to sack the Inquisition, nor a Trojan horse ploy to capture Havana. Perhaps the backers of the Jewish-led armada learned their plans had been exposed and canceled them. Or perhaps Fonseca's charges were nothing more than barroom talk—he claimed to be a former crew member. In either case, his statement affirms the mettle of Moses and his mates. Over card games, they drank rum, smoked cigars, and discussed their various enterprises—shipping sugar, selling slaves, smuggling silver from Potosí—and plotted the overthrow of the Inquisition empire.

As long as Johan Maurice was governor, New Holland thrived. The colony's disparate groups regularly condemned one another, but ultimately got along. Annual sugar production doubled, from fifteen thousand tons at the beginning of the seventeenth century to thirty thousand tons during Maurice's tenure. In the process, the retail price of sugar was halved, thereby spreading consumption from the banquet table of the rich to the penny candy counter.[40]

While the Cohen Henriques brothers and their friends were carving a niche for themselves in Brazil, their cousins in Amsterdam were growing rich importing and exporting goods from all over the known world. Dutch captains, trading illegally with converso agents in ports throughout the Spanish Empire, brought cargo direct to Amsterdam. In Peru, where Jews controlled the silver trade, ore skimmed from the mines was exchanged for silk from China via Mexico; pimento spice from Jamaica found its way into Holland's smoked herring; pearls from Venezuela were a viable currency most everywhere. Spanish traders could match neither the price nor the quality of the goods the *contrabandistas* (free traders) had to offer.[41] Jews in Amsterdam in contact with Sephardic merchants in Europe, the Mediterranean, and points east passed the New World's resources on to them, and their goods on to the New World. As middlemen in this commerce, Amsterdam Jews made profits to and fro.

In 1640, after sixty years of union with Spain, Portugal again achieved its independence, the result of a bloodless coup in Lisbon by followers of the Duke of Braganza. The duke, now reigning as King John IV, sent a delegation to Holland to sign a peace pact and form an alliance against Spain.

The resulting treaty created a peculiar situation in Brazil.

Holland was now an ally of Portugal, yet occupied a major part of her New World colony. Rather than acknowledge this anomaly, and perhaps award Brazil's Portuguese certain privileges in recognition of their new status, the States General instead ordered Prince Maurice to capture as much surrounding territory as he could. The prince lost no time in carrying out this Machiavellian move. While he was ostensibly negotiating a truce with leaders of adjacent provinces under Portugal's control, his soldiers occupied their territory. At the same time, he sent a naval force to Africa to capture São Tomé and the port of Luanda in Angola.

By 1642, New Holland ruled most of northeast Brazil and the African entrepôts that transshipped most of the colony's slave labor.[42] The colony was at its zenith, but not for long. When the prince's contract was up, the States General decided his administration was too costly, and did not renew it. Admittedly, New Holland had become the most expensive colony in the Dutch empire, but she also produced the most money. Nevertheless, in September 1643, the prince was notified to return to Holland forthwith. To no avail did the leaders of New Holland's religious communities formally request he remain. The Jews' letter praised his "wise and happy rule," and thanked him for "the protection he had granted [them]." If he stayed, they promised to triple his income with an annual annuity.[43] But if he had to go, they wished to buy his castle and make it their synagogue. The Calvinists objected strongly to this, and persuaded the governor to decline.[44]

Whatever compelling reasons the States General may have had, the move to recall Maurice was shortsighted. In retrospect, the States General apparently had not taken into account that Portugal would not honor a peace treaty the Dutch themselves had voided. As soon as the prince stationed troops in the neighboring provinces, Portuguese nationals in New Holland began plotting to regain their colony, and two months before his departure, he received news that a border state had fallen to Portuguese rebels. It was March 1644, the beginning of the end of New Holland.

The revolt was led by João Fernando Vieira, a leader of the Portuguese community, who vowed to put his life and property at the service of "the restoration of our fatherland."[45] He, along with eighteen compatriots, concocted an assassination plot. They would invite "our Dutch chiefs" to a June banquet at Vieira's home to celebrate a saint's birthday, and then murder them all. Among the conspirators was a covert Jew, Sebastian Carvalho, who passed word of the plot to the leader of the Mahamad, Dr. Abraham de Mercado. The doctor, in turn, gave a letter to Abraham Cohen detailing the conspiracy and signed it "A Verdade Plus ultra" (The Ultimate Truth). When Cohen informed Prince Maurice of the deadly scheme, the ex-governor asked him to aid in the capture of the traitor.[46]

Vieira, having learned his plan had been exposed, gathered his men and escaped into the forested countryside. Cohen armed some comrades to go after them. In a brief skirmish, two Jews were slain. Cohen and other prosperous Jews, pledging "the dead must be avenged," financed a government expedition to track down the guerrillas. Six hundred Dutch soldiers and three hundred Indians were soon on Vieira's trail. Confidently, they marched in formation into the bush, only to fall into a rebel ambush and be routed. So began a civil war that was abetted by a run of poor sugar harvests in 1642, 1643, and 1644 that gained the rebellion the financial support of the major Portuguese planters. Faced with economic ruin, they renounced their debts and sided with the rebels.

In the summer of 1645, a horrific incident took place, with major repercussions. Rebel soldiers, attacking an island off Recife, captured a Dutch militia that included a squadron of thirteen Jews led by a Jewish captain. Separating the Jews from the other Dutch prisoners, they hanged them all. To the rebel commander, the Jews were more than enemy soldiers: they were traitors. The Portuguese leader therefore felt no qualms about stringing them up and burning their captain alive.[47]

When news of the atrocity reached Recife, the Supreme Council sent a formal communiqué to the Portuguese commander that caustically asked: "Why are Jewish prisoners of war martyred unto death in so beastly a manner? Are they worse people than we?"[48]

In Amsterdam, the Jewish council, the Parnassim, led by Uriel da Costa's younger brother, Abraham, petitioned the States General, "With tears of blood running from [our] hearts, order the government in Brazil to insure that in all agreements with the enemy, members of the Hebrew Nation should be treated like other Dutch subjects." The Jewish soldiers, they wrote, had been volunteers "vigilant in their efforts against the rebels [and] their undying loyalty had been proven by their denunciation of the conspiracy headed by Johann Vieira which failed thanks to Abraham Cohen and Dr. Mercado."[49]

Appealing to the Calvinists' devout belief in the Old Testament, in which Israel is called the people of God, the petitioners reminded the States General that the Lord loved and protected His people "at all times and will help and deliver from all danger those whom He has named His people . . . because God rewards those who have acted kindly towards this poor, dispersed Nation." They concluded their memorandum, quoting Queen Esther's plea to King Ahasuerus: "If it pleases the king, give me my life—that is my petition! Grant me my people—that is my request!"[50]

Responding to the Parnassim, the States General issued the Patenta Onrossa (Honorable Charter) declaring Holland's Jews to be Dutch subjects, entitled to nearly all rights pertaining to the burgher class. This decree on December 7, 1645, represents the first charter of equality a sovereign state conceded to the Jewish nation in the Western Hemisphere.[51] The Supreme Council in New Holland was thereupon instructed:

> The Hebrew Nation in Brazil [is] to be protected from
> any damage to person or property, in the same manner
> as all the citizens of the United Netherlands . . . [and]
> we shall favor . . . the Jewish nation on all occa-
> sions . . . without . . . making any distinction . . . between
> them and those of our other nationals . . . The Jewish
> nation will thereby . . . be animated and encouraged
> to further the service in this state and that of the West
> India Company.[52]

Owing to the civil war, by the fall of 1645 many Dutch colonists had returned to Holland, and the 1,450 remaining Jews now comprised nearly half of the white settlers. Recife had come under siege. A German working for the Company, informed that a regiment of 350 Jews was among the city's defenders, reasoned: "The Jews, more than anyone else, were in a desperate situation and preferred to die sword in hand than face their fate under the Portuguese yoke: the flames."[53]

The chief rabbi would later write: "Rich and poor alike could not obtain food . . . we starved . . . there was nothing left. Any dried up bread was considered a delicacy."[54] The rebels gave the Dutch three days to surrender, and promised the Jews "quarter if they accepted the Lord Jesus Christ as their savior." The offer was rejected after a "fierce debate" when Abraham Cohen told his comrades not to delude themselves that the rebels would be taken in by a sham conversion, and warned "if they fell into Portuguese hands they would be burned at the stake."[55] Later, four Dutch fugitives who deserted the city told the rebels, "None were opposed to surrender more than the Jews . . . [who swore] to sell their lives dearly."[56]

Despite the Jews' loyalty, some clergy continued to fault them. When the siege began, they complained to the Supreme Council that "on the Lord's day," the Jews keep their stores open, send their children to religious school, and make their slaves work. The Jews, rather than assert that they observed a Saturday Sabbath, chose to appease the petty minds of the ministers and agreed to also honor Sunday as a day of rest. With the city under siege, they had more vital concerns than contending over the Lord's Day.

Cohen took up a collection of money that sustained the war effort until the following spring, when the long-awaited relief ships arrived from Holland. Not everyone was pleased by his action. Those who favored surrender accused Cohen of bribing the Supreme Council to continue what they saw as a Jewish war.[57] (After the siege, the charges were dismissed, and Cohen was honored by the Council for his deed.)

The Patenta Onrossa was put to a test two years later, when rebels seized ten Jews from a Dutch ship and sentenced them to die as "blasphemous apostates."[58] The States General protested to Portugal's King John with a demand that Jews be treated like other Dutch subjects. In August 1649, the king replied that the rebels assured him those Dutch Jews who had not been baptized would be set free, but added that he could not interfere in "heretical matters involving false conversos."[59] Among the latter was a cousin of the Cohen Henriques brothers, Abraham Bueno Henriques. Born and baptized in Portugal, he was declared a heretic and handed over to the Inquisitions; his sentence is unknown.

King John, at the time, denied supporting the rebellion while preparing to do just that. Moreover, in 1649, he secured the support of Portugal's New Christians by promising them a blanket pardon and trade concessions. Anticipating victory, one of Portugal's richest conversos, Duarte da Silva, arranged with the king to set up the Compania du Brasil on the lines of the Dutch West India Company. Once victory over the Dutch was attained, the company would deal in Brazilian sugar, dye-wood, and other imports, and supply the colony with wine, oil, and flour. No mention was made of the slave trade. In return, King John pledged that the estates of converso shareholders would be exempt from confiscation by the Inquisition, and he pardoned them for past offenses.

It is one of the sad ironies in the history of these beleaguered people that the cost of the reconquest and the destruction of the first open Jewish community in the New World was borne by Portugal's *gente da Nação* (people of the Nation). Da Silva assumed that he would head up the new company, but it didn't turn out that way. A year before "the war of divine liberty" was won, he was imprisoned as a Judaizer, and the business of Brazil became the province of the king.[60]

The final battle began on December 20, 1653, when a Portuguese armada—paid for by her New Christians—sailed into Recife. Although the few remaining settlers had enough food and munitions to hold out until Holland sent reinforcements, morale was understandably low. Two months before, Holland had recalled home the two warships guarding Recife to defend her ports against a possible sea attack by England.

In early January, Abraham Cohen informed New Holland's military commander that he had overheard Dutch soldiers say they would rather sack the houses of the city's rich Jews than continue fighting. This development so enraged the commander that he immediately mobilized everyone in the city and called on them "to protect themselves from their own troops." It was a futile move. All knew the desertion of the troops signaled the end.[61]

New Holland's historical record supports the notion that nothing of consequence happened in the colony without Abraham Cohen knowing and abetting it. When the Supreme Council decided to capture the guerrilla leader Vieira, they hired Cohen to spring the trap; when the Dutch ran out of money to pay troops, Cohen advanced the funds; when merchants looked to flee, he had the Supreme Council issue arms to Jews who vowed to stay. A sonnet composed by a Jewish poet of Amsterdam, Daniel Levi de Barrios (1625–79), celebrated Cohen's patriotic behavior.[62] It reads, in part:

Today Abraham Cohen enjoys the spotlight of the Empire . . . in nine years continuous, with great magnanimity [he] helped without number Jew and Christian alike in the atrocious misery with what they needed.

On January 26, 1654, New Holland surrendered. Two days later, Recife was occupied; agents of the Inquisition moved into Prince Maurice's castle, and Zur Israel was converted into an army barracks.[63] Jews were given three months to leave or be handed over to the Inquisition. Among the 650 Jews who remained to the very end were the Cohen Henriques brothers and their Amsterdam comrades. For twenty-four years, Recife had been a Rock of Israel. Now, threatened with the Holy Fire, the Jews were forced to hit the familiar Diaspora road again. The question that concerned them was, Where next?

While the Rock of Israel still stood firm on the Rock of Brazil, elsewhere in the New World, Inquisition flames blazed. In Peru and Mexico in the late 1630s and 1640s, the leaders of the empire's two major secret Jewish communities were arrested for conspiring to overthrow Spanish rule. In each case the Judaizers were charged with being part of La Complicidad Grande, the Great Conspiracy. Peru's Jewish leaders were imprisoned for three years before being burned at the stake, while those in Mexico were confined in "secret cells" for up to eight years before suffering the same fate.

The destruction of the New World's two major covert colonies of Jews weighed heavily on those about to flee Recife. To realize the Holy Terror's impact on the psyches of all pioneer Jews, we need to review the rise and fiscal dominance of these mercantile outlaws. The following accounts are condensed from the writings of noted historian Seymour Liebman on the Great Conspiracy in Peru and Mexico.[64]

The richest Jewish community in the richest colony in the New World began when a shepherd pulling up a weed bush saw, to his astonishment, that the stones sticking to the roots were actually chunks of silver. A mountain of silver had been discovered, and in its shadow a community of Jews evolved to manage it. From all over the New World, they came to deal in the precious metal that circulated as pieces of eight, the major currency of the period. The best became the silver merchants of Potosí.

With its silver mountain and gangs of Indian slaves, who kept the mine working nonstop, Potosí was a surreal combination of California during the gold rush and Pharaoh's Egypt. In 1622, the city was the largest in the New World (population 120,000, mostly Indian) and was reported to be "overrun" with Jews. The Inquisition report stated: "Potosí is filled with Portuguese, all of the Hebrew nation . . . the export of silver is almost exclusively in the hands of crypto Jews."

In the 1630s, before the arrival of the Grand Inquisitor and his white-hooded minions, the Jews in Recife, Peru, and Mexico were in regular contact with one another, their transactions fueled by the silver merchants. Jewish wealth and power in the New World was at its peak. But by the end of the decade, the mountain of silver had attracted holier-than-thou claim jumpers crying heresy, and Peru's secret Jews were targeted. Thousands of names are contained in the trial records of the Lima Inquisition. Chief Inquisitor Andrés Juan Gaitan, who presided over the trials, said that heresy and conspiracy, not greed, had caused him to act. Others questioned his motives when he began traveling about in a silver coach drawn by six horses in silver harness, sporting silver horseshoes.

Still, considering what happened in Brazil, where false conversos assisted the Dutch invasion, there is no reason to doubt that overthrowing Spanish rule, in league with the Dutch, was an option Peru's covert Jews considered. As previously noted, when the Portuguese authorities received the news, they immediately warned Spain's king that the capture of Brazil by Hollanders and Jews was "not so much to make themselves masters of the sugar of Brazil as of the silver of Peru."

In Lima, Peru's capital, the silver merchants' agents funneled silver skimmed from the mines out of the country, and soon were as wealthy as their suppliers. Not content to play by the rules of mercantilism, they avoided Seville and dealt directly with Europe. At the time of Peru's Great Conspiracy of 1636, their contraband trade with Europe was greater than Peru's legitimate trade with Spain. An informer's letter to Inquisitor Gaitan, as quoted by Liebman, charged:

> The city is thick with them. Everything goes through their hands. They are in absolute control of the traffic in merchandise ranging from brocade to sackcloth, diamonds to cumin seeds . . . to the most precious pearl and vilest Guinea black. They are the masters of commerce.

Jewish merchants reportedly regarded Spanish Christians as "interlopers" whose interest was "confined to the extraction of silver," and allowed them entry into the silver market only if they took on a Jewish partner approved by Manuel Batista Pérez, described in the Inquisitor's report as the city's "wealthiest and most cultured Jew." Born in Seville in 1593, Pérez moved to Lima with his wife and three children and a hefty bankroll to invest for his brothers-in-law back in Spain. Though Spanish, Manuel called himself Portuguese because, as noted, Spanish New Christians were not allowed in the New World.

The Inquisitors reported that Pérez had a huge library, "[was] well versed in theology . . . foremost in the observance of the Law of Moses, [and was] held as an oracle by the Hebrew nation." He owned silver shops, invested in banking, and owned a number of mule trains that carried the bars of silver on a thousand-mile journey across the Andes to Lima (and on the sly, via the Río de la Plata, south to Buenos Aires).

Pérez, addressed by fellow Jews as "the Great Captain," was tried as the head of La Complicidad Grande. He was accused of having raised funds to finance a Dutch invasion, and of plotting to assist the Dutch army. The conspiracy began unraveling when a Lima merchant was charged with "adhering to the Law of Moses" for refusing to trade on a Saturday. Tortured, he revealed names; additional arrests and tortures followed, revealing more names.

In two days, over a hundred Jews were arrested. More would have been taken except, as the Inquisition reported, "the prisons are full. For lack of space we do not carry out a number of warrants in this city . . . people no longer trust each other, but go about in constant astonishment at the charges against a friend or comrade of whom they thought so much." The city's "most Christian gentlemen" were arrested:

No one of the accused Judaizers is being taken into custody who did not go about loaded with rosaries, relics, images, the ribbon of St. Augustine, the cordon of

St. Francis and other devotions and many with horsehair shirts and disciplines; they know the whole catechism and they always say the rosary.

In Lima's public square on January 23, 1639, an auto-da-fé condemned sixty-one Jews, and consigned Pérez and eleven others to be purified by fire. Many of the rest were sentenced to serve as oarsmen on Spanish galleys, in effect a death sentence, as oarsmen usually died before their time was up.

Pérez's estates were auctioned off for the modern equivalent of nearly $20 million. And that amount was undervalued: Inquisitor Gaitan had his agents bid for the property, and it was probably not a good idea to challenge their bids. When leading merchants accused Gaitan of having used his powers for mercenary reasons, he justified the arrests: "First because they are Judaizing heretics. Second, they conspired with the invading Dutch to blow up the city of Guadalupe by which they had begun to bore a hole in the powder magazine."

Whatever the truth of the charge, a noted researcher concluded that Gaitan's primary motive was greed: "The real crime against these and the two thousand Portuguese residing at that time in the country was that they made great fortunes . . . a plot imputed to them to seize the Kingdom of Peru from Spain was a political pretext to go with a religious pretext. Branded Jewish revolutionaries, there was no escape for them."

In the aftermath of the great auto-da-fé of 1639, the money world of Peru was overturned, Lima's leading bank failed, and Old Christians became the new power brokers. Gaitan and his assistants "speculated with the money of the Holy Office, and waxed rich thereon, took mistresses and dressed like young bloods in silk and lace."

Some of Lima's Jews escaped to Mexico, including Manuel Pérez's cousin, who married into the "first family" of Jews there, headed by Simon Vaez and his wife, Juana Henriquez. But there was no escape. The following year the Inquisition descended on Mexico.

In a period of relative peace, before their eight-year nightmare, about three thousand Jews were secretly settled throughout Mexico. In Mexico City, there were three congregations that can be roughly classified as orthodox, conservative, and reformed. There were contacts between them, but each had its own social structure and business dealings that carried over into imprisonment. Their downfall came when a priest's servant claimed that he overheard four Portuguese speaking on a city street one summer night. They reportedly said: "If there were four more men as courageous as they in the city, they would set fire to the House of the Inquisition and the Inquisitors would burn."

On July 7, 1642, the resulting investigation announced: "The Kingdom of Mexico is in the hands of Judaizers!" Authorities sealed the borders, and Jewish leaders began disappearing. Seized after midnight, they were confined to "secret cells." Eventually more than four hundred Jews were imprisoned, overflowing the Inquisition prison and a convent next door (the nuns had to move).

Spies and tortured interrogations with the *porto* had the prisoners scrambling to keep their confessions in line with those of others in the community. The *porto* was Mexico's version of the rack: a naked prisoner lay faceup on an iron bedframe, tied by cords attached to handles on the side of the bed. Each turn of the handle tightened the cords' viselike pressure. The torturer was limited to six turns of a handle, as more would cause the cords to cut through to the bone, and it was against Inquisition rules to draw blood. At first each group resisted, confident that *they* would be released, that *their* connections or plan would work. But as time went on, and their expected release did not occur, confessions were made. Individual files, compiled over the decade, run to hundreds of pages. The torturous years produced extreme effects, including an alleged Messiah; when he proved not to be the one, another group looked to a baby born in an Inquisition cell; others said a lovely child they called "Little Dove" was to be the Madonna.

In 1646, four years after the first arrest, the trials began. Each year, from 1646 through 1649, an auto-da-fé was held and a few dozen Jews were tried and sentenced. The autos-da-fé were treated as a fiesta, and the whole country turned out for these Judgment Days in the capital. No prisoner knew until the eve of the auto-da-fé if he or she would be tried on the morrow. Some of the accused spent eight years in the secret cells before being brought to trial. Only four Jews were acquitted. The usual sentence was two hundred lashes and life imprisonment. Nearly a hundred were burned at the stake.

During this nightmare decade, the prisoners never stopped seeking their release: Rumors were hot—"the Portuguese are sending an Armada to conquer New Spain and liberate us." Plots were convoluted—one leader's uncle was married to the sister of the wife of the king's attorney . . . and a little more "George" (money) would do the trick. Wishful thinking was the order of the day—"The Holy Pontiff and the king will send a general pardon on the next flotilla because they would not permit such important families to go out in autos." But they did.

Portugal's independence at the beginning of the decade had halted the *penetración Portuguesa*, the flow of Portuguese Jews to Spanish colonies, and in the 1640s those who were there came under increasing scrutiny. King Philip no longer relied on Jews for assistance in his colonies, and without his intercession, the arrests and autos-da-fé in the aftermath of Mexico's Great Conspiracy destroyed the community.

By the time of the Brazil exodus, the elimination of these two enclaves once again made the New World off-limits to Jews. On the eve of their expulsion, their options were few: They might settle one of the small Caribbean islands,[65] return to Holland, or venture farther north to a colony known as New Amsterdam. Moses Cohen Henriques at this time was fifty-three and Abraham forty-nine. They and their mates had been championing Jewish rights most of their lives. Taking a cue from their childhood rabbi, who had shown that age was irrelevant when it came to continuing the struggle, Rabbi Palache's old boys were spurred into action. Although they had been defeated in Brazil, and were well into middle age, their determination, creativity, and courage over the next two decades would win most of the freedoms that Jews in the West enjoy today.

Chapter Seven

EXODUS TO HERETIC ISLAND

In February 1654, Abraham Cohen bade a solemn farewell to friends and family at the Recife dockside. After a decadelong civil war, Dutch Brazil was no more; Jews had until April to quit the land or be turned over to the Inquisition. Cohen and the remaining hundred or so Jewish families would depart the following month aboard fourteen ships sent from Holland to carry them to Amsterdam. All hoped to meet again in another New World sanctuary, but for now their futures were unclear.

Two ships embarked that day—one to Curaçao, the Dutch island north of Brazil, the other to a faraway island in the northern climes purchased by a Dutch settler thirty years before for twenty-four dollars' worth of trinkets and named New Amsterdam by its optimistic owner. Aboard the Curaçao-bound ship were Cohen's twenty-four-year-old son Jacob, who would be attending the wedding of a namesake cousin,* and his brother Moses, who intended to return to his seafaring ways. Taking passage on the other ship, the *Falcon*, on the more ambitious voyage, were Cohen's cousin Benjamin Bueno Mesquita and his two sons, as well as a lifelong friend, the widower Abraham Israel and his son, Isaac.

The Curaçao sailing was uneventful. Not so the *Falcon*'s. Intending to put in at the French island of Martinique to drop off passengers and take on provisions, the ship ran into a ferocious storm. For ten days, gale-force winds, howling out of the northeast, blew the *Falcon* far off course into the western Caribbean. By the time the storm let up, the refugees found themselves in enemy waters "driven against their will by adverse winds to the island of Jamaica."[1]

Jamaica lay in the middle of the shipping lanes linking the New World with the Old. With its surrounding waters frequented by pirates lying in wait for Spain's treasure-laden ships and cargo vessels, all foreign boats were suspect. In late April, the *Falcon* was spotted off Jamaica's southeast coast, and an armed squadron was dispatched to bring it to port. Although its captain, Jan Craeck, explained that his passengers—a few dozen Jews and a small congregation of Calvinists—were refugees fleeing Brazil, Jamaica's authorities refused to allow them to depart.

Despite the obvious truth of the captain's statement, the local Spanish leaders had a vested interest in rejecting it. Years before, they had devised a nefarious scheme to overthrow the island's owners, Columbus's heirs, and gain legal right to their

---

* This other line of the Cohen Henriques family would prove a source of confusion to later historians.

lands. As the island belonged to the progeny of the great explorer, no matter how large or prosperous a settler's estate, it was not his. The discoverer's family owned every inch, rendering the ranchers little more than legalized squatters. In order to obtain title to their estancias, they would first have to arrange for the Spanish Crown to reclaim the island. The arrival of an enemy ship with "suspect heretics" aboard enabled them to put into play their plan to oust the family.

The detained passengers had no way of knowing that they had become pawns in a century-long conflict that had been simmering since the island had been given away. While converted Jews, working with the Columbus family, operated the island as a profitable way station for ships of any nation, and as a transshipment port for cargo going to and from the New World, local hidalgos stewed over their legal status, and were determined to end it by any means. The Jews' protected status was about to change, but not the way the local Spaniards envisioned.[2]

From Jamaica's founding in 1511, its converted Jews had lived peacefully under the protective wing of the Columbus family. They called themselves "Portugals" and though their religiosity was suspect, no one could seriously question their bona fides while the family kept the island off-limits to the Inquisition. This prohibition ended in 1622, when an ecclesiastic coup transferred local authority over the Church to the archdiocese of Santo Domingo.[3] With a foreign bishop allied with Jamaica's hidalgos dictating policy, the Holy Inquisition was granted access to the island. Jamaica's big ranchers thereupon appointed themselves *familiars* of the Inquisition, and patiently awaited an opportunity to charge that the island was riddled with heresy. Such an accusation would give the Crown the excuse it needed to void its treaty with the family and take back Jamaica.

King Philip IV had been alerted from the start of his reign that the Columbus family was secretly mining gold and, working with the Portugals, ran the island as a major smuggling port. The capture of a heretic ship thus furnished the hidalgos with the excuse to summon the Holy Inquisitor from Colombia to investigate the suspect heretics and likewise expose the Portugals as Judaizers. No longer would Jamaica be subject to a feudal lord, and the hidden gold mine would revert to the king.

After the union of the Iberian nations in 1580, Jamaica's conversos had felt themselves secure. The Columbus family had not only kept the Inquisition from darkening Jamaica's shores, but had also kept out all high church officials. In 1582, a visiting cleric declared he was the first abbot to ever visit the island. Given Jamaica's patrimony, the island attracted few permanent settlers. In the final decades of the sixteenth century, with the island population at a low point, nearly half were Portugals, and two successive governors were themselves conversos.[4]

As the century drew to a close, so did the halcyon days of the covert Hebrews. In 1596, a lawsuit between two contending Columbus heirs put Jamaica's ownership on hold. With neither claimant having the right to appoint a new governor, Spain's king named his own man. Dire consequences followed. Within days of his arrival, the governor, Don Melgarejo de Córdoba, reported to the king that Jamaica was a rogue island, existing solely on "illicit trade": "The island is like a keystone, a convenient stopping place for corsairs & traders who infest the coast to fit out their ships and get provisions from its abundant store."

He was equally shocked by the lack of religious fealty: "The temples are ill-treated. No mass is said in the principal church because it leaks all over and the walls are falling down."[5]

The Portugals had no compunction about doing business with Spain's enemies. Trading with the Dutch and English ships was profitable, and their wares were more affordable than the manufactured goods and textiles carried from Spain, whose ships only stopped in Jamaica to take on provisions on their way to the rich cities on the Spanish Main. One illegal trader was the pirate known as Motta the Portuguese, whose Jewish descendants are prominent today in Jamaica and Panama. The governor charged that Motta and his partner Abraham, "a Fleming," regularly called on Jamaica from a base in Cuba where they "put up shops and [play] games of bowls, and people go there from the country to be cured." Apparently Motta and the Portugals shared a Judaic interest in literature, as the governor accused the pirate of trafficking in "prohibited books which sowed a bad seed among the natives and Negroes."[6]

Melgarejo, in his crackdown on illicit trade, initiated a sea patrol by a brigantine and two naval launches to discourage foreign ships. The Portugals, faced with a leader out to destroy their livelihood, turned on him. The governor complained to His Majesty:

> Lampoons are insolently made on me, saying that I should let them live and not oppress them. They say that some night they will send 100 Englishmen to take me prisoner. All these enmities arise from my defending Your Majesty's reputation and commands. I would punish these people but there is no strong jail, nor is

there anybody of whom I could ask assistance except the delinquents themselves and their relatives, for they are all over the country . . . I am very much in danger that these people may take my life.[7]

To secure his person, he recruited four hundred soldiers from Puerto Rico and quartered fifty of them in his home. His action was endorsed by Jamaica's Cabildo, a five-man governing body of wealthy planters. Although they also profited from what was known as the "silent trade," they saw its suppression as an opportunity to discredit the Columbus family. Eventually the divergent interests of the Portugals, loyal to the Columbus family, and the Cabildo ranchers, who stood to gain title to their lands only if the Spanish king reclaimed Jamaica, made a clash between the two groups inevitable.

Melgarejo ruled for ten years and accomplished much: he repopulated the island, built up its defenses, and suppressed piracy and illegal trade while holding off accusations he was heavily engaged in it.[8] But he came up empty in his search for Columbus's gold mine. In his final communiqué to the king, he wrote that he was sure the mine was secreted in the Blue Mountains, but the two expeditions he sent out had not found it.[9]

In 1622, an ill-suited Columbus heir, Don Nuño Colón, was confirmed as the island's ruler. However, before he was able to reassert his family's control over Jamaica, two leaders of the Cabildo engineered an ecclesiastic coup that threatened to expose the Portugals as Jews. Operating with the connivance of the Crown, their leader, Francisco de Leiba, the self-styled "King of Jamaica,"[10] together with his cousin, Sanchez Ysassi, plotted with Ysassi's eldest son, a member of the Church hierarchy in Santo Domingo, to wrest control of the Jamaican church. The occasion was the 1622 Synod of Caribbean Churches.[11] Philip III had died the previous year, and following the coronation of his son, Philip IV, the region's prelates called on the new king to sponsor a church conference in Santo Domingo to reformulate policy on issues of Christian doctrine.

During the ensuing four-month synod, hundreds of decrees were passed, including one in the final session that—unlike the others—received no comment. Details are not known, but the upshot of this particular ruling was to transfer jurisdiction over the Jamaican church to the archbishop of Santo Domingo and his suffragan (assistant bishop), who happened to be Ysassi's son. When the conference ended, the chief plotters, Leiba and Ysassi (whom Melgarejo had lauded as "the leading colonists who sustain, protect and defend the State"), were sworn in as officers of the Inquisition.[12]

With this, a new force entered Jamaican politics, one that opposed the Columbus family and its chief allies, the Portugals. Under the nose of Don Nuño Colón, an inept ruler who may not have even visited the island, members of the Cabildo began to use their power in support of secret moves by the Crown to reclaim Jamaica. Their maneuvers were given impetus by the king's loss in September 1622 of his gold ship, the *Nuestra Señora de Atocha*. Returning from Havana, the galleon was battered by a hurricane off the Florida Keys and sank with forty-seven tons of gold and silver that Philip desperately needed to pay his creditors. Whatever value Jamaica had, he now wanted.[13]

The Portugals, sensing their days were numbered, looked first for aid from Holland. Dutch privateers were active in the Caribbean, and regularly stopped at Jamaica's ports. But, like

Moses Cohen Henriques, they were individual corsairs whose specialty was capturing ships, not countries. The one Dutch group that could pull off a full-scale invasion—the Dutch West India Company—was then preoccupied with mobilizing for their two-front invasion of Brazil and Peru the following year.

Although the Dutch were not interested in capturing Jamaica, England was. In 1597, Sir Anthony Shirley, a privateer whose marauding was in part financed by Queen Elizabeth, invaded Jamaica. For two weeks, he occupied the capital, La Vega, and plundered the countryside, and afterward wrote: "We have not found in the Indies a more pleasant and wholesome place. It abounds with beef and cassava, & most pleasant fruits. It is a marvelous fertile island, & is a garden or store house for the Spanish Main."[14] English traders who frequented Jamaica's ports shared Shirley's enthusiasm. But however tempting the conquest, it would take the Portugals' promise of acquiring Jamaica's golden legend to lure the English to invade.

Early in the century, Englishmen had pioneered the New World's northern climes, maintaining barely surviving colonies in Virginia and Bermuda and a dissident settlement of Pilgrims in a land they called New England. But these places had neither gold nor silver, and were far from the trade routes that carried the New World's riches to the Spanish king. And so they looked south. As Sir Walter Raleigh wrote, "It is his Indian gold that indangereth and disturbeth all the nations of Europe."[15] Raleigh was another son of Devon, the home of John Hawkins and Sir Francis Drake, the English heroes who had exposed the vulnerability of the Spanish Empire and the wealth that awaited a daring adventurer. But, unlike them, Sir Walter was not interested in smuggling or piracy. Having squandered his fortune colonizing Virginia, it was Indian gold he sought.

Chief among the golden legends was El Dorado, a mythical city in the Andes with riches surpassing those of Mexico and Peru. It was said to be by a large lake, backed by a hill of gold. Twice during Elizabeth's reign, Raleigh set out to find the ephemeral kingdom. Like dozens of adventurers before him, all he found was jungle, swamps, pestilence, and hostile natives.

When James I became king in 1603, Raleigh was sent to the Tower of London on a trumped-up charge of treason, but due to his popularity, James waived his death sentence. For the next thirteen years, Raleigh languished in the Tower and dreamed of again attempting to find El Dorado. Two young royals who visited him often and shared his fantasy were James's son Charles and George Villiers, the king's favorite, who together managed to obtain their hero's freedom so he could again seek the golden city.

When Raleigh's expedition set sail, King James, in one of history's great betrayals, confided in the Spanish ambassador, Gondomar, what Raleigh was up to. In doing so, he hoped to mend fences with the ambassador, because relations had been strained since the Palache trial three years before. If Raleigh realized his dream, James would not have turned down his royal fifth, but just the same, he felt it prudent to distance himself from the deed by handing Gondomar "a precise inventory of Raleigh's ships, armaments, ports of call, even a chart of his proposed route."[16] When Raleigh arrived at the headwaters of the Orinoco River on the north coast of South America, the

Spaniards were waiting with loaded cannon and routed his expedition. Sir Walter limped back to England a broken man. Gondomar demanded an audience with James. Furious, he spat: "I will be brief. Raleigh and his captains are pirates and must be sent in chains to Spain to be hung in Madrid's Plaza Mayor."[17] The king promised satisfaction. Five weeks later, he sent Raleigh to the chopping block.

Raleigh lost his head, but his quest for legendary riches in the New World was taken up by the young royals who had befriended him. Rather than El Dorado, they would embrace another gilded fantasy that had been bantered about in court circles from the time the Admiral of the Ocean Sea returned from his voyages of discovery. Extraordinary legends about the New World abounded, and there was ample reason to be a believer, as the land was filled with riches. By 1600, Spain had gained triple the amount of gold that had been in circulation before Columbus's voyage, and Peru's silver mountain was mined for a hundred years in increasing amounts, only to be surpassed by the discovery in Mexico of yet another mountain of silver.

So it was that the legend of the lost gold mine of Columbus was taken up by the king's son and George Villiers. While perhaps not as seductive as Raleigh's El Dorado, nor as wistful as Ponce de León's Fountain of Youth, or as elusive as Coronado's Seven Golden Cities, Columbus's hidden mine, "not yet . . . opened by the King of Spain or any other,"[18] had its own magnetic attraction. It was said to be somewhere in the mountainous island of Jamaica, where the great discoverer had been marooned for a year. Its allure was such that when Raleigh was preparing for his final voyage, Gondomar (until James told him otherwise) thought Jamaica was targeted, and notified Madrid to alert the island to fortify and prepare for invasion.

In the summer of 1623, George Villiers, with young Prince Charles in tow, was in Madrid on a fanciful marital mission that he and Gondomar had hatched to wed the prince to Spain's infanta, seventeen-year-old Princess María. When it became apparent, through a succession of misdeeds, that the so-called Spanish Match would not materialize, a court spy, in contact with Jamaica's Portugals, got word to Villiers: In return for a successful invasion of the island, they would reveal to their liberator the concealed site of the legendary mine.[19]

The Spanish spy's offer appealed to Villiers, whose egotism knew no bounds. He had been presented to King James at a London theater ten years earlier, and had become lover and confidant to both the king and his son Charles, the reticent Prince of Wales. He had risen from royal cup bearer to become the Duke of Buckingham, and his swift rise bound him to no one but the king.

The "secret overture" was made at the Escorial Palace, where Villiers and Charles were encamped in adjoining suites during their mission to bring off the Spanish Match—a marriage that would avert a pending war with Spain and make Villiers the godfather of a united Europe. Unfortunately, when Charles attempted to woo the infanta in the royal garden—strictly off-limits to all but the royal family—the gentle, reverent girl ran off screaming that she'd "sooner enter a convent" than marry him.[20]

In the days that followed, the duke comforted Charles. They

would return home, declare war on Spain, and pursue a treasure that had been spoken of since the time of discovery: the lost gold mine of Columbus. He had gotten the idea from a clandestine report he received from the Spanish king's secretary, Don Hermyn, who saw in the apparent collapse of the match an opportunity to acquire a share of the mine for himself.

Hermyn's secret memo to the duke presented a detailed account of his experience the year before, when he had been sent undercover to Jamaica by the king and his first minister, Count-Duke Olivares, to find out about the mine from the Portugals, the only people thought to be privy to its secret location. Once he had gained their confidence, he was taken to an isolated valley in Jamaica's rugged interior: "where the earth is black, Rivulets discover the source of the Mine." The gold, he observed, "is found neere the superficies of the Earth and slides down in the Rivers . . . The Vayne between the Rocks is but two inches wyde." As proof he had been to the mine, Hermyn engraved his initials on a rock which he hid near the mine's entrance.

Delighted with his find—he had been promised a tenth part of the proceeds—he returned to Spain and reported his discovery to Olivares. To acquire the mine, he proposed that the Crown expose Jamaica's Portugals as heretic traitors to justify reclaiming the island. To his astonishment, instead of welcoming the news, Olivares had him imprisoned and he was released only after being sworn to silence by the minister, who warned that if he spoke of the mine to anyone it would mean his death.

Olivares rarely left Philip's side. From the time his royal charge was thirteen, he supervised his learning. In 1621, when sixteen-year-old Philip became king, Olivares sought to mold him in the grand style of Charles V. There was one major impediment: Spain was in debt. In order to restore its fiscal health, he needed to befriend the very people Hermyn proposed they expose.

Count-Duke Olivares was a sincere converso, a devout Catholic who wore a piece of the True Cross around his neck, and kept other relics with which he regularly prayed. However, his faith did not interfere with his primary goal: to revitalize Spain's economy by courting those he would later label, in defending himself from the Inquisition, "the most perfidious of all heretics—the Jews."[21]

New World silver fueled the Empire. Needing bridge loans until the annual silver fleet arrived, Olivares contracted Genoese bankers, who, to his chagrin, regularly raised the interest rate. After one excessive spike, Olivares declared he would not let Spain be held ransom by their collusion, and turned to converso financiers in Lisbon who offered lower interest. Although their allegiance to Christianity was suspect—some had been living as secret Jews for a century or more—Olivares encouraged them to move to Spain, promising a general pardon and other inducements.

The Lisbon bankers were one part of Olivares's plan to fund the empire; another was to attract those they dealt with: the merchants, traders, accountants, insurers, and commodity buyers, conversos all, who with their foreign agents dominated empire commerce. Olivares saw this exiled entrepreneurial class as unparalleled creators of wealth, and believed that their presence in Spain would generate new revenue. In the New World, they had helped implement the system that routed all registered trade through Spain, while at the same time setting up a parallel trade network that illegally funneled a large portion of New World wealth outside the empire. In Olivares's day, this unregistered commerce, called the "silent trade," siphoned off upward of 25 percent of the silver stream to pay for European goods and slaves brought illegally to the New World. In return, the converso entrepreneurs shipped goods from the New World directly to Amsterdam, Bordeaux, Leghorn, and other ports where Jewish merchants were welcome as long as they maintained a Christian facade. By encouraging these exiled conversos to move back, Olivares hoped to make Spain the home base for this heretofore illegal trade.

His master plan to co-opt the conversos included those in Jamaica. Beyond the island's link in the "silent trade" network, its strategic location was integral to his defensive plan for the Caribbean. As Hermyn had written, "Jamaica lies in the belly of the New Spanish Sea and commands the Gulf of Mexico . . . all the fleets which come from the mainland must pass in sight of it." To protect the shipping lanes, Olivares called for fourteen warships to be based principally in Jamaica to patrol the sea. It therefore did not bode well to implement his Caribbean defense and his courtship of conversos by adopting Hermyn's plan to unmask those conversos living in Jamaica.[22]

Rejected and imprisoned by his former patrons, Hermyn turned to Villiers, who agreed to grant him "the same conditions promised him by the King." But now, instead of exposing the Portugals, Hermyn proposed that Villiers ally with them to conquer the island for England. Jamaica's covert Jews, long safely settled as Portuguese conversos, had told Hermyn they were now being threatened with exposure by the Inquisition and offered to assist an invading army. Success was assured because Portugals made up "most of the island's 800 man defense force . . . [and] long for nothing so much as to be free from the Spanish yoke." Their hatred of the Spanish "was so great that they could never be brought to discover their secrets to them," but would reveal to their liberator the location of "the secret golden mine, which hath not yet been opened by the King of Spain, or by any other."

Hermyn told Buckingham he would go to Jamaica to prepare the ground for the invasion, but when the Englishmen left, the turncoat's ambitions were neutralized when Olivares had him poisoned.

After the Madrid fiasco, and the death of King James in 1625, the duke was involved in a succession of failed escapades that would terminate with his assassination. Over a four-year period (1625–28), he engineered England's foreign policy so as to avenge personal slights and advance momentary interests. The duke thought he could achieve his foreign aims by attacking boldly. He could surprise the Madrid court and make off with the infanta, invade Cádiz, Spain's home port, and seize the treasure fleet, relieve La Rochelle and free the Huguenots. His vision was heroic, but his campaigns were poorly equipped and ill planned. After every misadventure, his defeated men limped home.

Historians agree that at the time of his assassination in 1628, the duke was set to embark on another expedition to relieve the Protestants of La Rochelle. However, there is persuasive evidence this mission was a sham. This is revealed in an examination of a cache of state papers, compiled in 1668 by Charles II's chief minister, Lord Clarendon, and kept at the Bodleian Library. This collection, never more than footnoted by historians, includes Clarendon's transcription of Hermyn's fourteen-page "Secret discovery . . . to the Duke of Buckingham," a step-by-step plan for New World conquest using Jamaica as a base.

Additional evidence is found in Clarendon's translation of a signed treaty by Villiers and Sweden's King Gustav Adolphus, which reveals Villiers's plan to capture Jamaica, possess the gold mine, and proclaim himself absolute monarch. The treaty, in the form of a contract, written in Latin and signed in Stockholm, is dated March 28, 1628, just two months before Buckingham's murder. It concerns Gustav's promised assistance in the conquest and his share in the proceeds of the "secret golden mine."[23] The Swede pledges to recognize the duke as "Absolute prince and Sovereign" of Jamaica, and send along "four thousand foote and six Men of War each of five hundred Tunne with Cannon and Munitions." The flotilla's expenses are to be paid for "out of the revenue of the Territory and Golden Mines." Gustav pledges to defend the duke not only from Spanish attack, but interestingly, "from all Puritans from Barbados or other places." In return, "The Duke of Buckingham makes good unto us a tenth part of the profits [payable] monthly."

Twelve days prior to the duke's murder, Gustav's new warship, the *Vasa*, which would have taken part in the Jamaica invasion, was "heeled over by a stiff breeze just after launching." With the ship's gun ports left open to proudly display her sixty-four bronze cannons, the *Vasa* sank like a stone in Stockholm Harbor, drowning fifty of her crew.

Meanwhile, back in Jamaica, the Inquisition threat had cooled somewhat. In 1626, a new Columbus heir, known as the Admiral, was confirmed in his position, and appointed Francisco Terril, a strong governor who opposed the Cabildo. His "high handed ways" led to his recall, so in 1631, the Admiral appointed one he could trust: Juan Martínez de Arana, a descendant of Columbus's Jewish mistress Beatriz Enríquez de Arana, mother of Fernando. Although the Cabildo's power had diminished, the king's earlier dominion over Jamaica during the first quarter of the seventeenth century had whetted his appetite to recover the island. In 1635, he instructed the Royal Audiencia of Santo Domingo to "report secretly what benefits the Admiral has in the island of Jamaica and if it is advisable for His Majesty to take it." The report issued in 1638 recommended:

> Your majesty [should] take the island [because Jamaica]
> is an outlet for all ships that reach there and defraud
> Your Majesty's Royal Treasury . . . it is a large island
> with a great supply of provisions . . . it is sited so that
> all ships and fleets pass within its sight . . . If the enemy
> gets a footing there, none of our ships will escape from
> their hands and the fleets will run great risk.[24]

The report reflected the Cabildo's view and had been prepared with their counsel. Relations between them and the loyal supporters of the Columbus family were further aggravated in 1640, when, after a sixty-year union, Portugal regained its independence. When the news reached Jamaica, it split the colony. The Spanish ranchers, loyal to Spain, turned against the Portugals loyal to the Columbus heir, who as fate would have it was a distant cousin of Portugal's new king. As the Cabildo saw it, the protector of the Jews was now in the enemy camp. Through the ranchers' intervention, troublesome Portugals began to be expelled from the island.

By 1643, the state of affairs had become so inflamed that the Portugals welcomed an English pirate as their liberator. Captain William Jackson, a privateer in the tradition of Sir Francis Drake, sacked Jamaica and went home convinced England could count on the Jews there to assist an invasion. His report to the Colonial Affairs Committee noted:

> During our aboard in Town, divers Portugals who had been kept off by the Spanyards from coming into us, did Express great affection they had to the English & proposed to bring us where the Spanyards hid all their Plate & Treasure, which they affirmed to be greater than we could imagine, but we scorned to violate our former covenant . . . We understood what inward desire they had to change their old Masters and seemed greatly to rejoice when we told them we intended to shortly come and beat ye Spanyards from this Island, which fittingly corresponds with an old Tradition long rooted in them that they shall one day come under ye English.[25]

Jamaica's Portugals were ready then and there to assist in the seizure of the island, a course affirmed by Jackson's crew: "All our men allured desire to set up their station here and to that purpose moved our General to undertake ye settling thereof" (twenty-three of the crew deserted and remained in Jamaica). But Jackson wanted booty: "On the encouragement of Balthasar, a Portugal from Jamaica, we set sail for Rio de la Hacha [Colombia], a place very rich in Plate & Pearl. Balthasar persuaded our General to undertake this design which was very hopeful if ye success had proved as fortunate." But good fortune was not theirs. Bad weather forced Jackson to return to Jamaica. Balthasar, not wanting the English to depart empty-handed, proposed they seize a ship in the harbor. "By the direction of Balthasar, we took a Spanish Frigate in the harbour next to where we had formerly rode at Anchor, being laden with Hides, Sugar & other provisions, & was bound with passengers for Cartagena."[26]

Balthasar acted with the support of other Portugals. His help in the seizure of a Spanish ship was calculated to impress upon the English that their loyalty was not to Spain. This maneuver was not lost on the Cabildo, which, in all but name, governed the island. In the aftermath of Jackson's raid, the colony nearly self-destructed. In October 1643, the governor "died a prisoner without guards in his own house."[27] Within hours, the Cabildo attempted a coup and again appealed to the king to retake the island. One account refers to a civil war.[28] The charges are not detailed, but an early historian noted that as a consequence of Balthasar's traitorous deed "internal divisions were soon to prove . . . disastrous. The Spanish settlers quarreled with those from Portugal and some of the latter were expelled from the colony."

Among them was Balthasar, who went on to become a renowned pirate whose exploits and daring escapes were chronicled by the "Boswell of the Buccaneers," the buccaneer author John Esquemelin. Figures on the number of Jews who were expelled range from thirteen families to "almost all the colonists of that nation."[29] A decade later, when the British conquered Jamaica and entered La Vega (where most Portugals resided), they observed more houses than occupants: "The deserted houses in the capital proved a want of tenants . . . The town was thinly populated compared with former years."[30]

Captain Jackson submitted his report to the Colonial Affairs Committee, whose prominent members included Jamaica's future conqueror, Oliver Cromwell. Historians claim Jamaica was not part of his plan to invade the Indies, as Jamaica is not mentioned. But considering what transpired during Jackson's raid, and his lauding of Jamaica as a "Terrestrial Paradise . . . with the delight and plenty of all necessary conferred by nature," it is hard to fathom why Cromwell would not have targeted Jamaica. Indeed, as the next chapter shows, the Spanish had no doubt Jamaica's conquest was a prioritized aim of Cromwell's "Grand Western Design" to secure a toehold in the fabulously rich New World.

Such was the situation in April 1654 when the "heretic ship" from Recife was brought to port in Jamaica. The Cabildo detained the Jewish and Calvinist refugees aboard the *Falcon*, and sent a messenger to Cartagena, the nearest Holy Office, requesting a hearing to determine what to do with the suspect heretics. Apparently their answer was to avoid trouble with Holland: to free the Calvinists and any Jews who had not been baptized, as the Inquisition's jurisdiction was limited to *relapsos*—conversos who had openly returned to Judaism. In July, the Cabildo therefore released the Calvinists and twenty-three so-called born Jews (as many as seventeen were children). Those freed included Abraham and Isaac Israel, and Benjamin Mesquita's two sons, Joseph and Abraham, but Benjamin himself was detained. How many other families were separated is not known, nor is the number of those still held.

The extended Ysassi family dominated the Cabildo, and held powerful positions in Puerto Rico and Cuba. But in their home base, Jamaica, the Columbus family stymied them. As *familiars* of the Inquisition, they hoped to use its power to stir up trouble—enough, they hoped, to warrant the Crown to intervene and appoint their leader, Francisco de Leiba, the equivalent of what he was already calling himself, "King of Jamaica." The capture of a heretic ship furnished them with an excuse to summon the Holy Inquisitor from Colombia to investigate the suspect heretics and, once there, to likewise expose the island's Portugals as Judaizers. No longer would they be subject to a feudal lord, and the Jamaica gold mine would revert to the king.

In detaining the Jews, the Cabildo overreached. Their action proved a lethal miscalculation, one that stirred a renewed effort on the part of Jamaica's Portugals to overthrow Spanish rule. Fearful that any investigation of the refugees would spill over into an inquiry into their own lives, Jamaica's Jews once more looked to entice a foreign liberator with the promise of gold. Since no vessel sailed direct from Jamaica to Holland, their message was carried first to New Amsterdam and then to Holland by Abraham Israel, who had convinced the Cabildo he was "born Jewish."[31]

The *Falcon*, allowed to depart Jamaica, sailed to nearby Cape St. Anthony in Cuba, a well-known port frequented by ships to and from Mexico and the Spanish Main. The refugees' stay there involved no risk, as they had been cleared in Jamaica and had the necessary papers attesting to this. After a few weeks, they obtained passage to New Amsterdam on a small French frigate, the *St. Catherine*.

On September 7, 1654, when the refugee ship dropped anchor in New Amsterdam harbor, they were met by an odd figure, floridly dressed like a peacock and walking about "with great state and pomp" on a wooden leg wrapped with silver bands. It was Peter Stuyvesant, the colony's governor. Residents made a jest of his pretentious ways, calling him the "Grand Muscovy Duke," but he moved among them with a show of force that made them understand he was a person to be obeyed.

Governor Stuyvesant welcomed the Calvinists, but not the Jews. He wanted them out. The seven-month voyage—from

Recife, to Jamaica, to Cuba, to New Amsterdam—had left them destitute. They owed the ship's captain, Jacques de la Motte, more than their belongings were worth. Stuyvesant wrote to the Company: "The Jews who arrived, nearly all like to remain, but fearing that owing to their present indigence they might become a charge in the coming winter, we required them in a friendly way to depart."[32]

Stuyvesant went on to reveal his true feelings, which had nothing to do with their finances. Owing to their "customary usury and deceitful trading with Christians," he wrote, "we pray that this deceitful race—such hateful enemies and blasphemers of the name of Christ—be not allowed further to infect and trouble this new colony." His letter, dated September 22, 1654, corresponds with the sailing date of the first ship bound for Amsterdam since the *St. Catherine* arrived. Along with the letter, Israel was on board.

Nine months after Abraham Cohen saw his cousins off in Recife, he had heard nothing of them or the others on the *Falcon*. The feeling among his Amsterdam colleagues was that the ship was lost at sea. Alerted by the harbormaster that a ship from New Amsterdam was unloading, Cohen hurried to the wharf. Anxiety gave way to relief when Israel disembarked and assured him everyone was alive. But the rest of his news was not good: Cohen's nephews, the Mesquita boys, had been freed, but their father, Benjamin, and others were still held in Jamaica, and those who had made it to New Amsterdam were broke, in debt, and threatened with expulsion.

The next morning, after religious services, the reunited friends conferred with the six officers of the synagogue, the Parnassim. Because their brethren in Jamaica were Dutch nationals, it was decided that their detainment was illegal. They thereupon submitted a petition to the government contending the incident was "an international outrage . . . [and that] the release of the Jewish prisoners should be requested of the King of Spain, and the Dutch consuls in Cadiz and San Sebastian should intervene in this affair."[33]

The States General's response was both immediate and forthright. On November 14, they wrote their consuls, "This business [is] considered by us as very serious," and dictated an "urgent request" to the State Council of the king of Spain, "that Spanish authorities not allow the Inquisition or anybody else to molest [the Jews] . . . and permit them to return home . . . This request being in conformity with the treaty of peace existing between the King of Spain and the Dutch Government."[34] There is no record of the king's response, but he evidently ordered Jamaica to free the detainees, as none were there six months later when English forces captured the island.

Following their successful protest of the Jamaica affair, Cohen and four members of the Parnassim, including Bento Osorio, the aforementioned leader of the Brotherhood, and Uriel da Costa's brother Abraham, were confident that the Company in New Amsterdam would overrule Stuyvesant and authorize Jewish settlement. For years, the Company had encouraged others to settle there, even offering free transport, land grants, and tax exemptions. On the basis of the rights granted them in Brazil by the Patenta Onrossa, and the fact that all of them were major shareholders in the Company, they assumed that their people would likewise be welcome.

But although the States General acted quickly and forcibly to protest the detention of Jews in Jamaica, three months passed before the Company directors belatedly, and only reluctantly, rejected Stuyvesant's request. On February 15, 1655, they wrote him: "We would have liked to fulfill your wishes that the new territories not be infected by the Jewish nation," but citing pressure from Jewish shareholders and "the considerable loss sustained by this nation in Brazil," a go-easy policy was recommended.[35]

In the coming year (1655–56), in light of the Company's lukewarm endorsement, Stuyvesant, his sheriff, and the colony's Calvinist leaders opposed the Jews at every turn. In a series of lawsuits, the sons of Abraham da Costa, Abraham Israel, and Abraham Cohen—Joseph, Isaac, and Jacob respectively—carried on their fathers' fight. Ultimately the courts sided with them, winning basic rights for Jews in what in the future would be thought of as the land of the free.[36]

During their detention in Jamaica, Israel and Benjamin Mesquita learned of Columbus's mine from the Portugals. Believing that the Cabildo's real intent in sending for an Inquisitor was to have him expose their own covert Judaism, the Portugals confided in Israel that the island was ripe for takeover and offered to reveal the secret site of the mine as an incentive. Israel, therefore, not only carried news that Jamaica was holding Dutch Jews and that Stuyvesant wanted to expel them, he also told Cohen about the mine. This became evident eight years later, when the three of them—Israel, Mesquita, and Cohen—struck a partnership with the royal sons of Prince Charles I and George Villiers to fulfill their fathers' quest for Columbus's gold.

Chapter Eight

CROMWELL'S SECRET AGENTS

"llow Jews back in England and the Messiah will come." This, essentially, was the visionary promise that an Amsterdam rabbi shared with England's new, Bible-quoting ruler. The date was September 1654, the same month that New Holland's twenty-three Jewish refugees finally arrived in New Amsterdam, only to be told they were not welcome. The previous December, Oliver Cromwell had become Lord Protector of the Commonwealth, ending England's twelve-year civil war.

Soon after the Puritans' victory, Cromwell concluded his nation's two-year war with the Netherlands. Although the outcome of what is known as the First Anglo-Dutch War was inconclusive (the maritime rivals would fight twice again in the next two decades), the Dutch had lost 1,500 ships.[1] This blow to the republic's sea power, coupled with the loss of their Brazilian colony, left Holland in no position to war with Spain, let alone invade Jamaica. So while Cohen and the Parnassim persuaded the States General to formally protest Jamaica's detention of her Jewish citizens, the Dutch were not about to go to war over the incident.

Israel and Cohen, aware of this realpolitik, and knowing of the rabbi's discourse with Cromwell, looked to England. They were privy to Cromwell's plan to invade the New World and believed the two goals—the return of Jews to England and the liberation of Jamaica's Jews—could augment each other. Despite their allegiance to Holland, national loyalty took a backseat to the possibility of securing two new homelands for their people, in England and Jamaica.

With the Dutch war settled, Cromwell spent the summer of 1654 formulating what he called his Grand Western Design, an ambitious plan to carve out a Protestant empire in the Spanish New World. The stage was thus set for his positive reception of Israel and Cohen's proposal to invade Jamaica. There was only one hitch: they were too late. In late November 1654, as they were about to embark for England, one of Cromwell's secret intelligencers and a possible relation, Daniel Cohen Henriques, told them not to bother; Jamaica was already targeted.[2]

Israel and Cohen therefore turned their attention to the more immediate goal of securing Jewish settlement elsewhere in the New World. Over the next fifteen months, while they were thus successfully engaged, Cromwell's effort to allow Jews back into England would be spurred by the role of Jews in Jamaica's conquest, and the promise of their valued assistance to develop his New World empire. As strangers in a strange land, the wandering tribe of Abraham had acquired particular skills that Cromwell needed. To understand this development, we leave Israel and Cohen in Amsterdam, holding tight the secret site of Columbus's mine until Cromwell's demise, when the sons of the royals who first sought it—George Villiers and Charles I—were restored to power.

In August 1654, Cromwell summoned the Spanish ambassador and bluntly told him that friendship with Spain could continue only if Englishmen were granted freedom of trade and religion in the New World. The ambassador was shocked: "Impossible," he said. "To ask for these rights is to demand of my Master his two eyes."[3] To allow England trading rights in the New World was tantamount to recognizing England's right to settle there. Monopoly of trade and propagation of the True Faith were cornerstones upon which Spain developed its colonial empire, and His Most Catholic Majesty was not about to share it with anyone, least of all a Puritan devil.

Cromwell, reportedly taken aback by the ambassador's response, abruptly dismissed him. This was pure theatrics. Months earlier he had begun secret preparations to send an armed fleet to the Caribbean.[4] Freedom of religion and trade were the stated reasons, but securing a major chunk of the New World was his compelling desire. Thirty years before, England had colonized a few small, empty islands in the eastern Caribbean, outside the sea lanes. Barbados, Nevis, and St. Kitts were prospering, but a more strategic base was needed if Cromwell was to break Spain's hold on the wealth of the New World.

To Cromwell, a ruler who framed every decision as being in accordance with Scripture, the invasion's success was preordained: "The ships would sail in accordance with God's dictates . . . Its triumph would signify God's favor . . . more God's favor assured its success."[5] Cromwell was too confident, however—his vaunted plan would have failed if not for the advice of his Jewish intelligencers. With other advisers pushing Hispaniola, Cuba, Puerto Rico, or Trinidad, the leader of London's covert Jews, Antonio Carvajal, whose knowledge of Caribbean affairs was unmatched, counseled Cromwell to follow up on Captain Jackson's raid.

An English prisoner captured in Jamaica would confess: "The Grand Western Design was designed and financed by Jews who planned to resettle England and buy St. Paul's Cathedral and turn it into a synagogue." While there is no hard evidence this was true, the Spanish defenders believed it, "since the example of Brazil exhibits similar treasons & inequities committed by this blind people out of their aversion for us."[6] The prisoner, Nicolas Paine, was the interpreter for General Robert Venables, the co-leader of the invading force. He made this disclosure, recorded by the Spanish notary, after having "begged for his life in Spanish." Where did Paine hear it? Was it scuttlebutt among the crew or something he overheard the general say? If so, where did the general hear it?

However skewed Paine's admission, Cromwell would not have reached a decision about where to attack without first consulting Carvajal, who recommended Jamaica. One of the city's prominent merchants, Carvajal owned ships that plied the seven seas. He had agents in most major ports, and the political intelligence he gathered made him one of Cromwell's most valued advisers. But since exposure of his role might have led to the arrest of associates and relatives in the lands of the Inquisition, his consultations with Cromwell, via the ruler's trusted secretary John Thurloe, were kept secret.

Though King John had formally expelled the Jews from England in 1290, by the mid-1600s a handful of wealthy Jewish families had managed to resettle there and became major players in international commerce. They called themselves Portuguese, attended Mass in the home of the ambassador (also a secret Jew), and were not circumcised.

Carvajal was forty-six in 1635 when he rode up to London's city gates astride a white Arabian stallion, dressed in "fine armor" and leading a string of pack mules carrying gold bullion. Halted by the king's guard, he announced that he was a merchant from the Canary Islands and had come to London to join his sister, whose husband was Portugal's ambassador. Given his impressive appearance, he was allowed to proceed. Later it was revealed that he had departed the islands' capital Tenerife a step ahead of Holy Inquisitors sent to investigate him.

Like Pasha Sinan and Rabbi Palache, Carvajal was a man of "superb and florid" personality who soon established himself as the leader of London's covert Jewish community of thirty or so families. Though Carvajal dealt in many commodities, silver was his specialty. At a time when New World silver powered global currency, transporting it was a Jewish enterprise. Carvajal imported silver bars from converso merchants in Seville, who received them in turn from converso merchants in Peru and New Spain. From the time the ore left the mines and was melted into bars, his own were embossed with a particular stamp. He also imported annually about $1 million (in today's money) in silver pieces of eight.[7]

Jamaica marked the first conquest of the British Empire, and Carvajal, who hoped to persuade England's new ruler to allow Jews legally back into England, played a major role. While invasion plans were going forward, his associate, Simon de Caceres, who traded extensively in the Indies, confided to him that a secret Jew in Jamaica, Francisco Carvajal, headed the army there and could be relied upon to assist an attack. While there is no evidence that the two Carvajals were related, Jamaica's Carvajal helped cement the English conquest, and when news of victory reached London, Cromwell's intelligencer was amply rewarded.

In December 1654, the fleet departed Portsmouth under the joint command of Admiral William Penn—father of the future founder of Pennsylvania—and General Venables with an army of 2,500 men. Unlike the disciplined soldiers Cromwell led in the civil war, these recruits had been hastily rounded up, and in the judgment of one observer, were mostly "common cheats, thieves, cutpurses (pick-pockets), and such lewd persons who long lived by sleight of hand and dexterity of wit."[8] Their leaders were likewise described as "lazy dullards that have a large portion of Pride but not of wit, valor or authority."[9]

First stop was Barbados, where Venables tripled the size of his army by the beat of a drum in the public square and the promise "Any bond-servant who volunteers shall have his freedom." With little to lose and much to gain, four thousand indentured servants, comprising fully a fifth of the population, signed on. Twelve hundred more were recruited from St. Kitts, Nevis, and Montserrat. By the time the fleet embarked, Venables's army had swelled to nearly eight thousand men but carried supplies for only half that number.[10] The invasion plan called for the army to first attack Santo Domingo. Significantly, the fleet halted at the small island of Nevis, where Admiral Penn enlisted Campoe Sabada, the Jewish pilot who had previously sailed with Jackson.

This slovenly army was primarily made up of servants who

had signed on for freedom and plunder; accordingly, when the general announced that there would be no taking of booty, they threatened mutiny. Confronted by "an unruly and ignorant mass," he canceled the order. Meanwhile, it was obvious that the admiral had no respect for the general, who, to the annoyance of all, had brought along his new young wife and rarely left his cabin. Always contending for command, it was said, Penn snickered whenever Venables made an error, which Venables tended to do whenever he gave an order.

Rather than a direct assault on Santo Domingo, Penn favored a surprise attack, and landed the army thirty miles up the coast. Unfortunately, the site was a desert, and as Cromwell's brother-in-law, responsible for equipping the army, had forgotten to pack canteens, the soldiers had to march without water through hot, barren land without shade. They never reached the capital. Many collapsed from thirst; others were cut down by a cavalry charge of three hundred mounted Spaniards, who ran them through like knights of old with twelve-foot lances. Afterward, their leader boasted that had he had more "cow-killers" (as his men were known) he would have killed every invader. This singular breed of toughened Spaniard was a cowboy in reverse, expert not at herding cows, but at slaying them. It was later reported that during the attack, Venables hid behind a tree, "so much possessed with terror he could hardlie spake." With no water, no discipline, and pursued by the lance-wielding cow-killers, the invading army retreated to the coast. As Cromwell's relation also hadn't packed any tents, the demoralized troops had to huddle in the open when days of torrential rain followed. In one week, Venables lost a thousand men, while Spanish losses numbered forty.[11]

The two commanders were now so distrustful of each other

that the general refused to allow the admiral and his crew to board the ships ahead of his soldiers, suspecting they might sail away without them. At a council aboard ship, the officers rejected a further assault on the city, contending that any attack would have to be fought by them alone as "they could not trust their men to follow."[12]

What now? An attack on fortified places like Cartagena or Havana was out of the question, and if they simply retreated to London they could lose their heads. Historical accounts state that following the humiliating defeat at Hispaniola, the decision to invade Jamaica was first mentioned. However, this is disputed by a number of English prisoners. The first, an advance scout captured a day after the English landed, confessed, "Our purpose is to take this land . . . then pass on to Jamaica." Prisoners, taken later, confirmed this sequence. According to the Spanish account:

> [After the cow-killers] . . . killed more than 800 men and compelled the enemy to retreat . . . two captured Englishmen [said] they intended to go to another island they had been before. *In view of the prisoners' dispositions . . . his Lordship immediately arranged to send a warning to Jamaica since this was the island the prisoners designated* [italics added]. He sent it with all diligence to the governor, advising him of the form of fighting we employed [and] to use the same . . . He told him the enemy was badly used up, lost many men, and was short of victuals, in order that Jamaica might know the facts and be prepared.[13]

Since no account of the invasion plan mentions Jamaica, historians have followed in lockstep the contention that Jamaica was "an afterthought." Is this simply a case of historical confusion, or is something more convoluted involved? The island's location in the middle of the Caribbean made it a natural target. After Jackson's raid twelve years before, the local priest spelled this out in a letter to King Philip, wherein he called upon the Crown to reclaim Jamaica:

> The defense of the island is very poor . . . If the enemy takes possession there can be no doubt from it he will quickly infest all ports making himself master of their trade and commerce. As it lies in the way of the fleets voyaging from these kingdoms to New Spain and the plate galleons to Habana . . . it can be gathered how harmful it would be for ships in that trade if the enemy should take possession of this island.[14]

Captain Jackson's report to Cromwell's Committee on Colonial Affairs the previous decade had exposed a divided, lightly defended colony with a Jewish fifth column that would welcome an invasion.[15] With Carvajal's intelligence endorsing this analysis, Cromwell was fully cognizant of Jamaica's strategic site, poor defense, and the promised support of local Jews. These facts, along with the prisoners' confessions and the recruitment of Jackson's Jewish pilot who had previously led his ships into Jamaica's harbor, all point to Jamaica being a prima facie target. Why then was it kept secret?

The probable answer is revealing: When the fleet left Portsmouth, the commanders were kept in the dark as to their target. "We shall not tie you up to a method of any particular instructions," Cromwell told them, but ordered the attack plan kept sealed, only to be opened when the army reached Barbados.

Cromwell, already accused of selling out to Jews, apparently felt he would have been further tainted if even his advisers knew of their role in his Christ-ordained Grand Western Design. His far-reaching plan was to allow Jews back into England, both for economic reasons and because of his conviction that their return and mass conversion would hasten the Second Coming of Christ. But for now it was better to keep secret their role in his imperialist plans.[16]

On May 10, 1655, four days after leaving Hispaniola, the *Martin*, piloted by Sabada with the two rival commanders on board, led the fleet's thirty-eight ships into Jamaica's harbor. The invaders had lost a thousand men, but the army was still an overwhelming force, more than four times Jamaica's population of 1,500 Spaniards, 750 slaves, and a hundred or so Jews. (Following Jackson's raid, many Jews were expelled from the island.) If they could land without incident, conquest was assured. Defending the port was a small garrison with three mounted guns. After an initial salvo while the ships were still at sea, the defenders fled. Their report smacks of terror: thirty-eight ships had become fifty-six ships, and the seven-thousand-man army was reported as twice that number.

Unchallenged, Venables's army marched eight abreast on a wide road linking the port with the capital of Villa de la Vega, and set up camp outside the city. The next morning, two Jamaican officers rode up under a flag of truce. They had come, they said, in place of the governor (a syphilitic old man with festering sores all over his body) to find out what the English wanted. They introduced themselves as the current and former Sargento Mayor (army commander). But something else the two men shared turned out to be more significant. The officers, Francisco Carvajal and Duarte Acosta, were secret Jews.[17]

"We have come not to pillage but to plant," Venables told them. After some dickering, Carvajal asked Venables: "By what right do you claim the island? Spaniards have had possession of it for 140 years and it was given to them by Pope Alexander." Before the general could reply, his adjutant interjected:

"It is ours by the right of might. Just as the Spaniards had taken Jamaica from the Indians, so we English have come to take it from them. As for the Pope, he could neither grant lands to others nor delegate the right to conquer them." Besides, he added, only the weak get conquered: "Henry VIII offered England to any who chose to take possession, but none deigned to accept that gift." At that, the English officers "laughed long and heartily."[18]

The next day, Governor Ramariez, carried in a hammock by African slaves and escorted by Acosta and Carvajal, entered the English camp to negotiate terms. He was there for show. His Portuguese officers signed the surrender treaty, and reportedly drafted it as well. They got what they wanted: Portuguese were encouraged to remain while Spaniards were to be transported to New Spain. Venables later reported to Cromwell that the "Portugals [accepted] our invitation to stay."[19]

No account of the conquest mentions the advance warning from Hispaniola that "his Lordship . . . sent with all diligence to the governor . . . in order that Jamaica might know the facts and be prepared." Yet it was this warning that had spurred the Portuguese officers to be the first to meet with the invaders. With the ocean current favoring ships sailing west from Santo Domingo to Jamaica, the 480-mile distance would have been covered in four to five days. As such, Governor Ramariez should have received the warning more than a week before the English invasion. That he didn't is evidence the message was intercepted. Given what transpired, it would appear that when the ship arrived, Portuguese merchants in control of the port got hold of the letter, and rather than deliver it to Ramariez, revealed its contents to the two officers who then positioned themselves to negotiate Jamaica's surrender.

Cromwell's army had taken Jamaica, but the Cabildo, led by Francisco de Leiba, the self-styled king of Jamaica, along with his cousin Sanchez Ysassi and the latter's son, Arnoldo, marshaled their supporters and retreated to a sugar estate west of the capital. They hanged the two servants whom Carvajal and Acosta sent with the treaty and, loudly rejecting the surrender terms, cursed the two officers as traitors.[20] Arnoldo led a rebel group into the hills, where they formed a guerrilla force and ambushed soldiers who ventured outside the capital to hunt cattle.

Jamaica was English, but in July, when Cromwell also received the news of the disaster at Hispaniola, he was not pleased. Later that month, when first Penn and then Venables returned to England, each blaming the other for Santo Domingo, Cromwell called them quarrelsome incompetents, and confined them in the Tower for deserting their forces.

An opposite reception greeted Antonio Carvajal's "great friend," Simon de Caceres, who returned on the ship bearing Venables.[21] An international trader from Amsterdam with offices in Europe and Barbados, he had been visiting his two brothers in Barbados when the English fleet arrived. When the greatly enlarged army set sail, he volunteered to secure the extra provisions that would be needed, and was with the supply ships that caught up with the fleet in Jamaica two weeks after the conquest. Meeting with Carvajal, who had taken charge of the army's commissary, the two took stock of what was needed. Back in England he submitted a memorandum to Cromwell "on things wanting in Jamaica."

His "Proposal for Revictualing and Fortifying Jamaica" stressed the need to complete a harbor fort to defend against an expected counterattack from Cartagena. The report reads like a grand shopping list: 1,500 shovels, 1,000 pickaxes, 100 wheelbarrows, 2,000 hatchets, and so on. Further, "as an encouragement" for the fort workers, he recommended sending "plenty of brandy and wine . . . and fine linen stockings and handsome shoes [for the officers]." Self-interest likely played a part in these extra requests, as among the items he traded in were "shoes, linen, wine and brandy."[22]

De Caceres told Cromwell that before he left Jamaica, one Captain Hughes had begun fortifying the tip of the peninsula at the harbor entrance. (This was the beginning of the town of Port Royal that, in the next decade, would be known as the "wickedest city in the world.") After receiving his report, Cromwell shipped the necessary supplies and ordered Jamaica's commander to "study your security by fortifying."[23]

On August 17, 1655, with Penn and Venables in the Tower, Cromwell honored the one man who had correctly advised him on the invasion plan. Summoning Antonio Carvajal and his two sons to his office, Cromwell awarded them English citizenship, making them the nation's first legal Jews in 365 years.[24] Later Carvajal would warn Cromwell that the exiled Prince Charles had signed a secret treaty with the Spanish king, promising to return Jamaica for help in overthrowing the Commonwealth, and that Spain was outfitting a fleet to retake the island. So alerted, Cromwell's naval forces were able to smash the fleet in Cádiz harbor before it sailed.[25]

In 1658, Carvajal's imports accounted for 8.3 percent of London's customs revenue.[26] A description of him that year shows that (like Pasha Sinan and Rabbi Palache) age had not mellowed him. The occasion was his arrest. Custom officers had seized one of his shipments. Feeling his goods unjustly impounded, he broke into their warehouse, and holding the guard at sword point, threatened to run him through while his servant emptied the place. The police report described him as "of grizzled beard and fiery temper . . . and no 'prentice hand with the rapier," while his servant Manuel Fonseca "could double his fist with any Englishman." Charges were dropped when the man known as the Great Jew died later that year.[27]

In the fall of 1655, England's leader announced a settlement policy for Jamaica that is significant in what it omits: His proclamation opened Jamaica to every "planter or adventurer" without regard to religion or national origin.[28] He also granted citizenship in Barbados to a prominent Jewish refugee from Recife, Dr. Abraham de Mercado.[29] Like the Cohen Henriques brothers, de Mercado was one of Rabbi Palache's old boys. Considered the first Jewish physician in the New World, he proudly wore the title of doctor, but in spy circles went by the code name Plus Ultra, as when he tipped off Dutch authorities in Brazil that the Portuguese banquet they were to attend was to be an assassination party.

Cromwell's actions sent a message to Jews, albeit a circuitous one, that they might henceforth look to him as their defender. Cromwell evidently felt that for his Grand Western Design to succeed, he needed Jews in place. He is said to have looked on with envy at the boost they gave the Dutch economy.

Jews had helped make Amsterdam Europe's richest port, and as they helped Holland, he believed, so they could make London "the common warehouse of Europe."

Granting special favors was Cromwell's way of demonstrating his intentions. England's colonies were open to Jews. But not the mother country, at least not yet. However, in honoring Carvajal, Cromwell revealed his inclination to revoke the ban on Jewish settlement. Besides their business skills and trade, there was the matter of securing intelligence. As he confided to Bishop Burnett: "They are good and useful spies . . . skilled purveyors of foreign intelligence."[30] With England's exiled prince ready to strike, and Spain's declaration of war over Jamaica, Cromwell needed to work closely with London's Jews and their agents. They, in turn, were grateful for the opportunity to demonstrate their loyalty and economic clout.

The midseventeenth century was a time when True Believers ruled and every action was righteous and backed by Scripture. It was the politics of Holy Inevitability, and Cromwell liked to frame his policies in those terms. Along with commerce, and intelligence, Cromwell's religious convictions presented him with an irresistible motive for Jewish resettlement: Only when Jews were allowed back in England, he believed, would the Messiah return. His public expression of this religious rationale garnered him the fervid support of England's philo-Semites, who saw this as necessary for the redemption of the whole human race.

From 1607, when King James published an English translation of the Bible, the Old Testament had become required study among Puritans. Its influence was seen by their adoption of biblical references during the recent civil war: The Lion of Judah was inscribed on the Puritan banner; King Charles was referred to as Pharaoh, and his rule as the Egyptian Bondage. After Cromwell's victory, a messianic group called the Fifth Monarchists proclaimed the Puritan Commonwealth to be the so-called Fifth Empire prophesied in the book of Daniel, which was destined to usher in the thousand-year reign of Jesus Christ. (The other four were Babylon, Persia, Greece, and Rome.) They also quoted Deuteronomy (18:64) to argue that God would not reappear until his Chosen People were readmitted to England. The passage actually predicts that the Jews will be scattered to the "end of the earth," but Puritan clerics preached that since the French called England Angleterre, a phrase which Jewish medieval literature used to signify the "angle" or "end" of the earth, it was clearly God's will that they admit the Israelites, "so they might be brought to see the truth." Whatever the merits of this twisted reading of Scripture, for Cromwell the message was clear: Allow Jews back into England, and the Messiah would return . . . and so would trade.[31]

Meanwhile, in the Diaspora, homeless Jews favored any argument that would work. Their horizons were rapidly narrowing: New Holland was no more; in Spain and Portugal, Inquisition burnings were on the increase and the great autos-da-fé in Mexico and Peru had left the remnant of Jews in Spanish lands looking to move on. In New Amsterdam, they were engaged in a struggle to stay. In Eastern Europe, galloping hordes of saber-wielding Cossacks were killing Polish Jews by the tens of thousands.

In October, a Cabalist rabbi from Amsterdam arrived at Cromwell's invitation to discuss the divine argument proffered in his book *The Hope of Israel*. The religious sage was the former child prodigy Menasseh ben Israel, who it will be recalled stayed late at synagogue immersed in the mysticism of Cabala while the Henriques boys and their rebel pals frequented the docks, absorbing sailors' tales of exotic lands. Menasseh held that the Torah contained divine revelations which prophesied the coming of the Messiah, and in *The Hope of Israel* he identified England as the Promised Land to which the Jews must return before the Messiah appears. (He and Cromwell agreed on that, disagreeing only on whether or not He had been here before.) Menasseh, a pragmatic scholar, peppered his prophecies with a discourse on what Jews could do for England's economy.[32]

In December 1655, Cromwell called a conference of leading personages to debate the issue. The conference ended without making any recommendations, except to agree that there was no legal bar to Jewish resettlement. All that was required for readmission was for Parliament to approve it. Cromwell tried, but was unable to get Parliament to act. He was not deterred. As a royalist spy told Prince Charles, "Though the generality oppose, the Jews will be admitted by way of connivancy."[33] An opportunity presented itself when, shortly after Spain declared war, Parliament ruled that Spanish property would be confiscated. London's Jews, though calling themselves Portuguese, were considered Spanish subjects, and their goods were therefore subject to seizure. The situation came to a head in what is known as the Robles trial.

In February 1656, customs officials seized two ships in the Thames carrying wine from the Canary Islands and a safe with forty thousand ducats in gold. London's Jews were alarmed. The ships and strongbox belonged to Antonio Robles, a member of their community. If his property could be legally confiscated, their holdings could likewise be taken. What to do? With Carvajal and de Caceres leading the way, a decision was reached for the converso community to come out of the closet and declare that they were Jews, and loyal to England. On March 12, 1656, they confronted Cromwell with an either/or demand, saying in effect: "Your conference accepted that there is no legal bar to our admission. The issue is therefore between you and us: as you well know, we are not Portuguese Catholics; we are Jews and we want the right to worship and bury the dead in our manner." Not stated, but implied, was a threat—"otherwise we will look to Holland."[34]

Robles followed suit. He petitioned the court for the recovery of his ships and goods on the grounds that he was "of the Hebrew nation." He recounted how he had been on the run from the Inquisition that killed his father, tortured his mother, and burned at the stake many close relatives. He had come to England, he said, hoping to find a home among a people also considered heretics. In the course of the trial, ten London Jews sent in affidavits supporting his submission; others testified they knew Robles to be "of the Hebrew nation and religion."[35] When the six-week trial ended, the court declared Robles "a Jew borne in Portugal" and restored his ships, wine, and box of gold.[36]

On April 3, 1656, London's thirty-five Jewish families gathered in the Great Jew's home for Passover Seder to celebrate the Israelites' freedom from Egyptian bondage and their current liberation. After 366 years, England's Jews were no longer illegal aliens. Henceforth, as followers of the Law of Moses, they would seek their rights openly rather than hide behind a foreign identity and a Christian cloak. To consecrate this new day, Cromwell's chief intelligencer proudly changed his name to Abraham Israel Carvajal.

Although Cromwell, still facing opposition in Parliament,

never formally reversed the ban on Jewish admission, his religious convictions were sincere and only added to his desire for the mercantile skills and connections Jewish settlers would bring. As Bishop Burnett commented in his diary, "it was more on that account than in compliance with the principle of toleration that he gave them leave to build a synagogue."[37] Later that summer, their two leaders, Carvajal and de Caceres, rented a cemetery plot and a building for a synagogue, and sent to Amsterdam for a Torah.

In Jamaica, meanwhile, things were not going so well. With England's occupying army having tripled the island's population, there was not enough food to feed everyone. Weakened by hunger and "the bloody flux," the ranks suffered from malaria. Many soldiers rebelled when ordered to plant food crops. They had been promised freedom and booty, not bondage. As for the officers, the only thing they wanted was to return to England. In October 1655, six months after the conquest, nearly half the army was dead. Cromwell's newly arrived commissioner Robert Sedgwick wrote home:

> For the Army, I find them in as sad, and deplorable, and distracted a condition as can be thought of; their commanders, some having left, some dead, some sick . . . the soldiery many dead, their carcasses lying unburied in the highways and among the bushes . . . As I walked through town many that were alive lay groaning and crying out, bread for the Lord's sake . . . It is strange to see young lusty men, in appearance well, and in three or four days in the grave, snatched away in a moment with a confluence of many diseases. The truth is God is angry and the plague is begun, and we have none to stand in the gap.[38]

By January 1656, the mortality figure had risen to more than five thousand, and a month later included Sedgwick as well. Only the sailors aboard ship under Vice Admiral William Goodson, who had their own provisions, remained healthy. In these harsh circumstances, the Jewish pilot, now addressed as Captain Campoe Sabada, and known to be familiar with the island from his time with Jackson, was sent to reconnoiter the western end. In February 1656, he landed a hundred soldiers at Great Pedro Bay and captured the two rebel scouts who had been trailing them. The governor of Cartagena, they said, had got word to Ysassi that two galleons with a thousand men were being readied to join "an armada from Spain to come to Jamaica harbor to beat the English from the land."[39]

Sabada hurried back to so inform Admiral Goodson, who wrote Cromwell (March 12) that he was sending ships to Cartagena to intercept the galleons, and was equipping others to patrol for the armada. Goodson's letter went on to stress the advantages of strengthening island settlement and the need to complete fortifications:

> once well peopled [Jamaica] is so advantageous, being in the midst of the Spaniards' country, that having a considerable force here to make inroads upon the enemy, and a fleet to secure the seas, it might become the magazine of all the wealth in the Indies. To affect this we must have a considerable recruit of seamen, landmen and some commanders, to give life & vigor to the action; besides which, we must also hope for a good supply of provisions; those we have should last four months longer. In short, if your highness continues your resolutions to proceed in this great design, you must in a manner begin the work again.[40]

With the threat of a Spanish attack from without, and battling Ysassi's forces within, it was essential to find a defense that did not depend on recruiting reinforcements for a disgruntled and dying army. The answer was to be found on a small island off the northwest coast of Hispaniola, where a rough breed of men once eked out a living hunting wild cattle and hogs. How this came about, and how these men evolved from hunters of cattle to hunters of men, is worth taking time out from this narrative. We begin with the man thought to have recommended their recruitment, Carvajal's "close friend," on whom Cromwell relied for on-the-spot intelligence of "things wanting in Jamaica."

Though a generation removed from Rabbi Palache's old boys, Simon (Jacob) de Caceres was cut from the same cloth. The temper of the man, who at the Robles trial proudly testified, "I am of the Jewish nation of the tribe of Judah,"[41] is evident in a brazen proposal he submitted to Cromwell on the heels of his Jamaican shopping list. In it he offered to conquer Spain's New World empire with "people of my nation" as an advance guard for English forces. If Cromwell would give him four ships of war and a thousand men, he would sail around Cape Horn and attack the Spanish Main from the Pacific side, à la Drake, and invade the continent via Chile. In the meantime, anticipating Cromwell's favorable decision, he was off to Holland to recruit "young men of my own nation, [who] shall go as Englishmen for his Highness' service only." To finance the bold invasion, the would-be conquistador intended to capture Spain's silver fleet. Although Cromwell did not respond to de Caceres's grand scheme, there is evidence that he considered the Jew's strategy.[42]

A flamboyant character, de Caceres was described by a friend at the Robles trial as a "proud Jew who made no more ado about not being a Christian than how he had fought the dogs of the Inquisition on the Sea & Land."[43] He named his ship the *Prophet Samuel.* Like the prophet, he believed it was his godly duty to unite all Jews and was known to frequent the docks hoping to persuade newly arrived conversos to come out as Jews.

De Caceres was a successful international merchant, and Carvajal's friend (although twenty-five years his junior). He had offices in London, Amsterdam, and Hamburg, two brothers in Barbados, and relatives in Martinique and Suriname. Besides England's leader, he was on friendly terms with the king of Denmark and the queen of Sweden.[44] His plan to conquer the New World shows him as a man of militant vision, one that he likely followed with a further recommendation that set the course for Jamaica's immediate future.

With England's army dying and surrounded by enemy forces, it was not enough to build a fort. Cromwell knew that once he withdrew his army and navy, the colony would require a defensive force that could protect the colony, wage war on the Spanish, and at the same time feed itself. As a shipowner and illegal trader throughout the Indies, de Caceres knew precisely where to find such a force: the hunters of Hispaniola, a communal society of anarchists, exclusively male, who switched from hunting beef to robbing boats after the aforementioned cow-killers wiped out their prey. Crowded on a small offshore island, and now calling themselves the Brethren of the Coast, they were looking for new opportunities.

The challenge for Jamaica's survival was to intercept Spanish shipping on the high seas, and thereby cut the umbilical cord that fed the Spanish Empire. The Brethren could do this, and knowledgeable Jews, like Jamaica's Portugals, could both outfit and direct their attacks. From their extensive trade with fellow conversos in each colony, they knew what ship sailed, when it sailed, what it carried, and what the captain had hidden in his cabin.

De Caceres saw England's conquest of Jamaica as the first step in the liberation of his people. Step two was assuring that the Grand Western Design stayed afloat. Bring the Brethren to Jamaica, legalize them as privateers, and their attacks on Spanish shipping and land settlements would keep the Spaniards on the defense (and make their backers rich in the process).

This sort of game was not new to exiled Jews. From the time of their expulsion, Sephardim in North Africa had profitably backed the corsairs of the Barbary Coast.[45] De Caceres's friend Carvajal, who came from Las Palmas, a pirate port in the Canary Islands where conversos also had a sponsoring role, would certainly have endorsed his proposal.

"It is with the Jews that the connection with the buccaneers began . . ." is how Jamaica's foremost nineteenth-century historian, Robert Hill, links the two nomadic tribes whose alliance transformed the English colony into the pirate capital of the New World. Considering what de Caceres was up to, and the Sephardic involvement with the Barbary corsairs, Hill's statement rings true.[46] In any case, the strategy found favor with Cromwell, and by 1657, Jamaica was home to the formidable deterrent force known to history as the buccaneers of the West Indies.

In the first half of the sixteenth century, before the natives of Hispaniola died out, animal tending was Indian work. By the

1550s, with few Indians left, the animals ran free, and many settlers, lured by the attractions of the Main, quit the island. Those who remained abandoned the countryside for life in the city. Cattle, pigs, and horses, first brought by Columbus, returned to the wild, turning the island's northwest region into a vast animal kingdom.

By the 1620s, the huge herds had attracted a weird assortment of hunters, New World outcasts who settled, one by one, the small offshore island of Tortuga. They were misfits of every stripe and color: runaway bondsmen, ex-soldiers, marooned seamen, escaped slaves, heretics, criminals, and political refugees. Here they found the anonymity they craved: last names were discarded; each considered his former life "drowned." The hunters, mostly French and English, owed no allegiance to the Old World.

Unable or unwilling to return whence they came, they resigned themselves to a life of essentials. For a year or so, groups of six hunted with packs of dogs until they had enough hides and meat to sell. Known for the way they barbecued beef on a green wood grill called a *boucan*, they were called *boucaniers*, later Anglicized to buccaneers. Innocent enough, but to the Spanish across the island in Santo Domingo they were dangerous intruders.

By the 1640s, Tortuga had become a thriving settlement. Six hundred *boucaniers* moved between Hispaniola and Tortuga's fortified port of Cayano, where they bartered beef and hides to passing ships for guns, bullets, and brandy. With a secure base, they began raiding ranches on the north coast and set up two permanent camps there. To the hidalgos on the other side of the island, the situation was intolerable. The *boucaniers* had effectively annexed the northwest coast. Spanish pride would not allow this. However, rather than a direct attack, they conceived a seemingly ingenious plan: they would eliminate the *boucanier* by eliminating his prey. They reasoned that with no game to hunt, the hunters would leave, and Tortuga's raison d'être would cease.

In the summer of 1650, a mounted regiment of three hundred Spaniards, armed with twelve-foot lances, fanned out over the savannahs, running the cattle through on the gallop, and left the slain animals for the vultures. These were the aforementioned "cow-killers" who later routed the English on Santo Domingo. Within a year, the great herds of cattle had been wiped out, and in 1653 the Spanish delivered a coup de grâce. They invaded Tortuga in full force and deported the *boucaniers*. Though many returned when the Spanish withdrew to Santo Domingo to counter Cromwell's invasion, the day of the *boucanier* was over; the day of the buccaneer had begun.

Spanish policy had corrected a problem with an unanticipated result. By eliminating the cattle, they created a nation of rude warriors committed to vengeance. Deprived of their livelihood, the hunters of cattle became hunters of Spaniards, and within a year, Tortuga was a thriving pirate capital.

The buccaneers formed a guild, calling themselves Brethren of the Coast, and began by seizing small coastal and inter-island trading ships. With each success they grew bolder. When Pierre Le Grand and a small crew went forth in a canoe and returned with a treasure galleon, the sea was theirs. Something like the forty-niner gold-rush fever took hold. From all over, alienated adventurers flocked to join the outlaw nation. But the situation was tenuous. Tortuga was overcrowded, and when the invitation came to move to Jamaica, they gladly accepted and soon found ready recruits among the distressed soldiers of Cromwell's ragtag army.

Though lawless by disposition, the buccaneers adopted a stern code of discipline that welded them together into a dreaded fighting force. At first, they elected and disposed of their captains at will. Since their ship had usually been captured, the prize belonged to the whole company and the Brethren were equal partners. All plunder was divided by shares and disabilities—the loss of a right arm brought six hundred pieces of eight or six slaves; loss of a finger was compensated with a hundred pieces of eight or one slave; death in battle entitled one's heirs to a thousand pieces of eight. The captain received five or six shares and officers from one to three. Rewards were given to the first man who spotted the prize and the first to board her.

Later, once formally licensed as privateers by the government of Jamaica, they came under the leadership of stern captains such as Henry Morgan, and their ships were owned and outfitted by merchants who received the major share of the plunder, and were first in line to buy the remainder. So began the golden age of piracy.

The involvement of Jews in the conquest of Jamaica, and the promise of their continued assistance in expanding England's sphere of influence in the New World, convinced Cromwell to ignore the dissenters and grant London's Jews, and a few others, residency rights. But with no formal declaration for their readmittance, his sudden death in 1658 left them vulnerable and uncertain of the future.

Chapter Nine

THE GOLDEN DREAM OF
CHARLES II[1]

W here next?" This had been the challenge facing the leaders of La Nação after quitting Brazil, and Abraham Cohen helped determine the answer. Back in Amsterdam, he had taken a second wife, Rebekah Palache, the grandniece of Rabbi Samuel Palache, and fathered three children. Though he had lost most of his fortune when the Portuguese "beat the Dutch out of Brazil," in rebuilding his shipping business he became one of the chief architects in resurrecting another Rock of Israel in the New World.

Encouraged by Holland's initial success in Brazil, France and England had cautiously occupied a few small islands on the eastern rim of the New Spanish Sea. Their survival alongside an enemy empire required a special type of colonizer, and the refugee conversos fit the bill. Although the conversos were welcomed by these upstart colonies, because their mother countries were still closed to Jews, Cohen's first priority was to settle Holland's other New World possessions.

A natural choice was Curaçao, a small, rocky island off the coast of Venezuela, first settled by the Dutch in 1634. Cohen had been back in Amsterdam only a few months when his son Jacob returned from there. While attending the wedding of his namesake cousin, he became acquainted with David Nassy and Abraham Drago, two Amsterdam Jews who had been authorized by the Company to settle the island. They had been granted a license on their claim to have recruited fifty pioneering families, but it was an empty boast. When Jacob arrived, he encountered fewer than a dozen Jewish families.[2] Hoping to entice other settlers, Nassy and Drago enlisted his help.

Back in Amsterdam, Jacob, with his father paving the way, persuaded the Parnassim to sponsor additional settlers in Curaçao. However, while plans were going forward, Israel and his son arrived with news that put their enterprise on hold. With friends and family reportedly stranded in New Amsterdam, homeless, broke, and threatened with expulsion, immediate action was called for.

In February 1655, after the Company grudgingly approved Jewish settlement in the northern territory, Abraham Israel and Abraham Cohen made the decision to send their sons Jacob and Isaac to confront Stuyvesant. Joining them was Jacob's friend Joseph da Costa, the nephew of Uriel da Costa, who had served with him on Zur Israel's Mahamad. Stuyvesant fought them every step of the way, but by mid-1657, with the Company's reluctant but potent backing, they overcame the final hurdle and gained burgher status for Jews in the colony. They thereupon returned to Amsterdam.

Abraham and friends now focused on settling Holland's

Wild Coast colony, a sparsely inhabited region north of Brazil. Before the year was out, the States General, pressured by Cohen and the Jewish lobby, granted "the People of the Hebrew nation that are to goe to the Wilde Cust . . . [all] privileges and immunities" enjoyed by Dutch settlers.[3] Documentation of Cohen's settlement activities from Amsterdam's shipping records show that he recruited settlers and bought and transported slaves and goods to settlements along the "Wilde Cust."[4] Holland's pecuniary interest in encouraging Jewish settlement there was revealed in a confidential letter from England's agent in Italy to Cromwell's Jewish intelligencer Antonio Carvajal:

> It seems the States of Holland are making a planta-
> tion betwixt Surinam and Cartagena in the West
> Indies . . . aiming chiefly at trade with the Span-
> yard . . . who are in most extreme want of all European
> commodities. They have sent . . . about 25 families of
> Jews and granted them many privileges and immunitys.
> Spanish is the Jews' mother tongue . . . and they will
> be very useful to the Dutch . . . to converse with the
> Spanyard by reason of their civility. If our planters at
> Surinam took the same course it would be much to their
> advantage.[5]

The Jews' "privileges and immunitys" were consistent with those prescribed in the Patenta Onrossa, with one significant addition: The States General—as they had with Rabbi Palache and Moses Cohen Henriques—declared that Jewish settlers who so desired would be issued privateer licenses, "to capture and deliver to the Company Portuguese vessels."[6] Their names are not recorded, but there is no reason to doubt that a number of Jewish captains, having been legally empowered as privateers, sailed from the Wild Coast to plunder ships of enemy nations.

In the fall of 1658, Charles II was playing tennis in Belgium when a messenger rode up with news that ended the match: Cromwell had died "a sudden," and England was rejoicing. A period diarist commented, "None but dogs cried."[7] For a decade, Puritanism had dampened all pleasures—handholding was frowned on, theaters boarded up, singing and dancing forbidden; even Christmas was banned for being popish. "The populace had nothing to do but contemplate their sins and wail for forgiveness."[8]

The Protector had died of natural causes. At first, there was little change. His son Richard assumed power and an unnatural quiet descended on the realm, so that Thurloe wrote, "There is not a dog that wags his tongue, so great a calm are we in."[9]

Public apathy did not last. Under the Puritans, the nation's moral pendulum had reached an apex, balanced there for a time, and now swung back with increasing speed. Young Cromwell resigned after nine months and the ineffectual Parliament that replaced him came under increasing pressure to recall the king. No longer primed meekly to accept Puritan restraints, the populace looked to their absent monarch who lived by the axiom "I think no joys are above the pleasures of love."[10] Charles's ten-year exile in France, Scotland, Belgium, Germany, and Holland was that of a wandering king without a realm. Aside from many mistresses, he possessed little else.

Even so, at one point, he jokingly wrote that he only lacked "fiddlers and someone to teach the new dances."[11]

His was a false gaiety. When Cromwell's power was at its peak, Charles's fortunes were such that his housekeeper wrote he had not even laundry money. In this ebb, he turned to England's archenemy, Spain. For arms and money, he promised to join Spain's war against England, and upon his restoration, to revoke the anti-Catholic laws and return Jamaica.

But Cromwell's death and the public's clamor for his return had changed things. Charles, now in Holland and anticipating his return, pledged that he harbored no prejudices and that no one would be "disquieted or called in question" for religious practice that did not threaten the peace. His so-called Declaration of Breda, promising "a liberty to tender consciences," was read aloud in the House of Commons and a grant of fifty thousand pounds was approved to aid his return.

On May 28, 1660, Charles landed at Dover and the following day rode bareback into London on the flower-strewn route. It was his thirtieth birthday, and "the common joy," an observer noted, "was past imagination. The ringing of church bells that greeted his entry was scarcely heard above the din."[12] It was a magnificent homecoming that he compared to "the return of the Jews from Babylonian captivity."[13] But for all the pomp, Charles was broke. Despite Parliament's grant, he couldn't even pay the sailors who brought him home. The nation's debt was such that there was not enough money to run the country, much less fund a penniless king.[14] All this played into his recognition of Jews as a ready source of capital.

Since 1657, London's thirty-five Jewish families had been holding services in a house at 5 Creechurch Lane (near the present synagogue in Bevis Marks). They met openly, but their situation was tenuous, as there was nothing in the public record to show that the banishment decree had been revoked. They were reminded of this when, shortly after Cromwell's death, London merchants petitioned for their expulsion.[15] No action was taken, but their status remained insecure. In December 1659, six months before Charles's return, Thomas Violet, a London alderman, appeared in court arguing that Jewish settlement was illegal. When the judge put off his decision, citing the nation's unsettled political climate, Violet tried another ploy. He had given an associate a purse of counterfeit coins, instructing him to pass them on to the rabbi, thinking he would circulate the bogus money. He could then accuse Jews of plotting to bring economic ruin to the nation. But the plot was revealed when his confederate confessed the scheme to the authorities.[16]

Charles was back only a couple of months when London's Lord Mayor presented him with yet another merchants' petition which characterized the Jews as "a swarm of locusts [who] debauched English women [and] ruined trade" and called for their removal. Calling Cromwell "the late execrable Usurper," the merchants accused him of illegally admitting Jews to "a free cohabitation and trade [and] the right to practice their *Judaical* superstition." They asked Charles to enforce the former laws against the Jews, "and recommend that Parliament enact new ones for their expulsion . . . and to bar the door after them."[17] Violet, "a restless, meddling man," followed their petition with another. The Jews, he demanded, due to their "criminal proclivities," should be imprisoned and their properties confiscated until ransomed by rich brethren abroad.[18]

Despite such accusations, Charles's personal repute with

Jewish leaders was high, as noted by their rabbi in a letter to a friend in the summer of 1660: "According to what everyone says, the King's good will is such that no intermediary is necessary."[19] Charles's tolerant nature was one reason for their optimism; another was his lack of funds. In August he confessed he had less money now than when he first returned: "I must tell you, I am not richer, that is, I have not so much money in my purse as when I came to you."[20] Aware of the Crown's finances, in November, the Jew-obsessed Violet called for the Jews to be heavily taxed:

> Their usurious and fraudulent practices flourish so much that they endeavored to buy St. Paul's for a synagogue in the late usurper's time . . . suggest the imposition of heavy taxes, seizure of their personal property, and banishment for those without license.[21]

This last attempt at their expulsion was a final straw that spurred Carvajal's widow, María, to take action. As her husband had taken the lead in petitioning Cromwell, so María now stepped forward. Her own family had been victims of the Inquisition, so she knew well what was at stake. Learning of Violet's latest petition, she summoned her coreligionists to her home to compose and sign a petition for "his Majesty's protection to continue and reside in his dominions."[22] Charles forwarded their plea to the House of Commons with a note, requesting their "advice . . . for the protection of the Jews." Commons, sensing he wanted to protect rather than expel them, allowed the privileges Cromwell granted them to stand.[23]

On April 23, 1661, Charles was formally crowned at Westminster, and in the months thereafter demonstrated in no uncertain terms his support of the Jewish community. Before year's end, he naturalized nineteen Jews and approved the trading rights for de Caceres's brothers in Barbados.

When local merchants objected that "the Jews are so subtle . . . that in a short time they will engross all trade," Charles paid them no mind. His position was more in line with the planters in his colonies who wrote, "the admission of Jews and the accession of free trade will exceedingly tend to the advantage of the Colonies and His Majesty . . . If it were not for the Jews, [the merchants] would garner the whole trade, necessitating the planter to accept any prices they think fit."[24]

Charles's treatment of Jews in his realm was consistent with the tolerance he expressed in the Declaration of Breda. London's Jews, no longer having to disguise themselves or hide their wealth,[25] gathered each Sabbath in the rickety first floor synagogue in Creechurch Lane. Their place in society was endorsed by John Greenhalgh, a prominent Christian, who, having visited the synagogue in April 1662, observed in a letter to a friend:

> When I was in the Synagogue I counted about a hundred Jews . . . all merchants . . . not one mechanic person of them; most were rich in apparel, with various jewels glittering (for they are the richest jewelers of any). They are generally black and may be distinguished from Spaniards or native Greeks, their hair a more perfect raven black; they have a quick piercing eye and strong intellect; several of them are comely, gallant, proper gentlemen. I knew many who I saw daily upon the Exchange.[26]

Across the North Sea, four months earlier, Abraham Cohen and Abraham Israel decided the time was opportune to pay the king a visit. Their friend Benjamin Bueno Mesquita, just back from Jamaica,[27] had told them that the Jamaican Jews who first revealed the mine, namely Abraham Suares and Jacob Vilhoa, had followed his lead and kept it secret all these years. Now that Jews were legally settled in Britain and the colonies, and the king had shown himself an ally, the partners sailed for England to set in motion their long-delayed design to gain Columbus's mine. It was in this connection that in February 1662, Charles's agent in Reading alerted him of the arrival from Amsterdam of "certain Jews having knowledge of the gold mine which a Spaniard told His late Majesty existed in Jamaica."[28] They were on their way to London and were seeking a royal audience.

On March 5, 1662, Sir William Davidson, the king's agent in Holland, introduced to Charles the three Dutch Jews who claimed to know the location of Columbus's lost mine. They were Abraham Cohen, Abraham Israel, and the latter's son Isaac. The two older gentlemen, he said, were well respected in Amsterdam, where they were major players in Holland's colonial trade, and wealthy beyond need.

Israel recounted how he had learned of the mine from Jamaica's covert Jews when he was imprisoned on the then-Spanish island. He told the king they had confided in him because they feared their feigned Christianity would be exposed by the Inquisitors due from Colombia. Knowing he was about to be released, they asked him to use this knowledge to encourage a foreign invasion. But by the time he got back to Europe, Cromwell's army had already sailed, and Jamaica was already targeted. But rather than dicker with a contentious Parliament, they had waited seven years until the king was restored to his throne before coming forward.

Although Charles had earlier promised to return Jamaica to Spain, the prospect of the mine's supposed riches changed his mind. It is not known what the Jews said to convince him, only that, as stated in their contract, "reposing trust & confidence in ye abilities, [he was] well pleased and contented [to] grant [them] full power . . . and authority . . . in Jamaica . . . to search for, discover, dig, and raise . . . a Mine Royal of Gold . . . whether the same be opened or not opened."[29]

The Jews, at their expense, would command a two-year expedition to find and work the mine, for which the king was to receive two-thirds of the gold "gotten into wedges," and the Jews one-third. Once the mine was found, they would be awarded a trade monopoly in brazilwood and pimento spice, Jamaica's major exports. In addition, each miner (including slaves) would receive thirty acres. As a show of good faith, they were made English citizens, and when the draft of the contract was initialed, Charles, in an expansive mood, removed the gold necklace he was wearing and placed it over the head of Israel's son. With his friend George Villiers Jr., the second Duke of Buckingham, looking on approvingly, he told his Hebrew partners he was "bestowing a gold chain for their encouragement."[30]

Villiers, the orphaned son of the unfortunate first duke, had been taken into the king's household after his father's assassination and raised as a kind of surrogate brother to the young prince. From childhood, the two had known about the mine, which was first offered to their fathers as an inducement to invade. They knew that it was somewhere in Jamaica, but as the vein of gold was reportedly only "two inches wyde," finding it on a 4,500-square-mile island of thickly forested mountains was like searching for the proverbial needle in a haystack. Columbus's family reportedly kept the mine hidden to prevent others "from invading an island as weakly manned as Jamaica."[31]

Charles had accompanied his father during the first years of the civil war, but after the king's army was defeated in 1646, he went to live in France with his Catholic mother. Buckingham, after a three-year frolic in Italy, where his family had sent him, soon joined Charles, and the two immersed themselves in the pleasures of Paris. The bishop of Salisbury, one of their six tutors (among them was Thomas Hobbes) blamed the eighteen-year-old duke for introducing the sixteen-year-old prince to "all the vices and impieties of the age."[32] The two aristocrats shared a love of women, adventure, and theater, particularly actresses. They were fascinated as well by the era's scientific findings. Charles founded the Royal Society of Science in July 1662 to encourage serious researchers like Sir Isaac Newton, while Buckingham's involvement was more dilettantish. In an early address to the Society, he promised to donate a unicorn horn.

This was the extravagant duo that contracted the Jews to fulfill the lifelong dream that had first galvanized their fathers.

In March 1663, HMS *Great Gift* put into Port Royal with a trio of fathers and sons on a mission to find and work the fabled mine. Disembarking were Abraham and Jacob Cohen, Benjamin and Joseph Bueno Mesquita, and Abraham and Isaac Israel, the last sporting a heavy gold chain.

With England, Holland, and France competing along the trade routes, Jewish merchant adventurers, particularly those from Amsterdam, were courted, and sometimes given credibility beyond their due. Was this the case with these so-called "gold finding Jews"? The harbormaster thought so. Suspicious from the start, William Beeston wrote in his diary:

> Six Jews arrived (with a rich cargo) under the specious pretext that they came in search of a vein of gold known to them during the Spaniards government . . . [but] this was basely a pretence for their design was only to insinuate themselves for the sake of Trade.[33]

As with Spain's exclusive trade policy, England's Navigation Act forbade foreigners from trading with her colonies. Beeston's judgment is supported by the fact that not only were the partners granted citizenship, but the second part of their contract awarded them a monopoly to ship "hollow ground pepper," aka pimento or allspice, for which the island is still famous. A year later, when no mine had been found, the Jews were accused of fraud. Charles revoked their privileges and ordered them expelled from Jamaica. In his pique, he further demanded that they return his gold necklace. But in May 1664, when his banishment decree reached Jamaica, the partners were already gone. The president of the Council of Jamaica wrote the king: "The gold finding Jew went hence a month ago . . . he has left here ore and direction to find the gold, but we are all infidels, because the miracle is to be wrought in our country."[34]

Every historian who has looked into this story has endorsed the harbormaster's derisive judgment that Cohen and his partners came "for the sake of Trade," and that the search for the mine was a ruse of these conniving Jews who spellbound a king with the promise of treasure. Later doings by the harbormaster reveal that he had a private reason for rendering his verdict. Even so, Beeston's bias didn't necessarily negate his charge. Further support was seen in a charge in 1664 that Mesquita was engaged in illicit trade with Cuba while he and his partners were supposedly looking for the mine.[35]

This cynical view has largely prevailed. However, a sheaf of seventeenth-century documents discovered by the author in the Island Record Office in Spanish Town, Jamaica's old capital, suggests that, to the contrary, the only fraud the partners may have perpetrated was in declaring they had *not* found the mine. This archival evidence is best understood in the context of events in Jamaica during this period, later memoralized as the golden age of piracy.

Chapter Ten

BUCCANEER ISLAND

In the decade after the English takeover, more people were dying than arriving in Jamaica. Cromwell's liberal policy to give "Encouragement to such as shall transplant themselves to Jamaica" promised English citizenship to every child born there, and an allotment of twenty acres to every male over twelve years (ten acres to each female).[1] But his stated resolve "to people and plant that Island" had few takers, as word seeped out that Jamaica was a land of famine and disease with enemies all about bent on reconquest. Cromwell's plan to send a thousand Irish boys and girls was stillborn; another to transport from Scotland, "all known idlers, robbers and vagabonds, male and female," was abandoned when he was warned "this would set the whole country ablaze."[2] Cromwell's appeal to fellow Puritans in New England also came up empty when their delegate returned from Jamaica "horrified at the mortality among the soldiers."[3]

Even his single success was short-lived. Responding to his offer, the governor of Nevis arrived with a party of 1,500 men, women, and children, and settled on the eastern end of Jamaica. Being farmers, the newcomers immediately set to work clearing and planting many acres. Soon they had a bountiful crop, but others had to harvest it: In the three months the crops took to mature, a thousand of them had died.[4] Reluctantly, Cromwell continued to send more soldiers and food supplies (termed "survival stores").[5] But this was no answer.

In 1657, he instructed Jamaica's commander, Colonel Edward D'Oyley, to extend a formal invitation to the buccaneers of Tortuga to call Jamaica home.[6] As they began to dispose of their wares, the "fair beginning of a town sprung up around the fort" that de Caceres had recommended to guard the harbor entrance. Occupying the tip of a long and narrow peninsula, the port town could only grow up, not out. Freshwater had to be brought in by boat, which was the only way to reach the town. However, the port's offshore depth was such that the biggest ships could unload at its wharfs, and hundreds more could anchor in the Caribbean's largest harbor, sheltered by the seven-mile-long peninsula.

At first, each buccaneer crew was a force unto itself, electing (and disposing) captains at will to cruise the sea for merchant ships and stray galleons. This changed in 1659, when Jamaica's naval commander, Commodore Christopher Mings, called them all together. Only a strong leader could unite men so fiercely individualistic, and Mings, who rose through the ranks from cabin boy, was a tough old sea dog who fit the bill. Rather than run down ships at sea, he proposed that they unite under his command and attack Spanish towns. On their first venture, Mings and his men plundered three towns on the

Main, and returned with a haul valued at 1.5 million pieces of eight. The sight dazzled the people. After a few days of raucous celebration, so much silver changed hands that one wrote, "Not a man in the island reaped not a benefit of that action."[7]

The higher-born English officers were offended at the wild frolicking and scoffed at Mings for having allowed his buccaneers to keep so much of the spoils. They called him "a proud speaking, vain fool and a knave in cheating the State and robbing the merchants."[8] This was sour grapes. There was no arguing with success. News of Mings's exploit brought other buccaneers, merchants, tavern owners, prostitutes, and assorted and sordid pleasure-seekers to the port, so that in a few years the Point, as it was known, grew from "a barren sandy spit, to the largest, most opulent town in the English Americas."[9] Mings's triumph paved the way for the golden age of piracy under the command of one of his young captains, known to history as the Buccaneer Admiral, Sir Henry Morgan.

In August 1660, news of Charles's restoration reached Jamaica. It was no longer a secret that he had promised to return Jamaica to Spain when he regained his throne. With the island's future in doubt, merchants in England and Jamaica waited nervously to see what their king would do. They need not have worried: Charles was quick to renounce his promise, saying he had made it solely to secure Philip's assistance to regain his crown, and as no help had been forthcoming, Jamaica would remain English.

This assurance, together with the defeat of Ysassi's guerrillas and the success of Jamaica's growing port, gilded by plunder and protected by buccaneers, put the island on a more secure footing. In the previous five years, Jamaica had been a burial ground for fully three-quarters of the nearly twelve thousand men, women, children, and slaves who had come to the island.[10] But now every ship arrived with new colonists, mostly from England. With the guerrillas no longer a threat, settlements spread inland. More acreage was planted and food was plentiful. Spanish silver, gained through plunder and contraband trade, poured into Jamaica. Now solvent, the colony began a regular trade with Boston, shipping hardwoods and cattle hides for fresh food and salt fish. Fort Cromwell was renamed Fort Charles, and the Point christened Port Royal.

Fed by plunder, nourished by merchants, and spiced with sensuous pleasures, Port Royal attracted English and French buccaneers, as well as men of no nation, or at least none they acknowledged. Here they found what they needed most: a ready market for Spanish loot, facilities to repair and equip their ships, and the ribald pleasures they sought between voyages. By the end of 1660, there were always "at least a dozen armed ships in the area."[11] Owing to their fearsome presence, Charles felt comfortable enough that Christmas to recall the fleet to England, and the following year disbanded most of the army.

Iberian Jews, welcomed by Cromwell and Charles II, now arrived in Jamaica from all over the New World and abroad. Here they could throw off their converso cloaks and live free and prosper. Together with brethren from Holland and England, the Jewish community included shipowners from Mexico and Brazil, traders from Peru and Colombia, and ship captains and pilots from Nevis and Barbados. Joining with

Jamaica's Portugals, their combined knowledge of New World trade (both legal and illegal) was unsurpassed.

An island census in August 1662 put Jamaica's population at 6,000 (including 552 slaves), and found that Port Royal was home to thirty "stout vessels" manned by three thousand buccaneers.[12] At the time, Mings was abroad with 1,500 of them, plundering Santiago, Cuba's second largest port, and sacking Campeche in Mexico. In December, he returned to a hero's welcome, and shortly after was recalled to England to be knighted by Charles and made admiral.[13]

When news of Mings's exploit reached Spain, Philip was furious. He wrote Charles demanding satisfaction. Hadn't he and Charles agreed to a truce only months before? Campeche was near Vera Cruz, where the *flota* was loaded with silver and other treasures. Fearing Vera Cruz could be next, Philip hurriedly dispatched an armada to escort the *flota* home.

Charles assured Philip that Mings's raids had been without his knowledge and that he would put a stop to it. He wrote Jamaica's governor: "Understanding with what jealousy and offence the Spaniards look upon our island and how disposed they are to make some attempt upon it . . . the king signifies his displeasures of all such undertakings and commands that no such be pursued for the future."[14] His condemnation not withstanding, the king's draft of his letter conveyed his truer feelings. While he called for a cessation of such attacks, he first wrote: "His Majesty has heard of the success of the undertaking which he cannot choose but please himself in the vigor and resolution wherein it was performed." His subsequent letters to Jamaica's governor indicated that, if given the right excuse, his orders to desist could be ignored.[15]

Versions of this episode were repeated again and again in the decades that followed. In a century that began with the Thirty Years' War, peace was a rarity. When Europe's rival powers agreed to a truce, more often than not it was so that the two signatories could jointly attack a third. At times the buccaneers would be reined in, and licenses to attack other nations' ships revoked. But these licenses, known as letters of marque, would soon be reissued on some pretext. Spain was the preferred target, but sudden shifts in alliances meant that, at times, the ships of Portugal, Holland, and France were also fair game. In 1665, the French and Dutch were at war with England. The Dutch bombarded Barbados, and the next year the French routed the English at St. Kitts and threatened Jamaica.

Publicly Charles castigated the sea rovers; privately he turned a blind eye. Governors were dispatched to Jamaica "with strict orders to keep the peace," but quickly learned to holler wolf: "The Spanish are coming!" An alleged need to preempt a foreign invasion was the usual excuse for unleashing the buccaneers. Besides, it was argued, if Jamaica denied them the freedom of Port Royal, they would resort to other havens, and perhaps even target English ships.

In March 1663, "the gold finding Jews" entered a town that had grown to near three hundred buildings. When they left the next year, another hundred had been built, all crammed together at the end of the otherwise barren peninsula. A visitor described Port Royal's crooked streets and narrow lanes, lined with shops, taverns, and warehouses topped with balconied homes, as having the look of "an English shire town perched on the end of a tropical spit."[16] At the time of the conquest, the site was "nothing but loose Sand [with] neither Grass, Stone, fresh water, Trees, nor anything else," and only used by the Spaniards to careen ships to clean their hulls.[17] A decade later, the land spit had morphed into the treasure house of the Indies, so dubbed for its plunder-filled warehouses along the wharves, packed high with cases of sugar, cocoa, dyewoods, precious stones, plate, bullion, and other commodities. With buccaneer ships unloading their spoils, while others waited in the harbor to disgorge their ill-gotten gains and rowboats plied passengers and goods to and fro between ship and shore, the waterfront was a noisy, nonstop scene of bustling human activity.[18]

The pirates captured the riches, but it was the merchants, both Sephardim and rival English, who profited most, buying the booty "dogge cheape" on the dock, and selling it dear abroad. Wrote one visitor: "The merchants live here to the height of splendor, in full ease and plenty, being sumptuously arrayed . . . not wanting anything to delight and please their curious appetites." Their elegant homes were spectacular, furnished with plunder—silver plate, crystal chandeliers, and other accoutrements that had once graced a noble's casa or a bishop's dining table. Not to be outdone, by 1663, twenty-two pirate captains had equally grand residences, and shod their horses with silver horseshoes, loosely nailed and carelessly dropped to show their disdain for hoarded wealth.

It is not known how Cohen and his partners spent their time in Jamaica. Inside of a year they were gone. Gone too, at least from the historical record, are the two Portugals who welcomed the English, Duarte Acosta and Francisco Carvajal. Sephardic names appear on the island's early land deeds, bills of lading, wills, lawsuits, immigration records, hostile petitions, and so on. Port Royal had a Jew Street and a synagogue. The port's leading Jewish merchants are named (15 from a list of 125 merchants), as are their enemies, the rival merchants who petitioned to expel "the crucifiers of our Lord . . . who eat us and our children out of all trade."[19]

Most ships sailed to England in accord with the Navigation Act; others snuck in and out to avoid registration. In Jamaica's public registry, the amount of cargo consigned to Jewish merchants is relatively small. As in Spanish Jamaica, the Sephardim dominated the so-called silent trade. It is in this undocumented trade with converso merchants in Spain's colonies that Jamaica's Sephardim specialized, supplying them with European goods at bargain prices.[20] Unregistered merchandise bound for Vera Cruz, Havana, Nombre de Dios, Cartagena, and Santa Marta left Port Royal and the surrounding mangroves on unmarked sloops in the dead of night. Archival records contain the names of ninety-six Jews who lived in Port Royal during this era. That there were more is certain, but their names are absent from the public record. With trade restricted to English citizens and Jews who had been naturalized, undocumented Jewish traders kept their participation secret.

How many illegal aliens were there, and how big was the silent trade? The Port Royal historians David Buisseret and Nuala Zahedieh do not even hazard a guess. Their detailed analysis of the port's public record simply notes that the trade's covert nature makes it difficult to quantify. However, an indication of the enormity of contraband trade throughout the New World may be gauged by the fact that while no Spanish galleons arrived for two years after Charles regained his throne, when the ships finally came loaded with goods in 1662, there were few buyers. Their wares, the colonialists said, were far too expensive, and the galleons "returned [to Spain] with most of their cargo unsold."[21]

In the 1660s, Port Royal was the busiest port in the New World, and the most expensive. Employment was plentiful, with wages three times higher than in England. Only in the heart of London were rents so dear.[22] The town's permanent residents (numbering four hundred in 1664) were artisans, merchants, tavern owners, and ladies of the night who catered to the port's transient visitors. Once the booty was shared out, the buccaneers made for the bars and bordellos—one for every ten residents. Each place offered its own brand of vice, and none were said to lack customers. In the cool of the evening, the unexpurgated fun began. The taverns threw open their doors and pipe-smoking, petticoat-clad courtesans strolled the lanes.

Next to the merchants, it was the owners of the pleasure domes who profited most from the free-spending wild men. It was said no true buccaneer would go to sea again until he had spent every last piece of eight "in all manner of debauchery." He gambled it away, drank it up, and spent it on the ladies. "Pieces of eight were thrown around and no man bothered to count his change."[23] For a vivid picture of "wenching on a grand scale," it is worth quoting a passage from the Dutch surgeon (and suspect converso) John Esquemelin, who served with Morgan. He wrote that as soon as a pirate received his share, all he desired was "strumpets and wine":

> Such of these pirates are found who will spend 3000
> pieces of eight in one night, not leaving themselves
> peradventure a good shirt to wear on their backs in the

morning . . . I saw one give a common strumpet 500 pieces of eight only that he might see her naked. My own master [Morgan] would buy on like occasions, a whole pipe of wine, and, placing it in the street, would force everyone to drink with him; threatening also to pistol them, in case they would not. At other times, he would throw these liquors about the streets, and wet the clothes of such as walked by, without regarding whether he spoiled their apparel or not, were they men or women.[24]

Such frantic moments ashore only partially reflect the complexity of men who began life in the Old World and ran away to the New. The stereotypical pirate with a kerchief round his head and a cutlass at the waist, singing "Yo ho ho and a bottle of rum!" doesn't begin to describe these untamed men who in Hispaniola had slept with their animals, "with no more estate than a knife, and a gun, the sky their coverlet."[25] The fellow behind the eye patch and the gold earring was a natural anarchist who followed his own way on an uncharted journey that eventually brought him to Port Royal. In Tortuga, he had found a refuge. In Jamaica, he found a home.

To maintain a semblance of order, Port Royal had two prisons, a cage, a ducking stool, and stocks. One jail was for sailors "and other unruly elements." The other was for women, "to allay the furie of those hott Amazons." A nightly roundup hustled into a cage those too drunk to make it to a bed. When not whoring, the buccaneers shot at targets and gambled at cards, dice, billiards, shuffleboard, cockfights, and on a beastly match that pitted a bull and a bear. It was a rum-soaked scene—tawdry, noisy, and violent. The taverns and brothels "sucked them in, sucked them dry, and then tossed them out to seek further gold."[26] A newly arrived cleric, shocked to his core, left on the ship he came in on, and afterward wrote: "This town is the Sodom of the New World, the majority of its population being pirates, cut-throats, whores and some of the vilest persons in the whole of the world."[27] Another visitor concurred: " 'tis almost impossible to civilize [the town]. Vile strumpets and prostitutes are a walking plague against which neither the cage, whip nor ducking stool prevails."[28]

The setting cries out for a good novelist. It is an interesting challenge, as characters previously introduced now show up in Port Royal: Moses Cohen Henriques, whose citizenship paper was signed by Henry Morgan, lived here with his wife, Esther; Campoe Sabada, the invasion pilot, was likewise awarded citizenship; and Abraham Lucena, one of the half dozen Jews who with Jacob Cohen and Isaac Israel fought Stuyvesant, eventually owned land at the port.

Then there is the interesting figure of Batholomew (aka Balthasar) the Portuguese, whose misadventures are part of buccaneer folklore. Expelled from Jamaica after having assisted the English invaders in 1642, he turned full-time pirate and was in and out of the port on roving excursions. His tale is told by his contemporary John Esquemelin.[29] Smarter and more persistent than most in his profession, the Jewish pirate didn't know when to quit. In 1666, his ship heavily outgunned and outmanned, he captured a "great vessel" off Cuba's south coast with a rich cargo of cacao beans and seventy thousand pieces of eight. Contrary winds prevented his safe return to Port Royal and he was intercepted by three Spanish men-of-war, which took him to a nearby port, Campeche. Bartholomew having previously escaped imprisonment there (for "infinite murders and robberies"), his captors decided to keep him aboard ship "fearing lest he escape out of their hands on shore."

Knowing he was to be hanged the following day, Bartholomew, unable to swim, fashioned a pair of crude water wings from two empty wine jars, killed his guard, and slipped overboard. Hiding in a mangrove swamp, he concealed himself from the search parties for three days in the hollow of a tree. Using nails salvaged from a board washed ashore, he built a raft of twigs and branches and floated downriver to a secluded harbor frequented by buccaneers. There he met up with a Jamaican pirate crew "who were great comrades of his own." Relating his "adversities and misfortunes," he promised them a share of the wealth if they gave him a small ship and twenty men to retake the great ship that had been his two weeks before. Entering the port undetected, he and his men were able to persuade those aboard that they were traders coming from the mainland. By the time the Spaniards realized their mistake, it was too late.

Bartholomew was again master of the ship where he had previously been held prisoner awaiting execution. Although the silver had been removed, the trade goods were still in the hold, and weighing anchor, he set sail for Jamaica "with extremity of joy." But south of Cuba, "fortune suddenly turned her back upon him once more, never to show him her countenance again." A "horrible storm" dashed the ship against the rocks, leaving him and his crew with only a canoe to return to Port Royal. Esquemelin concludes his monograph, noting that although Bartholomew survived to "seek his fortune anew . . . from that time on [it] proved always adverse to him."

Critics cite the earlier presence in Port Royal of Abraham Cohen's relative Joseph Bueno Henriques, and his purported knowledge of a secret Spanish copper mine, as evidence that Cohen's purported search was "a fraudulent scheme . . . to gain entry into the economic life and trade of Jamaica."[30] In 1661, Joseph petitioned "Your Majesty to obtain permission to go to Jamaica . . . [to] discover a copper mine . . . the Spaniards . . . found to be productive." He claimed that when he was living in Jamaica in 1658, an escaped Spanish prisoner "informed me of [its] whereabouts." He had the gall to offer Charles a niggardly 10 percent of the proceeds, and the king rejected his proposal.[31] However, Charles later granted him naturalization and in 1672 he is listed in a Port Royal census as one of sixteen Jewish merchants so certified.

The tale seems to validate the skeptics' view. But a reading of the royal contract clearly dispels the notion that Cohen and his partners really came "for the sake of trade." It states in no uncertain terms that the Jews will be awarded the right to export "all hollow pepper [pimento], *only in the event of the discovery . . . finding and working of the mine*" [emphasis my own].[32] Therefore, if their search was indeed bogus, and there was no mine, there would be no trade benefits.

The never-before-accessed documents found in the archival vault also supported the view that the search for the gold mine was real and that Cohen, if he did not actually find the site, at least believed he knew where it was. They show that Cohen, despite his lifetime banishment, returned to Jamaica sometime in 1670, and in January 1671 secured 420 acres in an isolated river valley at the headwaters of the Oracabessa River (an area today confirmed as a gold-bearing region by Jamaica's Ministry of Mining). Cohen's actions—leaving behind his new family in Amsterdam and journeying to a far-off island from which he had been banished in order to buy land in a hidden valley—only seems plausible if he believed it contained the site of Columbus's mine.

As for Beeston's view that the mission was a fraud, this too demands another look, not just because of Cohen's return, but also because Beeston's later actions show he was no friend of the Jews. Along with policing the waterfront, he was a rival merchant, and more than once tried to expel Jews: In November 1671, the harbormaster seized a Jewish-owned ship on the pretext that Jews were foreigners and had no right to trade.[33] The court overruled him, but when he became governor in 1700, he tried to drive Jews from the island. His means this time was to tax them in what they formally protested was "an extraordinary Manner hoping thereby to oblige [us] to quit the island."[34]

Beeston's unrelenting hostility was again evident in 1702, when Jews, citing unfair treatment, petitioned for voting rights. Beeston, with the Council of Jamaica concurring, declared their grievance "false and scandalous," and suggested they should be "imprisoned for their presumption." They weren't, but they were ordered to pay a tribute of two thousand pounds. When the Jews appealed the fine, the Crown sided with them, but not in regards to suffrage.[35]

The archival documents highlight what was going on in Jamaica when Cohen was expelled in 1664, up until his final appearance in 1675. Twice during that decade, he was in and out of the island, first to buy the valley land, later to develop it. What the documents do not reveal is what allowed him to return to buy land in 1670, and what made him suddenly leave the following year. Nor do they explain why in 1674 he felt it was safe to come back, ostensibly to work the mine, only to leave again in haste.

In June 1664, two months after the "gold finding Jews" left Jamaica, the island's new governor, Thomas Modyford, arrived from Barbados. Unlike Beeston, Modyford favored Jewish settlement. Weeks before, when he was still governor of Barbados, he testified "on the value of the Jewish Traders in the progress of settling the Colony . . . the Jews are our chief suppliers in Barbadoes, and would sell very cheap, and give one not seldom two years to pay, by which credit the poorer sort of planter did wonderfully improve their condition."[36] Modyford, at the time he assumed the Jamaica post, may not have been aware of the king's decree that banished Cohen and his partners, but he undoubtedly knew of it when he approved Cohen's land deed in 1671, and otherwise supported his presence.

Modyford ruled Jamaica during the heyday of piracy. From 1666 to 1670, the buccaneers and their leader Henry Morgan invaded the fabled cities of the Main and held its citizens for ransom. Using the same Inquisition tortures (and at times the same apparatus), they forced the Spaniards to surrender their wealth. In five years of nonstop plundering, Morgan, with Modyford as his patron and defender, and backed by Port Royal's Jewish merchants, "attacked and plundered 18 cities, four towns 35 villages and unnumbered ships."[37]

Morgan was born on a farm in Wales in 1635 to a prosperous family. An adventurous youth, he journeyed to Bristol, then the major port for the slave trade, and soon found himself caught up in it—literally. "Shanghaied" is a later term for what was referred to as being "Barbadoed"—kidnapped and transported to a foreign land to be sold as an indentured servant. So it was that the nineteen-year-old farm boy hanging around the docks was captured and put aboard a ship bound for Barbados. Sold to the owner of a tobacco plantation, he did not have to labor long. Cromwell's fleet arrived shortly thereafter, and with the promise of freedom he joined Venables's army and wound up in Jamaica. Nothing more is known of him until 1662, when he signed on with Mings. By then he had fought the "cow-killers" in Hispaniola and Ysassi's guerrillas in Jamaica, gaining combat experience that served him well in the coming years, and from Mings he learned important lessons that made him a brilliant strategist. That he was also courageous, dauntless, and cruel were no less vital attributes.

Modyford and Morgan were a perfect pair to shape the colony. Though in many ways opposites, they complemented each other. A descendant of Morgan later contrasted the two: "[Modyford] was cunning, mannered, elegantly dressed and extremely popular; his sexual tendencies leant toward homosexuality."[38] Morgan, on the other hand, was lustful, boisterous, and prideful. Rum was his elixir, and he usually could be found with his mates in the taverns of Port Royal, where in his cups, he loved to spin yarns. Both men were charming, ambitious, duplicitous, and Machiavellian.

For all his licentiousness and volcanic temper, Morgan was a great leader, and when required, a disciplined and brilliant tactician. Morgan did whatever it took to conquer a place and wring the last piece of eight from a prisoner. If he and his men had scruples, they kept them hidden: They slaughtered soldiers and priests, raped women and nuns, tortured adults and children, and blew up churches. Modyford, for his part, ran interference, calling Morgan's actions necessary for Jamaica's defense.

When Modyford arrived in June 1664 with strict orders to recall the buccaneers, Morgan was away, having left the previous November on a two-year expedition, during which he raided three towns in Central America. When he finally returned towing eight Spanish ships, all laden with riches, he persuaded Modyford that his action was necessary to forestall a Spanish attack. The governor did not need much convincing. Shortly before Morgan's return, he received the unsettling news that the Jamaica-bound ship his eldest son was on had been attacked by Spaniards. Reportedly the young man had been taken alive but was either first tortured before being murdered, or sent as a slave somewhere in the South Seas.[39] After conferring with Morgan, Modyford wrote General George Monck his reason for unleashing the buccaneers:

> I cannot but presume to say we should in any measure
> be restrained while [the Spanish] are at liberty to act
> as they please upon us, from which we shall never be
> secure until the King of Spain acknowledges this island
> to be his Majesty's, and includes it in the capitulations.[40]

Again in 1666, Modyford defended the buccaneers:

> The Spaniards look on us as intruders and trespassers
> wheresoever they find us in the Indies and use us ac-

cordingly; and were it in their power . . . would turn us out of all our Plantations . . . It must be force alone that can cut in sunder [their] unneighbourly maxim to deny all access of strangers.[41]

Modyford was a cunning politician. His dispatches mention neither booty nor personal revenge. Rather, he harps on the theme that Jamaica was in constant peril from a Spanish invasion and that only Morgan's attacks were a deterrent. Receiving and investing 10 percent of all the booty brought to port eventually made Modyford one of the richest men in the English Empire. Governing by proclamation, he ruled as an independent potentate, answering only to a king thousands of miles away, whose directives took months to arrive. Major military and judicial posts were given to family members, and he alone decided how to spend the island's revenue.

King Charles's excuse to King Philip that Morgan was acting contrary to his orders was scant satisfaction for Morgan's devastating raids, particularly when Charles had no problem pocketing his share of the plunder. At the beginning of 1670, the Spaniards took matters into their own hands. Privateers were fitted out by the governor of Portobelo to attack English merchant ships, and Philip dispatched six war ships to the Caribbean. Morgan said there were twelve, and complained that the armada had been sent "to take all the English they can light on . . . and with a frigate or two lying off the Point [of Port Royal] take all our ships and so ruin the place by obstructing our commerce."[42]

Morgan was restrained by a cautious Modyford, but then an incident occurred that he could not ignore. A Spanish privateer raided and torched a few farms along Jamaica's unprotected west coast, and in an act of unbridled arrogance nailed a contemptuous message to a tree. The audacious pirate wrote that only lack of time prevented him from sailing "to the mouth of Port Royal to proclaim by word: I, Captain Manuel Rivera Pardal come to seek Admiral Morgan . . . and crave he come seek me that he might see the valor of the Spaniards."[43] His insulting challenge enraged the buccaneers and all of Port Royal. Merchants, tradesmen, tavern keepers, and even the petticoat-clad ladies were loud in anger. In truth, however, they must have smiled at the pirate's boast that would serve as a casus belli to turn loose the buccaneers and renew the flow of Spanish silver. In July 1670, Modyford addressed an angry Council. Citing evidence of Spanish aggression and Pardal's challenge, he demanded, and they at once agreed:

> For the security of this Island and the Merchant
> Ships . . . that Admiral Morgan gather all ships of War
> belonging to this harbor . . . and put to Sea to Attain,
> Seize and Destroy all the enemies vessels that shall come
> within his reach . . . and that he shall have power to
> Land in the enemies Country . . . to perform all manner
> of exploits which may tend to the preservation and quiet
> of this island . . . and all the goods gotten to be divided
> according to their usual rules.[44]

Although the Council did not specify where Morgan was to attack, it was no secret that his destination was Panama. A year before, Morgan had threatened the governor of Panama that he would be back within a year. Next to Cartagena, Panama City, founded in 1517, was the largest city in the Indies. Separated from the buccaneers by a twenty-five-mile-wide isthmus of almost impassable mountains, rivers, and jungle, its citizens believed they were secure. However, the city's very security made it vulnerable to men fired by the promise of plunder. Its merchants, intent only on amassing gold, lived in lazy luxury in palaces of scented wood, intricately carved and of Moorish design, furnished with luxuries from Europe. As Morgan described it: "The famous, antient City of Panama is the greatest Mart for Silver & Gold in the World, for it receives the Goods that comes from old Spain in the King's great Fleet, and delivers to the Fleet all the Silver and Gold that comes from the Mines of Peru and Potosi."[45]

Modyford, aware that the repercussions of such an attack, however successful, would fall on his shoulders, sought to gain the support of those closest to the king. Hoping to secure England's blessing, he wrote his ally Lord Ashley, one of Charles's confidants, that he was "a petty governor without money" and had no desire to declare war on "the richest and powerfulest prince of Europe." But since Spain had declared war on him, he had no choice. Anticipating an order to desist, he pointedly added, "Yet I far more dread the censure of my friends and countrymen on this occasion than the sword of the enemy."[46]

He was prescient in this regard, as Charles was then in Madrid negotiating peace. Barely a week after Modyford approved Morgan's plan, the two sovereigns signed a "Treaty for Composing Differences Restraining the Depredations and Establishing Peace in America." In return for England outlawing piracy, Spain agreed to recognize her possessions in the New World. However, by the time Modyford received news of the treaty, Morgan had already sailed. He sent a boat after him with orders to return to port, but as he wrote the king, "the vessel returned with my letters, having missed him at his old rendezvous."[47]

It was during this period that Abraham Cohen clandestinely returned from Amsterdam to secure a particular piece of land in Jamaica's interior. On December 2, 1670, when Morgan was disclosing to his compatriots his plan "to take Panama . . . for the good of Jamaica,"[48] Cohen and his surveyor were trekking in an unexplored river valley on Jamaica's north coast. On January 11, when Morgan and a thousand men were hacking across the isthmus, Cohen's surveyor, wielding rod and chain, set the boundaries of a 420-acre property at the headwaters of the Oracabessa River. On February 7, while Morgan and his men were ravishing the Golden City, Modyford signed the deed approving Cohen's ownership of the land.

Although Modyford did not know it at the time, his action was technically illegal, not just because of the banishment decree, which was still in effect, but for the fact that Modyford himself was no longer governor. The previous month, when Charles learned that Morgan had not been recalled, he blamed Modyford and revoked his commission: "Whereas Sir Thos. Modyford, late Governor of Jamaica, hath contrary to the King's express commands, made many depredations and hostilities against the subjects of his Majesty's good brother the Catholic King."[49]

When the news of the burning of Panama reached Spain, the English ambassador reported: "The Queen spent hours on her knees, imploring God's vengeance; all Spain is in mourning."[50] Anticipating Spain's reaction, Charles appointed as deputy governor Thomas Lynch, a wealthy Jamaican planter living in London, and sent him to Jamaica to arrest Modyford and return him to England under guard. He did so, but with discernment. A few days after he arrived, Lynch invited the governor to dine aboard his ship. Only then did he tell Modyford of his orders to imprison and send him to England. So as not to make an enemy of the popular governor, he added, it was simply a political move forced on the king because of Panama, and assured him "his life and fortune were in no danger."[51]

Lynch had first gone out to Jamaica with Cromwell's army, and later served as Modyford's chief justice until the governor dismissed him. Though the two started out as friends, they fell out over the matter of the buccaneers. Lynch, a sugar planter and owner of "the best and richest settlement" in Jamaica, was the agent for the Royal African Company, England's slave-trading consortium. As such, he favored peace with Spain, as it would open her colonies to the lucrative slave trade. His return in the summer of 1671 plunged the island into factional strife. He and the planters were opposed by those favoring the buccaneers. Many small farmers had given up their plots to join the buccaneers and it had become evident that farming and freebooting were incompatible. As long as piracy was sanctioned, legal trade was off the table.

Lynch had hoped that in return for collaring the buccaneers, Spain's colonies would welcome his trade ships. In his initial address to the Council of Jamaica, he told the assembly that peaceful trade would be "infinitely more advantageous, safe and honorable" than privateering. In line with this, he ordered ship captains to go to the major Spanish ports under a flag of truce to propose open trade, but despite his peaceful and profitable offer, they returned with the news that the Spaniards would not buy "so much as an emerald."

Compounding this rejection, late that summer an order arrived from the king to arrest Morgan, explaining that Spain was threatening war unless this was done. Lynch, his trade overture rebuffed, was in a quandary. He wrote Lord Arlington, the king's adviser, that "to obey the order and [see] the Spaniards satisfied [he would] send [Morgan] home." But he cautioned that Jamaica's only defense force was the buccaneers, and to send away the one man who could lead them would leave Jamaica unprotected at a time when he had learned that Spain was marshaling forces to invade. "Certain merchants in Jamaica," he wrote, had shown him "letters from Holland and Spain [that] the Church and Grandees of Spain were gathering an army of 5,000 men and a fleet of 36 ships to recapture Jamaica."[52]

Lynch did not identify these merchants, but like Cromwell, who relied on members of London's Portuguese community for intelligence, Lynch likewise received reports from the Jewish traders in Port Royal, who were in regular contact with agents in Holland and Spain and engaged in what Lynch called "a little underhand trade" with the enemy. In October 1671, Lynch defended them when English merchants sought his intercession at the unfettered "Trading of the Jews." Alarmed at the "alien presence in Port Royal [of] a multitude of Jews," they demanded an exact census be taken, followed by "the expulsion of any Hebrews" who were there illegally. Lynch, in forwarding their petition to the king, justified their presence:

To keep up the credit if not enrich the island, His Majesty cannot have more profitable subjects than the

Jews. They have great stocks and correspondence; His Majesty cannot find any subjects but Jews who will so adventure their goods or persons to get a trade. Their parsimony enables them to sell the cheapest; they are not numerous enough to supplant us; nor is it in their interest to betray us. Hopes we will do as much as will keep up the credit if not enrich the island by keeping peace and obliging them.[53]

Despite Lynch's advocacy, the census was ordered. Only sixteen Jews were able to show "patents of naturalization," and were deemed legal traders.[54] How many others there were without papers is not known. The community's insecurity was heightened the following month (November 1671) when Beeston had the temerity to seize a ship owned by a Jew from New Amsterdam (now temporarily in English hands and called New York) on the grounds that Jews were foreigners and had no right to trade. Cohen, having secured his valley land and fearing exposure, hastened back to Amsterdam, leaving his brother Moses, protected by Morgan, to oversee his properties.

Cohen wasn't in Amsterdam long before his wife, Rebekah Palache, reported that he had died, and as his widow collected debts due him. But this was a subterfuge. He had faked his death to cover his forbidden trips to Jamaica. Leaving Amsterdam, he moved to Salé, the pirate republic in North Africa where he had many associates and where both he and his wife's family were well established.[55]

Port Royal's Jews, adhering to the basic survival principle their people had acquired in the Diaspora, had a foot in both camps: They outfitted the buccaneers, advised them of potential targets, and received priority to purchase spoils. But if piracy was outlawed, there was the lucrative 'Spanish trade. It made no difference that the trade was still illegal. Everyone wanted a piece of it, including Jamaica's new governor. In March 1672, Lynch wrote Arlington that the presence of the buccaneers had forestalled a Spanish attack, and he was no longer interested in pursuing legal trade with those he termed "the most ungrateful, senseless people in the world."[56]

Lynch was not as naive as he let on. When he first sent his emissaries, he had instructed them that if the Spanish rejected his offer of peaceful trade, they should try to establish ties with the local merchants, whose names Lynch had obtained from his intelligencers who specialized in the "silent trade." As long as such trade was illegal, the Sephardim of Port Royal were the preferred agents of foreigners of whatever religion. For a 10–15 percent commission, they would "adjust the cargoes, strengthen the crews, provide commercial information and accompany the vessels to Spanish markets."[57]

The English merchants' animosity toward those they labeled "descendants of the Crucifiers of our Lord" didn't let up. In June 1672, Lynch received a petition from seventy-two Christian merchants stating that they were threatened "by the infinite number of Jews who daily resort to this island and trade amongst us, contrary to all law and policy." Ironically, the merchants, like those in Recife, accused the Jews of engaging in what is today normal business practice:

> The great Mischief we suffer by them is that their trading is a perfect monopoly, for they are a kind of joint stock company, and not only buy the choicest and best goods, but frequently buy up whole cargoes, and un-

dersell petitioners, which they can better bear by their penurious way of living . . . His Honor must have [seen] in Europe how Jews do engross the whole trade where they are . . . Although their trading seems to give credit and reputation to the island, yet England receives no benefit for all their merchandizes come from Holland, where they will certainly transport themselves again with all their gains and his Majesty's island will be drained and subjects will suffer.[58]

In urging Charles to reject the petition, Lynch renewed his case in the Jews' favor. The king, in continual need of hard currency, approved a liberal policy toward them. Their buying power and experience as importers and exporters of precious metals, together with their commercial ties with Spanish America (which had the silver), and Holland (the leading bullion market) made their presence in Jamaica vital to England's capital flow, and the colony's continued prosperity. Lynch's views were adopted, and the King-in-Council recommended steps to encourage even more Jews to settle the island. In December 1672, Charles wrote Lynch, declaring Beeston's seizure of a ship the year before on the grounds that its owner "being a Jew was to be accounted a foreigner" was "undue and illegal," and that "said owner, Rabba Couty, ought to enjoy the benefit of a free citizen . . . and his ketch and the value of her lading be restored."[59]

Prejudice could not stand up to economics. The Jews' contribution to Jamaica and England's prosperity determined the Crown's position in their favor. In two decades (1656–76), in large part due to the role of these proven entrepreneurs in the "underhand trade" and their dealings with the buccaneers, Jamaica funneled to England an estimated four million pounds of silver. England's Committee of Accounts noted that the island had become "the base for the greatest flow of silver and gold [and] more bullion is yearly imported from thence than from all other of the King's dominions laid together."[60]

Morgan had heard nothing from the Crown since he returned under guard to London in the spring of 1672, "to answer for his offences against the King, his crown and dignity."[61] Apparently Charles thought it was sufficient to recall him and let it go at that. A year would pass before the king summoned him. Unfortunately there is only a salacious hint of his time in London. If only Pepys had kept up his diary, we might have an unexpurgated account of Morgan's carousing there while London's dilettantes and ladies thrilled to host a live swashbuckler. While Morgan gallivanted around London, Modyford languished in the Tower, satisfying the Spanish ambassador that he was confined to "a cold, damp, stone room."[62] When he was finally released, it was thought his day had passed. But Morgan had not forgotten his arbiter.

Anxious letters from Lynch informed the king that Cuba's governor had licensed privateers to capture British ships, and Jamaica's outlawed buccaneers, having deserted to Tortuga, were now sailing forth with French commissions. Lynch declared that he had used his own money to store up the island's defense, and had come to appreciate Modyford's policy of keeping the buccaneers on a short leash. Without the threat of them as guard dogs, the Spanish had no interest in keeping the peace with the despised Protestants who had stolen their island. Lynch was blunt in his assessment: "I fear all may be lost if we have not a frigate or two to defend the island."[63]

In response to his governor's warning, Charles sent for Morgan to advise him how best to defend the island. Impressed by the pirate's counsel, the king decided to recall Lynch and return Morgan to Jamaica as deputy governor. Cocksure as ever, Morgan agreed, providing he was first made a knight and that his friend Modyford join him as chief justice. Charles consented. When Lynch learned of this turnabout, he was shocked, and predicted trouble: "Spaniards are much alarmed at the noise of the Admiral's favor at Court and return to the Indies. [His] appointment will fuel the Spanish fire." As for himself, he was happy to relinquish his post and was looking forward to returning to England: "None can come to the Government with such joy as I shall quit it."[64]

On March 6, 1675, Sir Henry Morgan arrived at Port Royal, and the following day took a carriage to Spanish Town to meet with Lynch and the planters and merchants who made up the Council. To a man, they wanted peace and feared the return of the notorious buccaneer. Their main interest lay in the slave trade—not just to buy for themselves, but also to sell to Spanish colonies. The last thing they wanted was a return to the days when Morgan's buccaneers made any chance of that impossible. Why should any Jamaican settler toil in the fields when he could join the buccaneers and reap the immediate reward of the "sweet trade"? As for the Spaniard, why should he chance inviting an English merchant into port who might turn pirate, as many unsuccessful trading ventures did? Simply put, piracy and trade were incompatible.

The Council members needn't have worried. Morgan, having discarded his old garb for the finery commensurate with his new status, and sporting medals and sashes befitting a knight, told the assembly that his orders were to continue to suppress piracy. This policy was seconded by Jamaica's new governor, Lord Vaughn, who arrived the following week. Vaughn, described by one who knew him as among "the lewdest fellows of the age,"[65] was also a poet and a patron of the arts. Preferring to rule over an enslaved island, rather than a wanton, undisciplined nation of licentious pirates, he sided with the planters.

They, meanwhile, were awaiting the arrival from Suriname of fellow English planters who were expert in sugar production. In 1674, when New Amsterdam was permanently deeded to England in exchange for Suriname, the English planters who had been living there had begun looking to move elsewhere, and in April 1675, three transport ships left England to carry their hundred or so families to Jamaica. Historians credit the Suriname planters with introducing the expertise that converted the island into a vast sugar plantation and the richest source of income in the British Empire. To accomplish this transformation, cheap labor was needed, and on May 11, the Council of Jamaica, composed mostly of planters, petitioned the Royal African Company, "demanding more slaves." The year before, the Company had sent "2,320 negroes to Jamaica," and in response to the request agreed to send "four more ships with 1660 slaves."[66]

Meanwhile, early in 1675, Abraham Cohen received news that convinced him it was safe to return. Modyford, his ally, was back in Jamaica. King Charles, he also learned, had authorized Suriname's Jews to settle in Jamaica. Since the king had rejected the Port Royal merchants' suit to exclude the Jews from trade, Beeston and others would have to pull in their claws and tend to their own affairs, and Cohen could lose himself among the new arrivals. However, when Cohen clandestinely returned to reclaim his properties, trouble arose—though not from the hostile merchants, but from his brother, who took him to court.

The reader will recall that in 1671, when Abraham returned to Amsterdam, he had asked Moses to look after his land. It must have seemed a good idea at the time. Although Moses was not one of the sixteen naturalized Jews in Jamaica, his presence there was not disputed and he and Sir Henry Morgan, as ex-freebooters, were longtime comrades. Ostensibly the case was brought over a claim of back pay for superintending Cohen's property. Settling the dispute in May 1675, Abraham acknowledged that he was "justly and duly indebted unto my brother Moses Cohen Henriques . . . for two years and seven months salary that he hath been employed by me."[67] In lieu of a hundred pounds sterling, Cohen agreed to give his brother forty cows and horses.

Although the suit was a minor matter, Modyford as chief justice presided and signed off on the settlement. Since both litigants were in their late sixties and wealthy, more than back pay was at issue. It appears that Moses had caught the gold fever and wanted a piece for himself. In any event, Abraham was dispirited: It was one thing to circumvent a royal ordinance, fake his own demise, and twice journey to a forbidden island while avoiding Beeston and his allies. It was quite another to find his own brother trying to horn in on a deal that he had been working on since he first learned of the mine twenty years earlier. A few months after signing off on the judgment, Cohen gave up the quest. He sold off the land, and that's the last we hear about the "gold finding Jews" and their search for Columbus's mine.[68]

In 1677, King Charles replaced Governor Vaughn with the Earl of Carlisle, a man more favorable to Morgan, who stayed on as deputy governor. Modyford, after two years as chief justice, retired to his estates. Jamaica's seesaw policy of alternately reining in and releasing the buccaneers continued until Modyford's death in September 1679. Afterward, Carlisle returned to England, and for the next two years Morgan was acting governor. Finally in a position to revive Port Royal as a pirate capital, he instead turned prosecutor. He had become a major landowner and, in his newfound allegiance to the status quo, no longer tolerated piracy. Retiring privateers, he announced, would be pardoned and given land to cultivate. Any caught violating his new directive might end his days rotting from a noose at Gallows Point.

One old privateer seeking an official pardon "upon the oath never to indulge in such practices again" was Moses Cohen Henriques. Well into his seventies, he likely hadn't been at sea for years, but apparently wanted to be pardoned for his earlier roving. So it was that Morgan, on November 18, 1681, acting on "the humble petition of Moses Cohen," signed the document granting him naturalization, that quasi-citizenship that was the best that a Jew could then aspire to. At the same time, Moses, like his brother Abraham, now foreswore his Spanish name. The document reads in part:

[I, Sir Henry Morgan] do graciously give and grant Moses Cohen his heirs and successors from this day forward in the island of Jamaica to be fully and completely naturalized and do hereby confirm to him and his heirs forever all the rights, privileges and immunities granted in this said act as fully and completely as our natural born subjects do have or enjoy or as if said Moses Cohen had been born in any of our dominions. Witnessed, Sir Henry Morgan, Knight Commander in Chief of the Island of Jamaica.[69]

As for the alleged gold mine, Morgan knew of it, but had no knowledge of its location. Still, when the Duke of Albemarle obtained from the king the sole right to search for Spanish gold in the Caribbean, Morgan lured him to Jamaica with tales of sunken treasure and the lost gold mine. Although Albemarle brought along "Miners to search for Mines," and the two men were successful in salvaging sunken treasure, the legendary mine was never found. After Albemarle's death, a near contemporary noted that the duke's prospectors "under the Pretence of search for Mines, instead went to Planters houses, & Got Drunk."[70]

The Great Earthquake of 1692 brought a climactic end to the pirate port, when the sea swallowed two-thirds of Port Royal. Beeston, who owned the waterfront land across the harbor that became Kingston, did not let his animosity toward Jews prevent him from taking their money. After the earthquake, he sold sixteen of the first lots to Jewish investors.[71]

From an infamous pirate capital, Jamaica, by 1698, had become a sugar island worked by forty thousand slaves, and after 1713, "the centre for slave distribution in the Caribbean and North America." It was then that England's Royal African Company was awarded the *asiento*—the monopoly right Spain granted to conduct the slave trade with Spanish America. A few Jamaican Jews did participate in the trade, but most dealt in dry goods. This fact was noted in a London petition in 1735 that protested the ongoing effort of rival merchants to exclude

Jews. Their defenders (ninety-two Jewish and non-Jewish merchants) wrote: "The Jews [in London] are almost the only persons that send any dry, fine goods to Jamaica, at their own risk, and on their own account . . . for the supply of the inhabitants of the island, and for making proper sortments of goods for the Spaniards."[72]

As Jewish involvement with piracy petered out in the Caribbean, the rovers and their Sephardic sponsors disbanded, only to reunite in the following century when a budding new nation would enlist them in its fight for liberty. In the American Revolution, a dozen prominent Jews sided with the rebels as privateers. Celebrated as founders of early Jewish congregations, these men owned and operated more than a few of the pirate ships that captured or destroyed over six hundred British ships and took cargoes and prizes with an estimated value of $18 million in today's dollars.[73]

Finally, no discussion of Jewish piracy should leave out the Jewish heritage of the famous pirate known to Americans as a hero of the battle of New Orleans. In a handwritten note, stuck in his family Bible, Jean Lafitte wrote: "I owe all my ingenuity to the great intuition of my Jewish-Spanish grandmother, who was a witness at the time of the Inquisition." Elaborating on his ancestry, Lafitte wrote in his journal:

> My mother died before I can remember and my maternal
> grandmother, who lived with us, became a mother to
> me . . . My grandmother was of Spanish-Israelite . . . My
> mother's father had been an alchemist with a good
> practice and patronage in Spain. He was a freethinking
> Jew with neither Catholic faith nor traditional adher-
> ence to the Jewish synagogue. But this did not prevent

him from dying of starvation in prison for refusing to divulge the technical details which the Inquisition demanded from all Jews. Grandmother told me repeatedly of the trials and tribulations her ancestors had endured at the time of the Spanish Inquisition . . . Grandmother's teachings . . . inspired in me a hatred of the Spanish crown and all the persecutions for which it was responsible—not only against Jews.[74]

Here our story ends. It is the history of Iberian Jews, disguised as Christians, who pioneered the New World as explorers, conquistadors, cowboys, and pirates, transformed sugar cultivation into an agro-industry that they introduced to the Caribbean, and created the first trade network spanning the seven seas. Figures are imprecise, but it is estimated that conversos numbered around ten thousand in the midseventeenth century, or 5 percent of the 200,000 settlers in the New World, and up to 15 percent in the islands. As they were an underground community, we only know about those targeted by the Inquisition or otherwise exposed. With a heritage of denying their Judaism, most of their descendants eventually abandoned their religion. Of the thousands or more Spanish and Portuguese names listed in the Jamaican telephone book, the island's declared Jews today number less than two hundred.

The Cohen Henriques brothers and their comrades came of age in Holland, a tolerant oasis in a hostile world. They had heard about the horrors of the Inquisition from their elders, who fled Iberia to settle in Amsterdam. Emulating their mentor, the pirate rabbi Samuel Palache, they were inspired to combat their people's enemies. In their twenties, using force and diplomacy, they gained a temporary homeland in Brazil, and in their maturity, when the Dutch colony was overrun, they parlayed their trade connections and skills in the production and marketing of sugar and other commodities to ensure their welcome in the islands of the Caribbean. Their economic power in turn enabled them successfully to lobby the Dutch West India Company in support of their children in New Amsterdam, and to secure the intervention of the States General to free their other comrades held in Jamaica. Finally, in Port Royal, as merchants and shipowners they used the buccaneers to wage a successful surrogate war on the lands of the Inquisition that effectively ended Spain's hegemony in the New World, and in the process they reaped the rewards, both legal and financial.

The Sephardic Diaspora of 1492 was nothing new in the history of a people who for more than two millennia had been wandering the known world. Since the expulsion of the twelve tribes in 722 B.C., the exiled Jews had been forced to develop particular talents that would be welcomed in foreign lands. The Iberian expulsion, far from destroying them, assured their survival. Concurrent with the Age of Discovery, they settled the newly discovered lands, and as world trade grew in importance, so did theirs. Trading with their brethren around the globe, they developed the markets and acquired the secret intelligence national leaders craved as they competed for lucrative trade routes. Menasseh ben Israel, in his appeal to Cromwell, quoted Amos 9:9: "I will sift the house of Israel among all the nations as corn is sifted in a sieve," and cemented his argument with an economic promise: Welcome us and we will make you rich. Today, centuries later, it is this promise of entrepreneurial wealth that still protects the People of the Book in an indifferent and often hostile world.

The search for the "lost gold mine" of Columbus was a last hurrah of the Jewish merchant adventurers, an adventure that failed. Not so the cause to which the Cohen brothers and their peers had devoted most of their lives. In 1675, the very year the brothers were battling each other in court, Jewish houses of worship were opened in Amsterdam and London, and the following year in Curaçao, Barbados, and Jamaica. It was thanks largely to their efforts spanning most of the seventeenth century that the barriers to Jewish residency and commercial rights were surmounted and Jews were finally free to be Jews in both the Old World and the New.

EPILOGUE: *SEARCHING FOR* THE LOST MINE OF COLUMBUS

I was in Jamaica's archival vault, a cavernous, dimly lit room, with row upon row of ceiling-high shelves filled with leather-bound ledgers dating back three and a half centuries. Perusing an early index of Sephardic names, I came across an obscure reference to a land deed assigned to Abraham Cohen. It was dated February 7, 1671—seven years after the king banished Cohen "off Our said Island never to reside or trade there again."[1]

The date didn't make sense; was the deed misdated? I took down the appropriate ledger for the years 1670–75, and there it was, or rather there *they* were, for along with Cohen's deed was another document, so remarkable I got chills reading it. Cohen's land title was indeed dated seven years after his banishment for failing to find the legendary mine. So he had come back to the island; but why? In 1670, Cohen was in his sixties and living in Amsterdam with a second wife and three young children. He was wealthy beyond need, so why had he crossed thousands of miles of ocean to an island from which he'd been expelled? As I pondered this, I turned to the back of the ledger to see how far it ran. A few pages before the end, the book fell open to a curious entry labeled "Cohen vs. Cohen," dated May 1675. I read the opening passage; I then read it again because I could not believe what I was reading. There before me, on crumbling parchment, was the settlement of a 1675 lawsuit that identified Abraham Cohen as the brother of the pirate Moses Cohen Henriques.

I had followed the careers of Abraham Cohen and Moses Cohen Henriques for years, but no historian or document I consulted had previously linked them in any way. This was the first time I became aware these two Jewish pioneers were brothers. Equally startling was the discovery that in their old age they were both in Jamaica apparently arguing over land that possibly contained Columbus's lost gold mine. The discovery also meant that the very man sponsoring my research was, unbeknownst to him, the brothers' descendant, and if the gold hunt proved successful, a rightful claimant to Columbus's mine.

A year before, Ainsley Henriques had given me a grant to research Jamaica's early Jewish history. He was then chairman of the Jamaica National Heritage Trust. In conversing with him, I had talked about the fantastic deeds of the pirate warrior Moses Cohen Henriques, how he had sailed with Piet Heyn in the capture of the Spanish silver fleet, then led the Dutch invasion of Brazil and afterward commandeered an offshore island for his marauding. When Ainsley told me that he too was a Cohen Henriques, I was surprised, but thought it possible that when Moses was forced out of Brazil, he wound up in Jamaica during the heyday of piracy and begat some offspring. I later found his wife's name in a list of graves of the island's oldest Jewish cemetery. She had died in Port Royal, around the time of the 1692 earthquake, and her tombstone read, "Snr. Moses Cohen Henriques (Esther)."

Although this finding linked my sponsor to Moses, there was nothing in the historical record that identified Abraham Cohen as an Henriques, much less as the brother of the notorious pirate. As noted, Cohen never used his Portuguese name. A sworn enemy of Spain, he had dropped his oppressor name in favor of his ancestral one, and signed his name in Hebrew whenever possible. In every period document dealing with his activities in Amsterdam, Brazil, and England, he is identified simply as "Abraham Cohen." Apparently only in a legal dispute with his brother was he required to disclose their relationship.

Going by different names, the siblings at first belonged to different synagogues in Brazil. Abraham Cohen was an officer of Recife's Zur Israel, while Moses founded Magen Abraham on his private island. Their attending separate synagogues, as well as the earlier absence of anything linking the brothers, might be indicative of an estrangement. Although Abraham's leaving his land in Moses's care could point to a reconciliation, the sad truth is that when Cohen returned four years later, whatever positive feelings may have been rekindled between them were squashed when Moses took his brother to court.

An amateur genealogist, Ainsley knew his family was long resident in Jamaica. Previous to these findings, he had traced his line to an ancestor coming out of Amsterdam in 1740. We now agreed that his Dutch forebear had apparently emigrated to Jamaica to join relatives already there.

In the court settlement, Abraham agreed to give Moses forty

farm animals for watching over his other property on the Rio Cobre during his absence. Strangely, a lower court did not adjudicate what should have been an insignificant case. Instead, the verdict was rendered by Jamaica's chief justice, the island's former governor Thomas Modyford. What did all this portend? Moses was never part of the gold mine deal. Was he trying to horn in on his brother's action? After a lifetime fighting their people's foes, the brothers were in their twilight years; in 1675, Moses was seventy-two, and Abraham two years younger. A few months later, Cohen sold both the valley and river land. Was brotherly discord the reason?

Since then, Jamaica's Ministry of Mining has reported that soil samples from Cohen's valley register "significant anomalies for gold." This finding led me to consider that Cohen, banished for his failure to find the mine, either had found it, or *believed* he had. But not satisfied to divide it with his partners, he had come back to claim it for himself.

There were two significant objections to my thesis. Edgar Samuel, chairman of the Jewish Historical Society of England, raised them when I sent him my findings in hopes the JHSE might publish them. Back in 1936, his father, Wilfred S. Samuel, had written the first well-researched account of this episode, one that basically concurred with Beeston's judgment. His son now asked me: How could Cohen bypass Jamaica's authorities to both secretly mine the gold and transport it off the island? These were pertinent questions that at the time I could not answer. Instead, I consigned them to the recesses of my mind until, on a recent visit to the Jamaica Archives, I again struck pay dirt in the form of previously overlooked documents that definitively answered one of his questions, and allows me to speculate on the other.

I still have no conclusive answer as to how Cohen thought he could operate the mine without attracting unwanted attention. However, the hidden valley was unoccupied and undeveloped, and the area surrounding it was sparsely settled and largely abandoned after a slave rebellion in 1676. In addition, Cohen's neighbor, Solomon de León, was another Jew who may have been in league with him.[2] These facts may have allowed Cohen to believe he had sufficient privacy to pursue a mining operation.

What troubled me more was Edgar Samuel's other question. How would it have been possible for Cohen to clandestinely transport the ore across the island from the mine to the sea? I found the answer in the archival vault, in a site map of the aforementioned riverfront property that Cohen bought at the same time he purchased the valley land. Its northern border was on the Rio Cobre, a major waterway that runs from Cohen's northern valley to the southern sea. When I walked the land I found it was on a deep bend in the river, perfectly sited for a pier to transfer the ore.

On this book's Web site (www.JewishPiratesOfTheCaribbean.com) are the documents that support my thesis: (1) Lord Clarendon's transcription of the Spanish spy's note to Buckingham locating the mine in the area of Cohen's land; (2) The 1662 contract Cohen and Israel signed with Charles II to discover and work the mine for one-third of the gold; (3) Charles's 1664 banishment decree expelling Cohen and his partners from Jamaica for not finding the mine, and demanding the return of his necklace; (4) Cohen's 1671 deed for land in an unsettled region of Jamaica; (5) Cohen's 1671 deed on a bend in the river running south from the valley to the sea; (6) Jamaica's Ministry of Mining test findings verifying gold deposits.

I don't know if the mine exists or not. But as the Spanish governor of Jamaica wrote to King Philip IV after the English conquest:

> Although it is not known now where the mine is, it is a well-established fact that when His Excellency the first Admiral of the Indies [Christopher Columbus], discovered this island, he extracted much and of big karat, and today on the island there are still some old jewels made from that gold·. . . and some old pits of that gold are still there.[3]

Such endorsements as this persuaded four kings and their ministers that the legendary mine was real and was to be found somewhere in Jamaica. Abraham Cohen's covert return to the island, his purchase of land in a river valley in an area that was once the province of Columbus's Indian ally, and the Ministry's finding there of "significant anomalies for gold" give credence to the legendary mine's existence. Cohen certainly believed it was there. His descendant Ainsley Henriques is more skeptical: "The gold is in the story," he says. Perhaps, but just in case, Ainsley and I recently took out a mining license for the valley to see if, as the Spanish spy disclosed to Buckingham, where "the Earth is black, Rivoletts discover the source of the Mine."

In Lord Clarendon's transcription of Don Hermyn's confidential report, the mine's location is disclosed in the following paragraphs in geographical and numeric code:

> The Secret golden Mine which hath not yet been opened by the King of Spain or any other [is] Two leagues from the Sea which faceth the gulf of Mexico in Jamaica

on the point which faces Hondura leaving the island
of Cuba at the eight hand the great Coast of the land
towards Nombre de Dios at the left turning your back.
Its at the point equally betwixt Cuba and Hondura
the Earth is black, Rivoletts discover the source of the
Mine . . . The gold is found neere to the superficies of the
Earth and slides downe in the Rivers or is found in the
Rocks. The Vayne between the Rocks is but two Inches
wyde and is for the most parte towards the East.

The spy advised Buckingham:

[Enter the island] at an open land near a 01: 94: 01:
a. 01. on the coast of 01 . aa . 94 . 66 a of right against
the Island a a .01 . 94 . 61. 01 . 94 66. 13 . 01 The prime
formula which are to be called upon by word 24. 19. p.p.
000. nl pp . pp . 66. pp are the 11 . 61 94 . 61. 91 1 or 22
. 4. 85. or they [the Portugals] will show you there . 61 .
61 . 01 . 60 . nl 85 and Treasures! which I have seen and
shall personally attend to discover when I shall be put
on the place and secured of proposition which I do present therein according onto agreement.

We leave it to the reader to decipher these codes, and invite
the first who does so to join our quixotic search for the legendary gold mine of Columbus.

ACKNOWLEDGMENTS

*T*his book could not have been finished without the unflagging support of my sisters Mary Freedman and Helen Kritzler, and my Jamaican family Ainsley and Marjorie Henriques. I am indebted to the editorial advice of cousin Alan Wellikoff; lifelong friends Russell Karaviotis and Charles Shapiro for backing me with bucks; my ex-wife, Wendy Orange, for her continued encouragement; noted Sephardic author Jane Gerber for giving my research the necessary credibility and recommending my book to Doubleday; my agent, Mildred Marmur's unstinting loyalty; my editors, Adam Bellow, Daniel Feder, and Melissa Danaczko, and publicists Chastity Lovely and Liz Hazelton at Doubleday. Other friends I want to thank are Jeffrey Phillipson for his unabated enthusiasm for my book; Allan Gordon, my role model for a Jewish pirate; and Vladimir Epelboym, my e-mail pen pal, who gave me many leads. Finally, when I look back over my life, I give thanks for the influence of Alan Freed, who fathered my rock 'n' roll generation; foreign correspondent Bernard Diederich for showing me a life path; college newspaper editor Jules Older, who welcomed my adventure articles; Gabe Levenson, the dean of Jewish travel editors, for his unflagging support; and my Latin American history professor Larry Birns, raconteur extraordinaire.

All history books are written standing on the shoulders of other historians. In addition to those quoted, I would like to mention the writers whose works I found particularly valuable. For information on conversos in the New World: Seymour Liebman, Arnold Wiznitzer, Hugh Thomas, Irene Wright, Isaac Emmanuel, Zvi Loker, and Mordecai Arbell; for New World pioneers, the best reads are the books of Germán Arciniegas; the Jews in Dutch Brazil are documented by Arnold Wiznitzer and Anita Novinsky; for Spanish history, my favorite authors are Jane Gerber, J. H. Elliott, and Salvador de Madariaga; Samuel Tolkowsky writes most entertainingly on Jewish maritime heroes; the Sephardic Diaspora is documented in the voluminous works of Jonathan I. Israel and Daniel M. Swetschinski; pirates of the Caribbean are best covered by Dudley Pope, Alexander Winston, Anthony Gambrill, C. H. Haring, Stephen Talty, and buccaneer author John Esquemelin; the heyday of Port Royal by Robert F. Marx, Nuala Zahedieh, and David Buisseret; England in the seventeenth century is the specialty of Antonia Fraser; and the Jews of England are documented in the books and articles of Cecil Roth, William and Edgar Samuel, and Lucien Wolf. For Jamaica's Jewish history, the best source is Jacob Andrade's *The Jews of Jamaica.*

CHRONOLOGY

1492: Columbus sails on the historic 9th of Ab (August 2), the same day Jews must leave Spain.

1494: Columbus discovers Jamaica on second voyage.

1497: Forced conversion of Portugal's Jews; Jewish children exiled to São Tome.

1500: Cabral with Jewish pilot discovers Brazil.

1502: Conversos barred from Spain's colonies.

1503: Converso Fernao de Noronha granted monopoly to develop Brazil's dyewood industry.

1503–1504: Columbus marooned in Jamaica, defeats mutiny; leaves his gold with *cacique* ally.

1505: Columbus returns to Spain; no record of gold mirrors.

1506: Columbus dies.

1508: Cuba's bishop writes, "Practically every ship [is] filled with Hebrews and New Christians."

1509: Seville conversos bribe king to trade in colonies; Henry Hudson discovers Hudson River.

1510: Diego Columbus sends Jewish loyalists to Jamaica to retrieve gold medallions.

1511: Formal settlement of Jamaica–Nueva Sevilla de Oro.

1513: Balboa discovers Pacific.

1521: Cortez's army in Mexico includes 100 conversos; Charles V named Holy Roman Emperor.

1522: Verrazano captures ship loaded with Aztec gold; sails into New York harbor three years later.

1528: First auto-da-fé in New World in Mexico (Hernando Alonso).

1534: An eventful year: Charles V licenses conversos to settle Jamaica; São Tome Jews introduce sugar agro-industry to Brazil; Pizzaro conquers Peru; Cartier discovers Canada; Suleiman captures Persia with trusted Jewish physician Moses Hamon, who maintains a yeshiva in Salonika; Luther publishes German Bible; Henry VIII establishes Church of England.

1535: Charles V conquers Tunis; Barbarossa and Sinan, "the famous Jewish pirate" escape.

1536: Crown cedes Jamaica to Colon family; Inquisition commences in Portugal.

1568: Crown charges Columbus heir with importing goods for illegal export to the Main.

1568–1579: Conversos with Sir Francis Drake and Sir Walter Raleigh: *Simon Fernando* pilots Raleigh's four voyages to America; *Nemo da Silva*, captured by Drake off Brazil in 1579, is abandoned fifteen months later in Mexico, where he is arrested by Inquisition as a *judaizer*.

1580–1640: Union of Spain and Portugal; resurgence of Inquisition; more conversos to Jamaica.

1597: English privateer Sir Anthony Shirley invades Jamaica and occupies it for two months.

1600: Melgarejo takes over Jamaica; institutes reforms and repels pirate "Motta the Portuguese."

1609–1621: Spain and Dutch declare twelve-year armistice.

1609: Sultans' envoy Palache signs trade and defense treaty with Dutch and secures Jewish rights.

1614: Palache arrested for piracy in England; Raleigh sails for El Dorado. Spain's ambassador calls them pirates and demands their death; James agrees on Raleigh but Palache is set free.

1616: Palache's state funeral in Amsterdam attended by William of Orange.

1618: Raleigh loses his head.

1618–1648: Thirty Years War: Catholic vs. Protestant; Jews sell arms and make loans to combatants.

1620: Pilgrims land at Plymouth Rock—one of the continent's first permanent settlements by Europeans.

1621: Dutch West India Co. formed; Pilgrims celebrate Thanksgiving modeled on Sukkoth.

1622: Ecclesiatical coup in Jamaica transfers power over church to the Bishop of Hispaniola.

1623: Jamaica's Portuguese encourage Buckingham to invade with offer of gold mine.

1624–1625: Dutch temporarily capture and occupy Bahia, Brazil.

1624: Uriel da Costa excommunicated from Jewish community; Dutch settle New Amsterdam.

1628: Moses Cohen Henriques and Piet Heyn capture silver fleet; Buckingham assassinated.

1634: Dutch take Curaçao and Jews allowed to settle.

1635–1639: Lima Inquisition destroys Jewish community.

1640: Portugal regains independence; Columbus heir in Jamaica related to ruling Braganza line; "Bartholomew the Portuguese" assists invading English pirate; Uriel da Costa commits suicide.

1642–1649: Mexico Inquisition destroys community—only 13 of 109 victims escape execution.

1644: Converso Antonio de Montezinos claims he found Lost Tribes of Israel in Ecuador.

1648–1650: Ukrainian peasants led by Bogdam Chmielnicki slaughter 100,000 Polish Jews.

1650–1651: Menasseh Ben Israel's book *Hope of Israel,* based on Montezinos' claim, argues Messiah won't come until Jews readmitted to England; Thurloe invites Ben Israel to England.

1654: Portugal recaptures Brazil; Dutch Jews aboard one refugee ship are "detained" in Jamaica as suspect heretics; eventually twenty-three "proven Jews" are set free to sail to New Amsterdam.

1655: DWIC authorizes Jewish settlement in New Amsterdam.

1655: England captures Jamaica; Cromwell opens Jamaica and Barbados to Jewish settlement.

1656: Robles trial in England; accused of being a Spaniard, Robles is freed when London's Portuguese merchants come out as Jews and declare he is one of them. In Amsterdam, Spinoza is excommunicated for denying angels, the divine root of the Torah, and the immortality of the soul.

1657: In England, London Jews open a synagogue in a house on Creechurch Lane.

1657: Buccaneers of Tortuga invited to call Jamaica home.

1661–1662: Charles on throne rejects petitions to expel Jews; backs "gold finding" Jews.

1663: Six Jews arrive in Jamaica "on a royal mission to find a gold mine known to them."

1664: Jews banished; mission declared a fraud and Isaac Israel ordered to return king's necklace.

1664: New Amsterdam becomes New York.

1665: New York Jews obtain freedom of worship and other advantages of English citizenship.

1670: Morgan takes Panama; Madrid treaty recognizes English conquest; Cohen back in Jamaica.

1671: Cohen buys land in isolated river valley.

1672: Merchants try to expel Jews; Beeston charges Jews are aliens and seizes a Jew's ship; Charles establishes Royal African Company for slave trade.

1674: Surinam Jews petition to come to Jamaica.

1675: Cohen vs. Cohen: Brothers' Revealing Lawsuit.

1675: Grand opening of Amsterdam synagogue, still used today.

NOTES AND SOURCES

Introduction

1. Fernand Braudel and Sian Reynolds (trans.), *The Mediterranean and the Mediterranean World in the Age of Philip II* (Berkeley, Calif.: University of California Press, 1996), 823.

2. Antonia Fraser, *Cromwell: The Lord Protector* (New York: Grove Press, 2001), 566.

3. Arnold Wiznitzer, *Jews in Colonial Brazil* (New York: Columbia University Press, 1960), 60.

Chapter One: Columbus and Jamaica's Chosen People

1. Kirkpatrick Sale, *The Conquest of Paradise* (New York: Alfred A. Knopf, 1990), 192n: The youths outnumbered adult seamen fifty-seven to forty-two; most stayed loyal to Columbus, but it is not known how many were conversos.

2. Quoted in Salvador de Madariaga, *Christopher Columbus, Being the Life of the Very Magnificent Lord Don Cristobal Colon* (New York: Christopher Columbus Publishing, 1967), 187.

3. S. E. Morison, *Admiral of the Ocean Sea* (Boston: Little, Brown, 1942),

quotes the royal chronicler's account of Santangel and his plea to the queen.

4. Simon Wiesenthal, *Sails of Hope: The Secret Mission of Christopher Columbus* (New York: Macmillan, 1973), 166.

5. http://www.sephardicstudies.org/decree.html

6. M. Hirsch Goldberg, *The Jewish Connection* (New York: Steimatzky/ Shapolsky Publishing of North America, 1986), 87. In the *Zohar* (Book of Splendor), Moses de León (1250–1305) opined almost two hundred years before Columbus that "the earth revolves like a ball . . . when it is day on one-half of the globe, night reigns over the other half."

7. Zvi Dor-Ner, *Columbus and the Age of Discovery* (New York: William Morrow, 1991), 104, 105.

8. Benjamin Keen, ed. and trans., *The Life of Admiral Christopher Columbus by His Son Ferdinand* (New Brunswick, N.J.: Rutgers University Press, 1992), 264–65. Fernando's description comes from his book, written years later when he was fifty as a brief in support of his family's lawsuit to recover rights granted Columbus: "No longer able to keep the ships afloat, we ran them ashore as far as we could, grounding them close together board and board, and shoring them up on both sides so they could not budge."

9. Ibid., 241–57.

10. Padron Morales, *Spanish Jamaica*, trans. Patrick E. Bryan (Kingston, Jamaica: Ian Randle Publishers, 2003), 20: Fernando writes the view of St. Ann's Bay from the caravel deck "seemed to [Columbus] the most beautiful of all those he had seen in the Indies."

11. John Boyd Thacher, *Christopher Columbus: His Life, His Work, His Remains As Revealed by Original Printed and Manuscript Records*, vol. 2 (New York: G. P. Putnam's Sons, 1904), 633–34: A copy of the letter was found among Spanish papers in 1655 when the English captured Jamaica. The original, never recovered, was said to belong to a Jamaican Jew whose ancestor was marooned with Columbus.

12. Ibid., 634n.

13. Ibid., 635n.

14. Ibid., 635n.

15. Washington Irving, *The Life and Voyages of Christopher Columbus*, vol. 2 (New York: G. P. Putnam's Sons, 1896), 582.

16. Ibid., 634.

17. Samuel Eliot Morison, *Journals and Other Documents on the Life and Voyages of Christopher Columbus* (New York: Heritage, 1963), 192.

18. Washington Irving, *The Life and Voyages of Christopher Columbus*, vol. 2, 614; Columbus, when questioned about the gold of Veragua, maintained he brought home no treasure, because, as he wrote, "I would not rob or outrage the country since reason requires that it should be settled, and then the gold may be procured without violence."

19. At the start of Columbus's voyage two years before, Ovando refused him shelter in Hispaniola despite an approaching hurricane, and when the rescue ship arrived back in Hispaniola, Ovando freed the Poras brothers and threatened to punish the loyalists who had slain some of the rebels.

20. Irving, *The Life and Voyages of Christopher Columbus*, vol. 2, 567; Irving quotes his contemporary biographer Bartolome de Las Casas, *The History of the Admiral*, lib. 2, cap. 32: "To cheer and comfort those who were loyal [Columbus] promised on his return to Spain to throw himself at the feet of the Queen, and represent their loyalty and obtain for them rewards."

21. Keen, *The Life of Admiral Christopher Columbus*, 272–73: the full story of the eclipse. A copy of R. Abraham Zacuto's tables with the marginalia of Columbus is in the Colombian Library in Portugal.

22. William B. Goodwin, *Spanish and English Ruins in Jamaica* (Boston: Meador Publishing Co., 1938), 13.

23. Clarendon State Papers, vol. 1, Bodleian Library, Oxford University, 14, no. 237. Clarendon's handwritten translation of a spy's "secret discoveries" to the Duke of Buckingham in 1623 to encourage him to conquer Jamaica assisted by the island's Portugals.

24. Hugh Thomas, *Rivers of Gold: The Rise of the Spanish Empire from Columbus to Magellan* (New York: Random House, 2003), 210. Juan d'Esquivel's parents were the conversos Pedro d'Esquivel and Constanza Fernández de Arauz.

25. Myrna Katz Frommer and Harvey Frommer, "Melilla: A Bit of Spain That Jews Never Left," *The Philadelphia Jewish Exponent*, August 29, 1996. Since 1497, Jews have been living in Melilla, having never been forced to choose between exile and conversion, and until many left after World War II, each extended family had its own synagogue.

26. Irving, *The Life and Voyages of Christopher Columbus*, vol. 2, 587.

27. Morales, *Spanish Jamaica*, 18. Francisco Poras would return to hold

a post in government. The Poras brothers were themselves conversos and had been placed on the fourth voyage by Columbus at the request of the treasurer of Castile, Alonso de Morales, who was amorously involved with their aunt.

28. Irving, *The Life and Voyages of Christopher Columbus,* vol. 2, appendix, 642. "Ferdinand had been receiving reports that the mansion Diego was building was actually a fortress and Diego designed to make himself 'sovereign of the island.' " Reportedly Diego paced back and forth on the patio "awaiting news from Esquivel of the discovery of gold in Jamaica [that] he might declare himself Emperor of the Americas." Irene A. Wright, "The Early History of Jamaica (1511–1536)," *The English Historical Review* 36, no. 141 (January 1921), 73. The king writes Diego (February 23, 1512) that he is informed that Esquivel has found more gold than he reported.

29. Frank Cundall and Joseph Pietersz, *Jamaica Under the Spaniards,* abstracted from the Archives of Seville (Kingston: Institute of Jamaica, 1919), 2.

30. From a letter referenced in Francis J. Osborne, S.J., *History of the Catholic Church in Jamaica* (Chicago: Loyola University Press, 1988), 482 *n*31: Peter Martyr to King Charles, September 9, 1526.

31. Ibid., 3; Goodwin, *Spanish and English Ruins in Jamaica,* 204.

Chapter Two: Adventuring in the New World

1. Samuel Tolkowsky, *They Took to the Sea* (London: Thomas Yoseloff, 1964), 103–6. An excellent contemporary account of Zacuto and King Manuel.

2. Irwin R. Blacker, ed., *Hakluyt's Voyages* (New York: The Viking Press, 1965), 24–38.

3. Tolkowsky, *They Took to the Sea,* 119–24; Louis B. Wright, *Gold, Glory, and Gospel: The Adventurous Lives and Times of the Renaissance Explorers* (New York: Athenaeum, 1970), 92–99; Paul Herrmann, *The Great Age of Discovery,* trans. Arnold J. Pomerans (New York: Harper and Brothers, 1958), 80–84.

4. Tolkowsky, *They Took to the Sea,* 122.

5. Samuel Eliot Morison, *The European Discovery of America: The Southern Voyages* (New York: Oxford University Press, 1974), 219–20.

6. J. M. Cohen, ed. and trans., *The Four Voyages of Christopher Columbus*

(Harmondsworth, U.K.: Penguin Books, 1969), 220–21. In a letter to Isabella, Columbus wrote: "I believe that earthly Paradise lies here, which no one can enter except by God's leave." Later the well-watered country of the Orinoco would be renamed Venezuela, Little Venice.

7. Wright, *Gold, Glory, and Gospel*, 103; Charles David Ley, ed., *Portuguese Voyages 1498–1663* (London: Everyman's Library, 1965), 41–59. Report of discovery sent to King Manuel from Brazil May 1, 1500, by the notary Pedro Vaz de Caminha.

8. Wright, *Gold, Glory, and Gospel*, 106–7; Ley, *Portuguese Voyages 1498–1663*, quotes notary's account in Hakluyt Society, series 2, vol. 81 (London, 1898).

9. K. G. Jayne, *Vasco da Gama and His Successors 1460 to 1580* (Whitefish, Mont.: Kessinger Publishing, 2004, reprint of 1910 edition), 58.

10. Germán Arciniegas, *Amerigo and the New World* (New York: Alfred A. Knopf, 1955), 123.

11. Tolkowsky, *They Took to the Sea*, 123.

12. Morison, *The European Discovery of America*, 288–96.

13. Arciniegas, *Amerigo and the New World*, 204–7; Tolkowsky, *They Took to the Sea*, 119–25; Morison, *The European Discovery of America*, 227, 233, 272–312; Arnold Wiznitzer, *Jews in Colonial Brazil* (New York: Columbia University Press, 1960), 3–5.

14. Tolkowsky, *They Took to the Sea*, 125–27; Wiznitzer, *Jews in Colonial Brazil*, 5–9; Arciniegas, *Amerigo and the New World*, 246–48; Daniel M. Swetschinski, "Conflict and Opportunity in Europe's Other Sea: The Adventure of Caribbean Jewish Settlement," American Jewish Historical Society (December 1982), vol. 2, 217. Portugal's upper class looked down on the mercantile profession, which they relegated below the seven "mechanical arts" (peasant, hunter, soldier, sailor, surgeon, weaver, blacksmith). Conversos, only 10 percent of the population, constituted nearly 75 percent of the business community.

15. Irene Wright, *Early History of Cuba, 1492–1586* (New York: Macmillan, 1916), 27; Dagobert D. Runes, *The Hebrew Impact on Western Civilization* (New York: Philosophical Library, 1951), 730: "Jews were considered to be especially proficient as crossbowmen, and in some countries were admitted in considerable numbers to the noncommissioned ranks."

16. Manoel da Silveira Cardozo, *The Portuguese in America, 590 B.C.–1974:*

A Chronology and Fact Book (Dobbs Ferry, N.Y.: Oceana, 1976); Harry Kelsey, *Juan Rodriguez Cabrillo* (San Marino, Calif.: Huntington Library, 1986): There is also a statue of the explorer at Point Loma in San Diego, maintained by the National Park Service, and in 1992 a stamp was issued in his honor; Seymour Liebman, *New World Jewry 1493–1825: Requiem for the Forgotten* (New York: KTAV, 1982), 6: "The term Portuguese Jews was used by the inquisitors in the New World after 1528 for all Jews . . . despite the fact that many had been born in Spain decades after the Expulsion." Only Old Christians possessing Limpieza de Sangre certificates—proof they were free of Jewish blood for four generations—were allowed to settle Empire lands.

17. Cecil Roth, *A History of the Marranos* (New York: Harper Torchbook, 1966), 56–62: On March 19, 1497, it was decreed that all Jewish children ages four to fourteen were to be baptized the following Sunday; families who did not appear had their children seized by officials and baptized by force. Parents who didn't also convert could leave Portugal but their children would remain and be given over to Christian families to be raised in the True Faith. It was in this manner that Isaac Abarvanel lost his twelve-year-old grandson.

18. Swetschinski, "Conflict and Opportunity in Europe's Other Sea," 216–18; Jan Glete, *Warfare at Sea, 1500–1650* (New York: Routledge Press, 2000), 86: "The commercial expansion was regarded as a threat to the established social order"; Anita Libman Lebeson, *Pilgrim People* (New York: Harper and Brothers, 1950), 4–7: As capitalists they invested in voyages, owned and captained oceangoing ships, and traded with fellow Jews and conversos settled in farflung seaports.

19. Hugh Thomas, *Rivers of Gold: The Rise and Fall of the Spanish Empire from Columbus to Magellan* (New York: Random House, 2003), 495–97.

20. Seymour B. Liebman, "Hernando Alonso: The First Jew on the North American Continent," *Journal of Inter-American Studies* 5, no. 2 (April 1963), 291–96; Seymour B. Liebman, "They Came with Cortes: Notes on Mexican-Jewish History," *Judaism* 18, no. 1 (Winter 1969), 91–92; G. R. G. Conway, "Hernando Alonso, a Jewish Conquistador with Cortez in Mexico," Publications of American Jewish Historical Society (1928), 10–25. The informer's tale referenced an earlier incident in Hispaniola involving Alonso's first son, noting Alonso then drank

the wine he had poured over the child. Threatened with torture on the rack, the Judaizer confessed he had done so "in mockery of the sacrament of baptism."

21. Hugh Thomas, *Conquest: Cortes, Montezuma, and the Fall of Old Mexico* (New York: Simon and Schuster, 1995), 266.

22. Ibid., 529, 777: Thomas quote ("Adventurous women went gaily to men still in their quilted armor") is from Miguel Léon-Portilla, *La Vision de Los Vencidos* (Madrid, 1985); pages 148–64 consist of a reprint of Manuel da Silveira Cardoz, "Relacion de la conquista por imformantes anonimos de Tlatelolco."

23. Hugh Thomas, *Who's Who of the Conquistadors* (London: Cassell, 2000), 193. Juan Ponce de Léon II, the son of Juan González, and the son of Antonio de Santa Clara, Juan's friend from his early days in Cuba, authored on orders from the king the *Relación de Puerto Rico* of 1582, the first chronicle of the island. See an English translation at http://www .mlab.uiah.fi/simultaneous/Text/eng_puerto_rico.html.

24. Thomas, *Conquest*, 359, 399.

25. Ibid., 636.

26. For Alonso, see http://www.geocities.com/lonogria_37/aBastard.htm; for Marina Gutiérrez Flores de la Caballeria, see http://pages.prodigy. net/bluemountain1/estrada1.htm.

27. See www.Sephardim.com.

28. A number of conversos in this chapter are identified in Thomas's three acclaimed books on the period: *The Conquest, Rivers of Gold*, and *Who's Who of the Conquistadors*. The source for many of his disclosures is from the monumental work of Juan Gill, *Los Conversos y la Inquisición Sevillana*, 5 vols. (Seville: University of Seville y las Fundacion El Monte, 2000–2002).

29. Seymour B. Liebman, *The Jews in New Spain* (Miami: University of Miami Press, 1970), 46.

30. Judah Gribetz, Edward L. Greenstein, and Regina Stein, *The Timetables of Jewish History: A Chronology of the Most Important People and Events in Jewish History* (New York: Simon and Schuster, 1993), 162.

31. Liebman, *The Jews in New Spain*, 46, quotes Spanish historian Salvador de Madariaga: After 1,500 years on the Iberian Peninsula, Sephardim were as much Spanish as Jewish: "The Jews of the Expulsion left behind a deeply judaized Spain, and went abroad no less Hispanified."

1. Frank Cundall and Joseph Pietersz, *Jamaica Under the Spaniards,* abstracted from the Archives of Seville (Kingston: Institute of Jamaica, 1919), 10–11.

2. Ruth Pike, *Enterprise and Adventure: The Genoese in Seville and the Opening of the New World* (Ithaca, N.Y.: Cornell University Press, 1966), 60, 89: In the 1530s, the Genoese were licensed to procure African slaves "to supply the needs of the expanding sugar industry on the islands," and in 1535 transported a thousand slaves. Nowhere is it reported that Portuguese were sent. Irene Wright, "Sugar Industry in the Americas," *American Antiquity* 21 (1916), 755–82; Irene Wright, "The History of the Early Sugar Industry in the West Indies from Documents of the Archives of the West Indies in Seville," *Louisiana Planter and Sugar Manufacturer Journal* 54 (1915), 14–15: In 1527, New Seville's sugar mill is described as "a good one, producing good sugar."

3. Alexandre Herculano, *History of the Origin and Establishment of the Inquisition in Portugal,* vol. 1, trans. John C. Branner (New York: AMS Press, 1968), 376–78, 380–81: A further indication that Manzuelo's request for "Portuguese" settlers was for Spanish conversos is the fact that in 1534, when Charles received the communiqué, Portugal's New Christians were not allowed to emigrate. From 1532 to 1536, Portugal's king had reversed his policy that for a price permitted conversos to settle his colonies.

4. J. H. Elliott, *Imperial Spain: 1469–1716* (London: Penguin, 1963), 52–53.

5. Laredo is Spain's port on the Bay of Biscay. Hayward Keniston, *Francisco de los Corbos, Secretary of the Emperor Charles V* (Pittsburgh: University of Pittsburgh Press, 1960), 161: "It was rumored that they were offering 50 ducats for each pregnancy with boy babies to remain in Spain and girls to return with them to Amazonia."

6. Dudley Pope, *The Buccaneer King: The Biography of the Notorious Sir Henry Morgan, 1635–1688* (New York: Dodd, Mead, 1978), 29–30: Charles's average of 3.5 tons of gold each year was equal to the amount the queen of Sheba gave Solomon. In the sixteenth century, Spaniards "found, looted or mined three times the amount of gold and silver which had been in circulation" before Columbus sailed.

7. Antonio Dominguez Ortiz, *The Golden Age of Spain, 1516–1659* (New York: Basic Books, 1971), 47: Jacob Fugger loaned him half of the one-million-florin cost of the election.

8. Germán Arciniegas, *Caribbean Sea of the New World* (New York: Alfred A. Knopf, 1946), 118–21; Henry Cruse Murphy, *The Voyage of Verrazzano: A Chapter in the Early History of Maritime Discovery in America* (New York, 1875): an appendix includes letters to Charles informing him of Verrazano's deed and continued threat.

9. C. H. Haring, *The Buccaneers in the West Indies in the XVII Century* (Hamden, Conn.: Archon Books, 1966; reprint of 1910 edition), 30; Arciniegas, *Caribbean Sea of the New World*, 118.

10. "Correspondence and Itinerary of Charles V," ed. William Bradford (London: Bently Publishers, August 31, 1850), 439, 367.

11. Miriam Bodian, *Hebrews of the Portuguese Nation, Conversos and Community in Early Modern Amsterdam* (Bloomington, Ind.: Indiana University Press, 1997), 11. In 1391, hundreds of thousands of Jews of Spain were forcibly converted or sentenced to death. "This huge influx of New Christians exacerbated social and racial suspicions and eventually led to what would become known as Toledo's *limpieza de sangre* or 'purity of blood' statutes of 1449 to limit the rights of the new class of Christians. Those who maintained Jewish blood or lineage deriving from Jewish ancestry were classed as 'impure' and excluded from positions of power and prestige, and universities. These laws were applied in Seville in 1515, and Santo Domingo in 1525."

12. William B. Goodwin, *Spanish and English Ruins in Jamaica* (Boston: Meador Publishing Co., 1938), 13: "[Jewish] descendants of these Portuguese settlers are found in many parts of the island today."

13. On July 14, 1534, the sultan's cavalry of fifty thousand horsemen conquered Tabriz in northern Persia, but rather than moving on to threaten Charles's eastern empire instead turned east and captured Baghdad that October.

14. Neil Grant, *Barbarossa, the Pirate King* (New York: Hawthorn Books, 1972), 8–9: The bulky ships of Spain and Genoa were easily outmaneuvered by the corsairs' galley, a long, slender vessel, driven by massive oars with one main triangular sail called a lateen. The pirates would attack an enemy ship by ramming it with its iron bow (resembling a long beak). The corsairs then leaped on board and a hand-to-hand fight would ensue.

15. Ortiz, *The Golden Age of Spain*, 52–58.

16. Sir Godfrey Fisher, *Barbary Legend* (Oxford, U.K.: Clarendon Press,

1957), 55: Barbarossa as "General of the Sea" rarely left the land—his functions as admiral were primarily administration and "his naval duties were performed by a lieutenant, until later in the century they were entrusted to a separate officer [Sinan] who, as the local Captain of the Sea, [was] directly responsible to the sultan."

17. Samuel Tolkowsky, *They Took to the Sea* (London: Thomas Yoseloff, 1964), 174: On August 16, 1533, Henry VIII's ambassador in Rome informed his king that a few days earlier "the famous Jewish pirate" was cruising with a strong Turkish fleet of sixty ships off the southern coast of Greece to attack the Spanish fleet defending the western Mediterranean; J. S. Brewer, J. Gairdner, and R. H. Brodie, eds., *Letters and Papers, Foreign and Domestic, of the Reign of Henry VIII* (London, 1862–1932), vol. 6, 427: Sinan was referred to in 1528 by the Portuguese governor in India as "the great Jew," who he mistakenly thought had been sent by Suleiman to assist the king of Calicut to fight the Portuguese; Benjamin Arbel, *Trading Nations: Jews and Venetians in the Early Modern Eastern Mediterranean* (New York: E. J. Brill, 1995), 181, lists many Venetian sources from 1530 that refer to Sinan as "the Jew."

18. "Correspondence and Itinerary of Charles V," 349.

19. Keniston, *Francisco de los Corbos*, 170.

20. E. Hamilton Currey, *Sea Wolves of the Mediterranean: The Grand Period of the Moslem Corsairs* (New York: Frederick A. Stokes Company, 1914), 108.

21. "Correspondence and Itinerary of Charles V," 358–59: Charles's unshakable courage is epitomized in one of his later battles, when, gout having immobilized his neck and made his feet lame, he had himself tied to his horse and galloped into the heart of the thickest action. Grant, *Barbarossa*, 46–48; Currey, *Sea Wolves of the Mediterranean*, 107–9.

22. H. Z. (J. W.) Hirschberg, *A History of the Jews of North Africa*, vol. 2, ed. Eliezer Bashan and Robert Attal (Leiden: E. J. Brill, 1981), 480, quotes the contemporary historian R. Josef Ha-Kohen's account of the aftermath of the battle: "The Jews of whom there were many, in part fled into the desert, hungry, thirsty and completely destitute, and the Arabs plundered everything they brought with them; and many died at that time."

23. Keniston, *Francisco de los Corbos*, 176.

24. Cundall and Pietersz, *Jamaica Under the Spaniards*, 12.

25. Padron Morales, *Spanish Jamaica*, trans. Patrick E. Bryan (Kingston, Jamaica: Ian Randle Publishers, 2003), Appendix 6, 278–79: In Feb-

ruary 1537, the king gave in to her demand for power over the church: "Upon our consideration . . . that the resolution of these lawsuits is in doubt . . . on behalf of Dona Maria de Toledo . . . and Admiral Don Luis Columbus, her son . . . we grant leave to thee and thy successors whereby thou mightst appoint persons to the Abbacy, including its revenues, as well as to other offices in the churches on the aforesaid island."

26. Ibid., 65: The royal edict also granted the family twenty-five square leagues in the province of Veragua, where Columbus had obtained the sixty-three gold pendants, but the land proved to be "swampy and unprofitable" and nineteen years later Don Luis gave up Veragua in return for an annual payment of seventeen thousand ducats.

27. Cundall and Pietersz, *Jamaica Under the Spaniards*, 13.

28. *The Jewish Encyclopedia* (JewishEncyclopedia.com), "Antwerp" (by Richard Gottheil): "Antwerp became the center of Portugal's East Indian trade, and many of the rich merchants and bankers of Lisbon had branch houses there. In 1536, according to a document in the Belgian state archives, Charles V directed the magistrates of Antwerp to allow conversos to settle Antwerp."

29. Tolkowsky *They Took to the Sea*, 203.

30. Hirschberg, *A History of the Jews of North Africa*, vol. 2, 9.

31. Christopher and Jean Serpell, *Elba and the Tuscan Archipelago* (London: Jonathan Cape, 1977).

32. In his remaining years, Charles made a series of abdications that left the Hapsburg dominions divided between Austria and Spain. By 1555 he had given his son Philip Naples, Milan, and the Netherlands, and in 1556 retired to the monastery of Yuste.

33. Christopher Hare, *A Great Emperor: Charles V, 1519–1558* (New York: Charles Scribner's Sons, 1917), 199.

34. Gertrude Von Schwarzenfeld, *Charles V, Father of Europe* (Chicago: Henry Regnery Co., 1957), 278–79: On his bedside table were a Bible, his favorite heraldic romance *Il Cortegiano*, and Machiavelli's *The Prince*. On penance days, he "beat himself with the rough pieces of a knotted rope till he had worn away the knots."

35. Tolkowsky, *They Took to the Sea*, 183.

36. Jane S. Gerber, *Jewish Society in Fez* (Leiden: E. J. Brill, 1980), 166–69.

1. The family's rabbinical lineage goes back to the tenth century, when Moshe ben Chanoch, a famous Talmudic scholar from Babylon, was captured by pirates and taken as a slave to Córdoba. Redeemed by the community, he became its rabbi, married into the Palache family, and along with his son established Spain as a center of Torah study. Down to Samuel's time, family members rose to prominence as rabbis in Italy, Turkey, and Greece. *Jewish Encyclopedia*, "Palache"; Hirschberg, *A History of the Jews in North Africa*, vol. 2, 212n (extensive note on Palache rabbis).

2. Mercedes García-Arenal and Gerard Wiegers, *A Man of Three Worlds: Samuel Palache, a Moroccan Jew in Catholic and Protestant Europe*, trans. Martin Beagles (Baltimore: John Hopkins University Press, 2003), 24–25.

3. The roving rabbi's influence on the boys brings to mind the uncle in *Death of a Salesman*.

4. H. Graetz, *Popular History of the Jews*, vol. 5, trans. Rabbi A. B. Rhine, ed. Alexander Harkavy (New York: Hebrew Publishing Company, 1937), 55: David Jesurun, "the boy poet," gave the city the sobriquet "New Jerusalem" when, on the run from the Inquisition, he reached the safety of Amsterdam and, inspired, wrote his paean to it.

5. H. I. Bloom, *The Economic Activities of the Jews in Amsterdam in the 17th and 18th Centuries* (Williamsport, Pa.: Baynard Press, 1937), 78n23: "The Jews of Amsterdam are so expert that, after disguising the merchandise by mingling it with other goods, or packing it in another way or remarking it, they are not afraid to go to certain Portuguese ports and resell the goods there."

6. García-Arenal and Wiegers, *A Man of Three Worlds*, 5: The duke wrote that even if they did seduce a few New Christians they were less a threat to His Majesty than the many Barbary Jews in his domain who were spies and should be expelled.

7. Ibid., 6.

8. Ibid., 5.

9. Ibid., 10.

10. Ibid., 11.

11. Isidore Harris, Jewish Historical Society of England, "A Dutch Burial Ground and Its English Connections," 113.

12. Henrich Graetz, *History of the Jews*, vol. 4 (Philadelphia: Jewish Publication Society of America, 1941), 663.

13. John J. Murray, *Amsterdam in the Age of Rembrandt* (Norman: University of Oklahoma Press, 1967), 21.

14. García-Arenal and Wiegers, *A Man of Three Worlds*, 56.

15. Ibid., 55.

16. Ibid., 76.

17. Ibid., 77.

18. Hirschberg, *A History of the Jews in North Africa*, vol. 2, 214–15.

19. García-Arenal and Wiegers, *A Man of Three Worlds*, 72.

20. Odette Vlessing, "Samuel Palache: Earliest History of Amsterdam Portuguese Jews," in *Dutch Jewish History*, vol. 3 (Jerusalem: The Institute for Research on Dutch Jewry, 1993), 52.

21. Ibid., 50; *Jewish Encyclopedia*, "Palache."

22. Hirschberg, *A History of the Jews in North Africa*, vol. 2.

23. David Carrington, "A Jewish Buccaneer," *Jewish Chronicle*, November 4, 1955: Palache obtained from the Netherlands permission to "levee and raise so many mariners and seafaring men as he shall have need with license from the States General . . . to Barbary where Palache went up to the King . . . and [received] a commission from him to go to sea and take all Spaniards that he could meet with."

24. García-Arenal and Wiegers, *A Man of Three Worlds*, 85.

25. Ibid., 77–79. In February 1612, Sidan sent an urgent plea to Samuel to hurriedly come to his aid with two ships and a thousand men. The sultan was desperate. His brother, Ibn Abu Mahalli, a radical Islamist warlord hoped to rid the nation of Jews who were overrunning his realm. Mahalli was given undue credibility in July when Morocco's Dutch ambassador recommended the States General recognize the self-styled "new king" as Morocco's ruler. When his report reached the Netherlands, Samuel's brother Joseph and nephew Moses refuted the ambassador's claim. The following year, Mahalli was killed by an ally of Sidan, and the Dutch diplomat, charged with treason, was briefly imprisoned. Sidan was again recognized as Morocco's supreme ruler.

26. García-Arenal and Wiegers, *A Man of Three Worlds*, 85.

27. Vlessing, "Samuel Palache," 52.

28. García-Arenal and Wiegers, *A Man of Three Worlds*, 88–89.

29. Ibid., 90.

30. Ibid., 91.

31. *Jewish Quarterly Review* 14 (1902), 358, reprints, letter from London, dated November 4, 1614, from John Chamberlain to his friend Sir Dudley Carleton, the British ambassador at Venice: "Here is a Jew Pirate arrested that brought three prizes of Spaniards into Plymouth . . . he shall likely pass out of here well enough for he has league and license under the King's hand for his free egress and regress which was not believed till he made proof of it." See also the Acts of the Privy Council, December 23, 1614, Privy Council to Sir William Craven, Alderman: "The Lordships give order for the restraint and safe keeping of Samuel Palache, a Jew, lately arrived at Plymouth [charged with] committing piracy and outrage upon the subjects of the King of Spain . . . Palache hath alleged that he is a servant unto the King of Barbary, and by him employed as his agent unto the States United, and that from the said King his master he had received commission for the arming and setting forth of ships of war, by virtue of which commission (together with license of the States United) he pretends the fact to be justifiable and no way with the compass of piracy."

32. Robert P. Tristram Coffin, *The Dukes of Buckingham: Playboys of the Stuart World* (New York: Macmillan, 1931), 73.

33. García-Arenal and Wiegers, *A Man of Three Worlds*, 92–93.

34. Ibid., 87: When Sidan thought the Dutch were going over to Mahalli and he was near to losing his kingdom, he had Samuel offer Medina Sidonia the Mediterranean port town of La Mamoa in exchange for military support. When the duke passed the offer on to Philip, the king, suspecting Samuel was a double agent, told the duke not to deal with him.

35. Ibid., 80–82.

36. J. A. J. Villiers, "Holland and Some of Her Jews," *Jewish Review* 7 (1912), 10–12: The day after the funeral, the States General noted: "His Excellency [Prince Maurice], and the State Council accompanied the body of Senor Samuel Palache, Agent of the King of Barbary, as far as the bridge in the Houtstraat."

37. García-Arenal and Wiegers, *A Man of Three Worlds*, 62.

38. Bloom, *The Economic Activities of the Jews*, 14, 15n70: "Six months after the demise of Palache his nephew, Moses representing the estate sold two Torah scrolls to Neve Shalom for 1,000 guilders."

1. On the 1605 pardon, see H. P. Salomon, *Portrait of a New Christian, Fernão Álvares Melo, 1569–1632* (Paris: Fundação Calouste Gulbenkian, Centro Cultural Portugués, 1982), 43–46; Wiznitzer, *Jews in Colonial Brazil*, 33–34: "The assessment of 1,700,000 cruzados was divided among all the New Christians of Portugal . . . And New Christians could not leave Portugal without proving that they had paid their part of the assessment or given the necessary guarantee for its payment . . . After the expiration of its one year term, the Holy Inquisition resumed the prosecution of Judaizers among the New Christians . . . any New Christian who tried to leave port without paying the assessment was to forfeit his possessions in favor of the crown. And the person denouncing the offender was to receive one third of the recovered proceeds."

2. Benjamin Arbel, *Trading Nations: Jews and Venetians in the Early Modern Eastern Mediterranean* (New York: E. J. Brill, 1995), 180–81; H. I. Bloom, *The Economic Activities of the Jews in Amsterdam in the 17th and 18th Centuries* (Williamsport, Pa.: Baynard Press, 1937), 93n70: The Spanish had a different explanation for aliases. In 1654 the Spanish consul in Amsterdam wrote the Spanish ambassador: "The president of the Synagogue signs himself Cortez instead of Corticos, . . . his real name . . . It is the custom of members of his nation to take as many names as they please, . . . so as not to jeopardize their parents or relatives who are known by the name in Spain." Daniel Swetschinski, "The Portuguese Jews of 17th Century Amsterdam: Cultural Continuity and Adaption," in *Essays in Modern Jewish History*, ed. Frances Malino and Phyllis Cohen Albert (Rutherford, N.J.: Fairleigh Dickinson University Press, 1985), 58–60: Ninety-one percent of the community men were named after patriarchs. The favorite first names (in order of preference) were Abraham, Isaac, David, Moses, Joseph, Samuel, Aaron, Benjamin, Solomon, Daniel, and Emanuel.

3. Joachim Prinz, *The Secret Jews* (New York: Random House, 1973), 70–74.

4. Seymour B. Liebman, *The Jews in New Spain* (Miami: University of Miami Press, 1970), 589; Gerber, *Jewish Society in Fez*, 63; Jan Stoutenbeek and Paul Vigeveno, *A Guide to Jewish Amsterdam* (De Haan: Jewish Historical Museum, 1985), 13: In 1616, Jews were forbidden "physical communion with Christian wives or daughters in or outside

the state of marriage even though these women themselves might be of bad reputation." Bloom, *Economic Activities of the Jews*, 20: In 1616, Jews were forbidden to employ Christian servants.

5. Graetz, *History of the Jews*, vol. 4, 57.

6. Prinz, *The Secret Jews*, 74: In 1660, Isaac Orobio de Castro described the situation in Amsterdam. "There are those . . . who undergo circumcision as soon as they arrive, love God's law and are eager to learn that which they and their ancestors had forgotten during their years of their imprisonment . . . There is another group who indulge in the idolatry of logic . . . they are full of vanity, haughtiness and a sense of superiority because they believe they know everything . . . They place themselves under the happy yoke of Judaism . . . but their vanity and so-called superiority prevents them from accepting our teachings . . . The trouble is that the young . . . admire them and follow suit. They all land quickly in the abyss of atheism and apostasy."

7. Odette Vlessing, "Samuel Palache: Earliest History of Amsterdam Portuguese Jews," in *Dutch Jewish History*, vol. 3 (Jerusalem: The Institute for Research on Dutch Jewry, 1993), 52.

8. Simon M. Schama, "A Different Jerusalem: The Jews in Rembrandt's Amsterdam," in *The Jews in the Age of Rembrandt*, ed. Susan Morgenstein and Ruth Levine (Rockville, Md.: The Judaic Museum of the Jewish Community Center of Greater Washington, 1981), 3.

9. Swetschinski, "Conflict and Opportunity in Europe's Other Sea: The Adventure of Caribbean Jewish Settlement," American Jewish Historical Society (December 1982), vol. 2, 216–17: "Old Christian Portugal traditionally disdained the mercantile profession . . . It was therefore natural for many New Christian outcasts to assume a position in that segment of Portuguese society that was numerically understaffed and socially underrated . . . New Christians constituted about 65%–75% of the total Portuguese mercantile community while hardly totaling more than 10% of the population."

10. John J. Murray, *Amsterdam in the Age of Rembrandt* (Norman: University of Oklahoma Press, 1967), 49.

11. Schama, "A Different Jerusalem," 8: "There was a willingness to use Jews in high risk areas of the economy where more prudent or nervous investors were reluctant to venture." Jews were only let in on Holland's more speculative ventures like invading the New World and

attacking the Spanish silver fleet. When these paid off the brothers were set, big-time: on page 642 Schama quotes Elie Luzac, *The Wealth of Holland*, vol. 1 (1778), 63, 501: "It was only in 1612, in imitation of certain Jews who had taken refuge among them, and who had it was said set up counting houses everywhere, that the Dutch began to set up their own and to send their ships all over the Mediterranean."

12. Vlessing, "Samuel Palache," 53.

13. Ibid., 54, 62–63: From the time they entered Amsterdam, Jewish merchants dominated the sugar trade. In an address to the States General, Amsterdam's Portuguese merchants wrote: "During the 12 year truce, thousands of cases of sugar were brought each year to Holland in our ships . . . shipping and commerce increased so considerably that each year 12 to 15 ships were built and added to the trade . . . We were so successful that we drove all the Portuguese caravels that used to carry the sugar from these waters." The merchants wrote of other benefits Holland derived from their trade with Brazil: "The greatest benefit gained from this trade, namely, the sugar refineries . . . increased from three or four, 25 years ago, to 25 in Amsterdam alone, supplying Holland with sugar [as well as] France, England, Germany, and the East." Cornelis Ch. Goslinga, *The Dutch in the Caribbean and on the Wild Coast 1580–1680* (Asen, the Netherlands: Von Gorcum, 1971), 149: During the truce, the Dutch-Portuguese link controlled as much as two-thirds of the Brazilian trade with Europe.

14. Jonathan I. Israel, "The Changing Role of the Dutch Sephardim in International Trade, 1595–1715," in *Dutch Jewish History*, vol. 1, ed. Jozeph Michman (Jerusalem: Tel Aviv University, 1984), 33: "Dutch Sephardim overseas commerce is characterized by the primacy of dealings with Portugal and its colonies . . . via Lisbon."

15. Ibid., 36: "During the Truce years, the vast bulk of the freight-contracts signed by Dutch Sephardim were for voyages to and from Portugal."

16. Dorothy F. Zeligs, *A History of Jewish Life in Modern Times* (New York: Bloch Publishing Company, 1940), 109: In the seventeenth century the Dutch owned more than half the merchant ships of Europe.

17. Schama, "A Different Jerusalem," 6: "The Dutch Republic represented a prototype of that liberal pluralist socialist society—the imagined

arcadia of 19th century Jews—that would enable each faith to practice as it wished without having to . . . suffer the stigma of dual allegiance."

18. Daniel M. Swetschinski, *Reluctant Cosmopolitans: The Portuguese Jews of 17th Century Amsterdam* (Portland, Ore.: Littman Library of Jewish Civilization, 2000), 62.

19. Egon E. Kirsch, *Tales from Seven Ghettos* (London: Robert Uncombed & Co. Ltd., 1948), 182–83.

20. Bloom, *The Economic Activities of the Jews*, 19–20: "Philosopher and jurist Hugo Grotius . . . commissioned to draw up regulations regarding Jews . . . said they should be admitted but limited to three hundred families; they were not to hold political office nor marry the daughters of the land." Sabbath was respected and they could swear by "the Almighty who has . . . given His Laws through Moses"; 23–24: In 1632 magistrates ruled: "The Jews in this city who [are] or shall become burghers [are] forbidden to start a retail business." Also they could not join or form craft guilds.

21. Edgar Samuel, "The Trade of the New Christians of Portugal in the Seventeenth Century," in *The Sephardi Heritage*, vol. 2., ed. R. D. Barnett and W. M. Schwab (Grendon, U.K.: Gibraltar Books, 1989), 109.

22. Steven Nadler, *Rembrandt's Jews* (Chicago: University of Chicago Press, 2003), 28.

23. Ibid., 15–16, lists his Jewish neighbors.

24. Jonathan Israel, "Sephardic Immigration into the Dutch Republic, 1595–1672," *Studia Rosenthaliana* 23, no. 1 (1989), 51.

25. P. J. Helm, *History of Europe, 1450–1660* (London: G. Bell & Sons, Ltd., 1966), 234.

26. Israel, "Sephardic Immigration into the Dutch Republic," 51: Manuel Pimentel's will showed he had money invested in Venice, Constantinople, Spain, and Holland. His bookkeeper Hector Mendes Bravo, who reconverted to Christianity, was a spy who in 1614 submitted the names of 120 families from Amsterdam and the names of their correspondents.

27. Arnold Wiznitzer, *Jews in Colonial Brazil* (New York: Columbia University Press, 1960), 46–47.

28. Jane S. Gerber, *The Jews of Spain, A History of the Sephardic Experience* (New York: The Free Press, 1992), 10: The holding of Jewish slaves

was ruled illegal in the Talmud; therefore the slave who converted was immediately freed. Such conversions were commonplace since the Talmud prohibited Jews from keeping uncircumcised slaves; Eli Faber, *Jews, Slaves and the Slave Trade: Setting the Record Straight* (New York: New York University Press, 1998), 17: Regulation of Brazil's Zur Israel, the first synagogue in the New World: "A slave shall not be circumcised without first having been freed by his master, so that the master shall not be able to sell him from the moment the slave will have bound himself [to Judaism]."

29. Wiznitzer, *Jews in Colonial Brazil*, 47: In 1618, Alvaro Sanches informed the Inquisition's inspector in Bahia that a Jewish friend (Díego Lopes, a candy manufacturer) told him of the incident.

30. Schama, "A Different Jerusalem," 16.

31. Prinz, *The Secret Jews*, pp. 75–87; full account in autobiography of Uriel da Costa, *A Specimen of Human Life* (New York: Bergman Publishers, 1967).

32. Yosef Kaplan, "The Intellectual Ferment in the Spanish-Portuguese Community of 17th Century Amsterdam," in *The Sephardi Legacy*, vol. 2, ed. Haim Beinart (Jerusalem: Magnes Press, 1992), 295.

33. Five years after his brother's suicide, Abraham da Costa as head of the Mahamad authored the petition that led the States General to grant burgher rights to Dutch Jews, and a few years later, Joseph da Costa, the son of another brother, made use of this privilege in joining with other Jews in New Amsterdam to secure their civil rights.

34. Two other tortures commonly applied to *negativos* (prisoners who did not confess) were the *strappado* and water torment: For the *strappado*, a naked prisoner, with his hands tied behind his back and the rope connected to an overhead pulley, was raised to the ceiling, then let go, but before his feet touched the ground, he was jerked to a halt so that his arms were pulled from their sockets, dislocating both shoulders. This process was usually repeated for an hour. In the water torment, a wet cloth was placed over the open mouth and nostrils of a prostrate prisoner. Because a constant stream of water was poured into it, the prisoner could not help but suck in the cloth, which the torturer then suddenly removed, drawing with it the innards of the victim's throat.

35. *The Conversion & Persecutions of Eve Cohan*, a 1680 pamphlet found in Harvard University's Houghton Library for rare books and manu-

scripts. Donated 1780. The pamphlet states that after the death of his first wife, Abraham Cohen married Rebekah Palache, Samuel's grandniece, and two children from the marriage also married Palaches. The third child was Eva. The pamphlet is written by an ex-Jew about Eva's tribulations after running off and marrying the Christian servant of her elder stepbrother, Jacob Cohen Henriques.

36. Wiznitzer, *Jews in Colonial Brazil*, 171.

37. Odette Vlessing, "The Marranos' Economic Position in the Early 17th Century," *Dutch Jewish History*, vol. 3 (Jerusalem: The Institute for Research on Dutch Jewry, 1993), 173: From the time they entered Amsterdam, Jewish merchants dominated the sugar trade. This continued after the Dutch conquered Recife and considerably increased Brazil's sugar production.

38. http://www.yale.edu/lawweb/avalon/westind.htm; DWIC charter provisions XL and XLII grant the Company the right to build and garrison forts, and maintain warships.

39. Israel, "Sephardic Immigration into the Dutch Republic," 16: The States General protested to the king that "Portuguese citizens should not be treated any differently than other subjects and urged the release of the goods and money involved." Jonathan I. Israel, *Diasporas Within a Disapora, 1540–1740*, Brill Series in Jewish Studies (Boston: E. J. Brill, 2002), 140–41; Swetschinski, *Reluctant Cosmopolitans*, 114.

40. Wiznitzer, *Jews in Colonial Brazil*, 36.

41. Anita Novinsky, "Sephardim in Brazil: The New Christians," in *The Sephardi Heritage*, vol. 2, ed. R. D. Barnett and W. M. Schwab (Jacksonville, NC: Gibraltar Books, 1989), 443; Wiznitzer, *Jews in Colonial Brazil*, 41.

42. Anita Novinsky, "Sephardim in Brazil," 443.

43. Jane S. Gerber, *Jewish Society in Fez* (Leiden: E. J. Brill, 1980), 169–73: From the time of the Crusades, when the cane root was transplanted from Asia to the Mediterranean basin, the making and selling of sugar was dominated by Jews. Page 173: In the 1590s, England's Queen Elizabeth annually imported eighteen thousand pounds of Moroccan sugar for her household.

44. David Raphael, *The Expulsion 1492 Chronicles* (Hollywood, Calif.: Carmi House Press, 1992): More than thirty years later, the terrible scenes still lived in the mind of the old Bishop Coutinho who "saw

many persons dragged by the hair to the font. Sometimes, I saw a father, his head covered in sign of grief and pain, lead his son to the font, protesting and calling God to witness that they wished to die together in the law of Moses. Yet more terrible things that were done with them did I witness, with my own eyes." Afterward, King Manuel informed the Catholic kings of Spain, "There are no more Jews in Portugal."

45. Wiznitzer, *Jews in Colonial Brazil*, 10. São Tomé remains an open chapter. An early account of the forced exodus reported many of the seven hundred children drowned in the initial stormy voyage, and later others were ransomed. However, it is hard to square the accuracy of this account with the continued presence there of so many conversos. In 1632, a foreign visitor wrote that conversos of São Tomé numbered about half the population, and were still looked upon as Jews: "The island is so infested with New Christians that they practice the Jewish rites almost openly" (from Braudel, *The Mediterranean and the Mediterranean World*, vol. 2, p. 814, quoting J. Cuvelier, *"L'ancien Congo d'apres les Archives romaines, 1518–1640"* [Brussels: Royal Academy of Colonial Sciences, 1954], 498). For an excellent article on the island's conversos for the period 1492–1654, see Robert Garfield, "A Forgotten Fragment of the Diaspora: The Jews of Sao Tome Island, 1492–1654," in *The Expulsion of the Jews: 1492 and After*, ed. Raymond B. Waddington and Arthur H. Williamson (New York: Garland Publishing, 1994); see also Gloria Mound, "Judaic Research in the Balearic Islands and Sao Tome," in *Jews in Places You Never Thought Of*, ed. Karen Primack (Jersey City: KTAV, 1998), 60–63. How the descendants of those original kidnapped children were able to maintain their heritage is a mystery. Perhaps, like Moses's mother, their parents secretly emigrated with them. Estimating their average age at eight to ten years old, they would have been in their midforties when Coelho sent his recruiters. Some of their children would certainly have welcomed the chance to carve their niche in the New World.

46. Wiznitzer, *Jews in Colonial Brazil*, 12–14, provides a detailed list of dozens of heretical acts whose continued observance by conversos expose them as Judaizers. These include obvious ones such as circumcision and reciting Jewish prayers and obscure ones such as changing into fresh underwear on Friday evening and blessing children without making the sign of the cross.

47. Ibid., 57–58; Liebman, *The Jews in New Spain*, 213, describes the secret code used in Jewish correspondence.

48. Wiznitzer, *Jews in Colonial Brazil*, 47.

49. The secret organization was exposed by the historian Seymour Liebman, who spent much of his scholarly life translating thousands of Inquisition trials in the New World.

50. Seymour Liebman, *New World Jewry 1493–1825: Requiem for the Forgotten* (New York: KTAV, 1982), 80, 84, 92, 93.

51. Ibid., 94.

52. H. I. Bloom, *The Economic Activities of the Jews in the 17th and 18th Centuries* (Williamsport, Pa.: Baynard Press, 1937), 64–65n146, 86–87n55; Werner Sombart, *The Jews and Modern Capitalism*, trans. M. Epstein, (Glencoe, Ill.: The Free Press, 1951), 184: "Travelers admired the splendor and luxury of the houses of these refugees who dwelt in what were really palaces. If you turn to a collection of engravings of that period, you discover that the most magnificent mansions in Amsterdam were inhabited by Jews."

53. Cyrus Adler, "A Contemporary Memorial Relating to Damages to Spanish Interests in America Done by the Jews of Holland (1634)," American Jewish Historical Society, 45–47. Informer's statement: "Bento de Osorio, alias David Ossorio gives the orders & makes the plans for plundering and destroying, thinking by this means to destroy Christianity. It is with this object in view that they try to maintain so many spies in so many cities of Castile, Portugal, Biscay, Brazil & elsewhere."

54. Wiznitzer, *Jews in Colonial Brazil*, 49.

55. Ibid., 52.

56. Ibid., 51.

57. Ibid., 52.

58. Seymour Liebman, "The Great Conspiracy in Peru," *Academy of American Franciscan History* 28, no. 2 (October 1971), 182: The quote is from a letter from the Council of Portugal to Philip IV.

59. Wiznitzer, *Jews in Colonial Brazil*, 54.

60. Ibid., 54.

61. Ibid., 60.

62. Adler, "A Contemporary Memorial," 45–47.

63. Ibid., 45–47.

1. Cyrus Adler, "A Contemporary Memorial Relating to Damages to Spanish Interests in America Done by the Jews of Holland (1634)," *American Jewish Historical Society*, 48; Jonathan I. Israel, *Diaspora Within a Diaspora, 1540–1740*, Brill Series in Jewish Studies (Boston: E. J. Brill, 2002), 148–50.

2. Mendel Peterson, *The Funnel of Gold* (Boston: Little, Brown, 1975), 248–67.

3. Nigel Cawthorne, *Pirates: An Illustrated History* (Edison, N.J.: Chartwell Books, 2005), 29.

4. H. I. Bloom, *The Economic Activities of the Jews in the 17th and 18th Centuries* (Williamsport, Pa.: Baynard Press, 1937), 92: In 1655, the Spanish consul in Amsterdam with the aid of spies collected the names of Jewish merchants trading with Spain together with the names of their correspondents there. Leading the list was Bento Osorio. King Philip IV submitted the list to the Inquisition.

5. Information about the Spanish treasure fleet comes from Robert F. Marx, *Shipwrecks of the Western Hemisphere: 1492–1825* (New York: World Publishing Company, 1971); Dave Horner, *Shipwrecks, Skin Divers and Sunken Gold: The Treasure Galleons* (New York: Dodd, Mead, 1965): In April 1628, the *Tierra Firme* set sail for the New World. Skirting the north coast of South America, the galleons, after two months at sea, docked at Cartagena, where they unloaded trade goods and collected the treasures brought to port: gold and diamonds from Venezuela, pearls from Margarita Island, and gold and emeralds from the mountains of Colombia. The *Tierra Firme* then proceeded to Portobelo, on Panama's Caribbean coast, where the galleons filled their holds with Potosí silver that had been transported six thousand miles from Lima, first by ship to Panama, and then across the isthmus by mule train. After loading the silver, now converted into seventy-pound bars, the galleons returned to Cartagena to collect the remainder of the riches that had come in. For another month, the port took on the appearance of a tumultuous bazaar with merchants, peddlers, prostitutes, sailors, and adventurers gambling, drinking, playing, and trading for luxury goods and manufactured items from Europe. In August 1628, the annual *fiera* ended, and the *Tierra Firme* sailed north to Havana to meet up with the *flota*.

6. Adler, "A Contemporary Memorial," 45.

7. Arnold Wiznitzer, *Jews in Colonial Brazil* (New York: Columbia University Press, 1960), 59.

8. Ibid., 58. This was disclosed by the defeated Portuguese governor in his diary.

9. Wiznitzer, *The Records of the Earliest Jewish Community in the New World* (New York: American Jewish Historical Society, 1954), 3n2.

10. Bloom, *The Economic Activities of the Jews*, 129–30.

11. Wiznitzer, *Jews in Colonial Brazil*, 64.

12. Ibid., 62; Dudley Pope, *The Buccaneer King: The Biography of Sir Henry Morgan, 1635–1688* (New York: Dodd, Mead, 1978), 53.

13. Wiznitzer, *Jews in Colonial Brazil*, 59.

14. Jacob R. Marcus, *The Colonial American Jew 1492–1776*, vol. 1 (Detroit: Wayne State University Press, 1970), 70.

15. Wiznitzer, *Jews in Colonial Brazil*, 88.

16. Ibid., 74, 129.

17. Ibid., 63.

18. Ibid., 90–91.

19. Marcus, *The Colonial American Jew*, vol. 1, 77.

20 Wiznitzer, *Jews in Colonial Brazil*, 64.

21. C. R. Boxer, *The Dutch in Brazil, 1624–1654* (Oxford, U.K.: Clarendon Press, 1957), 115–16.

22. Bradford Burns, *A History of Brazil* (New York: Columbia University Press, 1970), 48.

23. Primary sources for this chapter are quoted from the works of Arnold Wiznitzer and Rabbi Herbert Bloom.

24. Anita Libman Lebeson, *Pilgrim People* (New York: Harper and Brothers, 1950), 43; Wiznitzer, *The Records of the Earliest Jewish Community in the New World*, 55. The street led to the Jewish Square; there was also a Playa de Judios (Jewish Beach).

25. Lebeson, *Pilgrim People*, 43.

26. Wiznitzer, *Jews in Colonial Brazil*, 83.

27. Ibid., 111.

28. Jacob Rader Marcus, *Early American Jewry*, vol. 1 (Philadelphia: KTAV, 1975).

29. From the top, the figures in this paragraph are quoted from Herbert I. Bloom, "A Study of Brazilian Jewish History 1623–1654, Based

Chiefly upon the Findings of the Late Samuel Oppenheim," Publications of the American Jewish Historical Society 33 (1934), 86; Wiznitzer, *Jews in Colonial Brazil*, 35; ibid., 69–70; Bloom, "A Study," 100.

30. Bloom, *The Economic Activities of the Jews*, 133.

31. Ibid., 133.

32. Wiznitzer, *Jews in Colonial Brazil*, 84.

33. Ibid., 72: From 1636 to 1645 the Company brought 23,163 slaves to Brazil, which they sold for 6,714,423 florins. After 1645, owing to the civil war the Company carried the slaves to Curaçao. The 26,000 figure is the estimate of Faber, *Jews, Slaves and the Slave Trade*, 21.

34. Faber's *Jews, Slaves and the Slave Trade* uses primary source material, and focuses on the British slave trade in the seventeenth and eighteenth centuries, which demonstrates "the minimal nature of Jews' involvement in the subjugation of Africans in the Americas."

35. Wiznitzer, *The Records of the Earliest Jewish Community*, 22; In 1643, Moses apparently changed professions. He is listed as a tax collector, indicating he had retired from the sea, but not necessarily from his plundering ways.

36. Ibid.; pages 1–107 reprint (with index) "The Minute Book of Congregations Zur Israel of Recife and Magen Abraham of Mauricia, Brazil." Invaluable work on these communities and their symbiotic relationship was done by Samuel Oppenheim, Herbert Bloom, and Arnold Wiznitzer. Much primary material is available, including the minute book of Zur Israel for the years 1648–53.

37. Bloom, "A Study," 91.

38. Wiznitzer, *Jews in Colonial Brazil*, 74–75.

39. Adler, "A Contemporary Memorial," 45; Yosef Kaplan, "The Portuguese Jews in Amsterdam: From Forced Conversion to Return to Judaism," *Studia Rosenthal* 15 (1981), 41–42. Quote from trial record: "Esteban de Ares de Fonseca was living in Spain in Pamplona when he met a cousin from Bordeaux . . . where covert Jews 'persuaded him to abandon the faith of the Lord Jesus of Nazareth and to adopt the Mosaic religion which is the true one and in which he will be saved.' . . . He arrived in Amsterdam in 1625 and was greeted by relatives who received him with 'great joy and told him that these were the wonders of God who brings those who live in the blindness of Christi-

anity to Judaism.' They immediately began to take care of him in order to turn him into a Jew because (they said) he was the child of a mother of Jewish origin. When he saw this, he did not want to be circumcised or become a Jew and they placed him in the company of a rabbi to persuade him to observe (this religion) and after he spent six months with him and could not persuade him, they excommunicated him so that no Jew would come in contact with him or speak with him. After 15 or 16 days in that position in which nobody spoke to him or helped him, he went (to them) and they agreed to circumcise him. After circumcising him they named him David." Kaplan writes: "It is doubtful we can rely on this as he sought to clear himself and present his conversion in Amsterdam as an act that was forced upon him against his will."

40. Richard Dunn, *Sugar and Slaves* (Chapel Hill: University of North Carolina Press, 1972), 61; Wiznitzer, *Jews in Colonial Brazil*, 88; Bloom, "A Study," 90.

41. Contraband trade via Amsterdam was so popular that in 1662 Spanish trading galleons, despite a two-year absence from the New World, went home with their holds half full.

42. Dutch territory in northeast Brazil included the provinces of Pernambuco, Itamaraca, Paraíba, and Rio Grande do Norte.

43. Wiznitzer, *Jews in Colonial Brazil*, 88–89 (transcript of letter in Wiznitzer's appendix).

44. Bloom, *The Economic Activities of the Jews*, 138, 138n.

45. Wiznitzer, *Jews in Colonial Brazil*, 93.

46. Ibid., 116–17.

47. Ibid., 95–96.

48. Bloom, "A Study," 94.

49. Wiznitzer, *Jews in Colonial Brazil*, 98.

50. I. S. Emmanuel, "New Light on Early American Jewry," *American Jewish Archives* 8 (1955), 11.

51. Ibid., 9–13: Abraham da Costa was the head of the Parnassim who signed the petition that resulted in the Patenta Onrossa. He was the younger brother of Uriel, who had killed himself after renouncing his heretic beliefs, and elder brother to Joseph, who would later refer to the Patenta Onrossa in the struggle to achieve civil rights in New Amsterdam.

52. Ibid., 43–44.

53. Arnold Wiznitzer, "Jewish Soldiers in Dutch Brazil (1630–1654)," *Publications of the American Jewish Historical Society* 46 (September 1956), 46.

54. Ibid., 48.

55. Bloom, "A Study," 126.

56. Ibid.

57. Ibid., 137.

58. Ibid., 130–31.

59. Wiznitzer, *Jews in Colonial Brazil*, 108–9, 210: text of King John's reply.

60. Roth, *A History of the Marranos*, 306: Portugal's reconquest of Brazil was due in large part to him. Da Silva "provided ships, supplies, and munitions to the army." After he was accused of judaizing, his trial dragged on for five years. Da Silva was finally freed after he appeared as a pentitent, and in 1662, the king sent him to England with Catherine of Braganza to administer her dowry. Though he remained in London, he never joined the now legal Jewish community.

61. Bloom, "A Study . . ." 136–37.

62. Simon Wolf, *The American Jew as Patriot, Soldier and Citizen* (Boston: Gregg Press, 1972), 449.

63. Wiznitzer, *The Records of the Earliest Jewish Community*, 55n44.

64. Liebman, "The Great Conspiracy in Peru," 176–90; Liebman, *The Jews in New Spain*, 225–35.

65. They could settle in the six small Dutch islands of Aruba, Bonaire, Curaçao, Saba, St. Eustacius, and St. Martin, and although France and England were still off-limits, they were welcome in the French Caribbean islands Guadaloupe and Martinque, and the English colonies Barbados and Nevis.

Chapter Seven: Exodus to Heretic Island

1. Arnold Wiznitzer, "The Exodus from Brazil and Arrival in New Amsterdam of the Jewish Pilgrim Fathers in 1654," Publications of the American Jewish Historical Society 44 (Philadelphia, September 1954), 80–97.

2. Captain Thomas Southey, *Chronological History of the West Indies* (London: Frank Cass & Co., 1968; reprint of 1827 edition): In 1568, the Crown accused the current heir, Don Luis Colón, of "blocking an investigation into charges the Admiral had used his private jurisdiction

on Jamaica to cover illegal trade." The charge was he imported more goods than the island needed for the sole purpose of exporting them to other colonies. This was in violation of the mercantile system that mandated first profits to the homeland, i.e., all goods had to come and go via Seville. Richard Bloome, *A Description of the Island of Jamaica with the other Isles and Territories in America in which English are Related* (London, 1672), 44: When the English conquered Jamaica, "the number of inhabitants did not exceed 3,000 of which half were slaves. And the reason why it was so thinly peopled was . . . chiefly because this isle was held in proprietorship by the heirs of Columbus who received the revenues and placed governors as absolute Lord of it. And at first it was planted by a kind of Portugals, the society of whom the Spaniard abhors."

3. Francis J. Osborne, *History of the Catholic Church in Jamaica* (Chicago: Loyola University Press, 1988), 84: The synod decreed the Jamaican abbot should come under the jurisdiction of the archbishop of Santo Domingo on February 15, 1624.

4. Frank Cundall and Joseph Pietersz, *Jamaica Under the Spaniards*, abstracted from the Archives of Seville (Kingston: Institute of Jamaica, 1919), 17: Miguel Delgado, one of the Portugals who founded La Vega (Spanish Town) in 1534, was lieutenant governor in 1583; Morales, *Spanish Jamaica*, 86: Diego de Mercado ruled from 1583 to 1597. Prominent Jamaicans who bore those names were all of Jewish ancestry. See Jacob Andrade, *A Record of the Jews of Jamaica* (Kingston: Jamaica Times, 1941).

5. Cundall and Pietersz, *Jamaica Under the Spaniards*, 21, 26.

6. Ibid., 30.

7. Ibid., 30–31.

8. Ibid., 17–34. Melgarejo's thirst for power exceeded his authority. Though loyal to the Crown, he had no qualms about feathering his own nest. After Philip II's death in 1604, six merchants petitioned Philip III, accusing the governor of corruption, and "prayed he might be recalled." They alleged he traded with foreign ships and pirates, "while taking for himself and his lieutenants all negroes and merchandise which entered the island." However, the king was pleased with Melgarejo's performance and appointed him to another term. When Melgarejo left office, Philip III, "on the petition of the people of Jamaica," pardoned the illicit traders.

9. Ibid., 24.

10. Ibid., 47, 48: Jamaica's governor tried, without success "to take from Francisco de Leyba Ysazi [sic] a tannery he has on the river which cause a lot of sickness being so near the town."

11. Osborne, *History of the Catholic Church in Jamaica*, Appendix C, 445–76, lists the synod decrees. Don Nuño's abbot, Mateo de Moreno, attended the synod, but the novice prelate was outmaneuvered by forces aligned against the Columbus family.

12. Cundall and Pietersz, *Jamaica Under the Spaniards*, 44–45; S.A.G. Taylor, *The Western Design: An Account of Cromwell's Expedition to the Caribbean* (Kingston: Institute of Jamaica and Jamaican Historical Society, 1969), 74.

13. Robert F. Marx, *Treasure Fleets of the Spanish Main* (Cleveland: World Publishing Co., 1968), 4–5. Charles impatiently waited for the galleons: "The importance of the treasure from the New World to Spain can be readily understood from the following dispatch sent by the Venetian ambassador in Spain to the doge in September 1567: . . . 'there was great anxiety all over Spain over the delay of the arrival of the treasure fleet from the Indies and, when the Genoese bankers informed the King that unless the fleet reached port shortly, that they would be unable to negotiate any further loans for him, Philip II fell into such a state of shock that he had to be confined to bed by his physicians . . . I am happy to inform you that news has just arrived from Seville that the fleet has made port safely and there is now great rejoicing not only here in the Royal Court, but all over the land as well.' "

14. Irwin R. Blacker, ed., "The English Voyages of Sir Anthony Shirley," cited in Richard Hakluyt, *Principal Navigations, Voyages, Traffics and Discoveries of the English Nation, 1598–1600*, vol. 3, 601 (New York: Viking Press, 1965), 294.

15. Shannon Miller, *Invested with Meaning: The Raleigh Circle in the New World* (Philadelphia: University of Pennsylvania Press, 1998), 158.

16. Robert Lacey, *Sir Walter Raleigh* (New York: Athenaeum Press, 1974), 344–45: James handed Gondomar "a precise inventory of Raleigh's ships, armaments, ports of call and estimated dates of arrival."

17. Antonia Fraser, *King James VI of Scotland, I of England*, (New York: Random House, 1975), 375: "Gondomar demanded . . . an immediate audience with James. Assuming a lofty and insolent tone, he declared

the King could not judge Raleigh as he had commissioned him and was surrounded by his friends. Rather Raleigh and his captains were pirates and must be sent in chains to Madrid to be hanged in the main square. James, angered by his friend's audacity, threw his hat on the floor, clutched his hair, and shouted that might be justice in Spain but not in England. Gondomar sneered that there was indeed a difference between England and Spain in regards to piracy, and abruptly left the room. Buckingham, who had been present, sided with Gondomar." Philip Gibbs, *The Reckless Duke: The Romantic Story of the First Duke of Buckingham and the Stuart Court* (New York: Harper and Brothers, 1931), 76: "[Gondomar's] most insolent demands had a tone of imperial dignity. His manner was that of a man who moved the world. His confidence in himself and in his country gave strength to his diplomacy and majesty to his deportment." Coffin, *The Dukes of Buckingham*, 71–72: After Raleigh's beheading, Gondomar and the king made friends. Next to Buckingham, Gondomar was "the most frequent visitor to the King's bed-chamber"; 73: "Although Gondomar had captivated James, beyond Whitehall he was despised. Once, while passing a group of Englishmen in the litter that Buckingham had made the vogue, Gondomar was cursed by one who shouted, 'There goeth the Devil in a dung cart!' " Fraser concludes (p. 375): He was "perhaps the most influential foreign ambassador ever to reside in England . . . With a folly bordering on madness James admitted to intimacy the most dangerous man with whom he ever had to deal."

18. Most references to Columbus's gold mine in Jamaica are found in Lord Clarendon's papers kept at Oxford University's Bodleian Library: Clarendon State Papers, vol. 1, no. 237, 14. Clarendon's transcription of Hermyn's "secret discoveries" includes a coded invasion plan of Jamaica, cryptic references to the location of the secret gold mine, and the promise by local "Portingals" to reveal this to their liberator.

19. Clarendon State Papers, vol. 1, no. 237, 14.

20. Roth, *A History of the Marranos*, 246. Although she said she would sooner enter a convent than marry a heretic, it is interesting to note "her confessor, Fra. Vincente de Rocamora, a Dominican friar famous for his 'piety and eloquence,' disappeared from Spain in 1643 and shows up in Amsterdam, under the name of Isaac, studying medicine and playing a prominent part in the general life of the Jewish community."

21. J. H. Elliott, *The Count-Duke of Olivares, The Statesman in an Age of Decline* (New Haven: Yale University Press, 1986), 232: "The most perfidious of all heretics condemned by the church—namely the Jews"; see page 10 for Olivares's Jewish ancestry.

22. Jonathan I. Israel, *Diasporas Within a Diaspora, Crypto Jews and the World's Maritime Empires (1540–1740)*, Brill Series in Jewish Studies, ed. David S. Katz (Boston, 2002), 148: Olivares' economic plan to recruit Portuguese conversos "had much to do with the absence of specific measures against Portuguese New Christians in the Indies in 1624." Jonathan I. Israel, *Empires and Entrepots: The Dutch, the Spanish Monarchy and the Jews, 1585–1713* (London: Hambledon Press, 1990): Accepting Olivares's invitation, more than four thousand Portuguese conversos settled in Seville and Madrid. Among them was Moses Cohen Henriques, who figures later in the Columbus gold mine venture. By 1640, the Portuguese expatriates in Seville constituted nearly a quarter of the population. "They had grown rich on legal and illegal trade, lived bejeweled lives, dressed in fancy clothes . . . Their ostentatious life style aroused the resentment of the Spanish merchants who viewed the Portuguese as *nouveau riche* foreigners. The Portuguese conversos occupied positions that made them easy to hate.

"Olivares' opponents said he had invited the wolves into the hen house . . . His financial advisor was a prominent ex-Jew from Amsterdam, and his council was dubbed his *sinogoga* . . . Right before his downfall, Olivares' own converso heritage was exposed. The king . . . threatened that should he return to court, 'the public will not be appeased unless you are turned over to the Inquisition.' With this change in climate, the grudging tolerance the conversos were accorded came to an end. Most of the community Olivares fathered soon departed for freer lands. For five years, Olivares kept the Inquisition at bay. In the free trade atmosphere of new business and fresh capital, Spain prospered. Innovative Portuguese letters of exchange and credit made capital portable and goods transportable to ports everywhere. But in the end, the Inquisition triumphed. An *auto da fe* on July 4, 1632 signaled the end to Olivares' scheme. Olivares looked on as six Portuguese confessed to *judaizing* . . . The Grand Inquisitor, from atop a platform at one end of the square, condemned the six (four men and two women) to the *quemadero* (the burning place) . . . later that month the nephews of Olivares' financial advisor disappeared into the secret cells of the Inquisition. Months later they . . . confessed under torture to *judaizing*. The message was clear: Spain was not ready to bring back her Jews."

23. Using Jamaica as his base, he intended to recruit additional settlers from the French islands and capture the rest of Spain's New World empire. Sweden's account of the treaty is found in Aron Rydfors, *De diplomatiska forbindelserna mellan Sverige och England 1624–1630* (Uppsala: 1890), 100–113, trans. on request by Hans Linton, Ministry of Foreign Affairs, Stockholm.

24. Cundall and Pietersz, *Jamaica Under the Spaniards*, 39–40.

25. V. T. Harlow, "The Voyages of Captain William Jackson 1642–1645," *Camden Miscellany* 13 (1923), 19.

26. Ibid., 20–21.

27. Cundall and Pietersz, *Jamaica Under the Spaniards*, 40: In October 1643, Governor Francisco Ladron de Zegama "died a prisoner without guards in his own house."

28. John Taylor, *Taylor's History of his Life and Travels in America and other parts, with An Account with the most remarkable Transactions which Annuallie happened in his daies*, vol. 2 (1688). See John Robertson, "An Untimely Victory: Reinventing the English Conquest of Jamaica in the 17th Century," *English Historical Review* 117 (2002), 14: "In St. Mary, the Spanish settlers built a nunnery to mark their victory in a civil war with their Portuguese fellow colonists."

29. Bryan Edwards, *History of the British Colonies in the West Indies*, vol. 2 (London: John Stockdale Pickadilly, 1801), 193. "The Jealousy occasioned by the revolution which had placed the Duke of Braganza on the throne of Portugal, caused the expulsion of almost all the colonists of that nation. When the British forces entered Spanist Town, they found 2000 houses but few inhabitants. The deserted house in the capital proved the want of tenants. This was due to the expulsion of Portuguese settlers."

30. Carol S. Holzberg, *Minorities and Power in a Black Society: The Jewish Community of Jamaica* (Lanham, Md.: North-South Publishing, 1987), 16n: "15 or 20 years before British invasion . . . 13 Portuguese families were expelled."

31. I first came across Israel's name in Captain Fonseca's 1634 testimony

before the Inquisition in Madrid. The spy listed Israel as "adjutant" (administrative officer) of the Recife-bound supply ships that allegedly were to stop off in Portugal, storm the Inquisition prison, and free the prisoners. Israel's name also appears in the testimony of Abraham Bueno Henriques, a young Dutch Jew taken prisoner in the fighting in Brazil and sent to Lisbon for trial. W. Samuel, "Sir William Davidson, Royalist (1616–1689) and the Jews," *Transactions of the Jewish Historical Society of England* 14 (July 1936), 49–50: In his confession to the Inquisitors, he noted that Abraham Israel was married to his niece. Since Israel's full name "de Pisa" identifies him with Italy, and since the Bueno Henriques family also had links with that country, Samuel suggests that despite the commonality of the name Abraham Israel (one likely assumed by conversos upon their reversion to Judaism), the young prisoner was referring to his near kinsman Abraham Israel de Pisa. This relationship Samuel reinforces in the testimony of Sir William Davidson, who in urging the endenization [naturalization, or some rights of citizenship] of Daniel Bueno Henriques, a Barbados Jew, notes that Daniel Bueno Henriques is "a neir kinsman of the Portingall Merchand who goes for Jamaica for the discovery of the Myne ye know of." However, the "neir kinsman" might just as likely have been Abraham Cohen, who was also an Henriques. My deduction is that all three were related. As Daniel M. Swetschinski has documented in his article "Kinship and Commerce: The Foundations of Portuguese Jewish Life in 17th Century Holland," *Studia Rosenthaliana* 15, no. 1 (1981), 65, the partners in most business dealings were "almost inevitably related."

32. Morris U. Schappes, ed., *A Documentary History of the Jews in the United States, 1654–1875* (New York: Citadel Press, 1950), 1–2.

33. Arnold Wiznitzer, "The Exodus from Brazil," 319–20: That some were left behind in Jamaica is documented in a "Letter of Protest of the States-General of the Netherlands to the King of Spain," dated November 14, 1654.

34. Ibid., 320.

35. Schappes, *Documentary History of the Jews,* 5.

36. When the ship bearing the Company's letter arrived in New Amsterdam granting the Jewish "boat people" admission, among its

passengers were the sons of Cohen and Israel, Jacob and Isaac. Each was around thirty years old. Looking beyond the borders of New Amsterdam, the two friends applied for a license to trade for furs with the Indians, and Israel journeyed down to South River to barter for skins with the Delaware Indians. He returned with pelts, but their license was rejected, and only approved after Calvinists added their signatures. Hints of their characters are apparent in the court records: Cohen was charged with smuggling eleven carts of tobacco, and Israel with "punching [another Jew] in the face." After securing rights for their people, the two wound up joining their fathers in Jamaica in the search for Columbus's lost gold mine.

Chapter Eight: Cromwell's Secret Agents

1. James Williamson, *A Short History of British Expansion: The Old Colonial Empire* (London: Macmillan, 1965), 249: The 1,500 ships were "double that of the English mercantile marine."

2. Albert M. Hyamson, *The Sephardim of England: A History of the Spanish and Portuguese Jewish Community, 1492–1951* (London: Methuen, 1951), 11: Daniel Cohen Henriques, aka Duarte Henriques Alvares from the Canaries, married a Jewess, Leila Henriques, in Amsterdam, and after their marriage they settled in England. "This was the first appearance in England of the well-known Sephardim family of Henriques."

3. Antonia Fraser, *Cromwell: The Lord Protector* (New York: Alfred A Knopf, 1974), 521.

4. Ibid. Fraser wrote that the preparations were so secret that "one Scottish soldier involved wrote, 'if he suspected his shirt knew of the plans, he would be compelled to burn it.' "

5. Ibid., 522.

6. Irene A. Wright, "The English Conquest of Jamaica," *The Camden Miscellany* 13, (1924), 11, quotes the Spanish captain Julian de Castilla's report on the invasion: "Among the prisoners taken was an English youth who begged for his life in Spanish. He stated he was General Robert's interpreter . . . He said his Protector . . . had received into London the greater part of the Hebrews of Flanders and sold them one of the best quarters in the city, with a church for synagogue. He understood that these Jews had urged the dispatch of this fleet and advanced a great

loan for its fitting out. It is not difficult to believe this, since the example of Brazil exhibits similar treasons and iniquities committed by this blind people out of the aversion they have for us."

7. Most information on Carvajal is from Lucien Wolf, *Transactions of the Jewish Historical Society of England* 2 (1894), 14–46; and Lucien Wolf, "Crypto Jews Under the Commonwealth," *Transactions of the Jewish Historical Society of England* 2 (1893–94), 55–88.

8. Fraser, *Cromwell*, 524.

9. S. A. G. Taylor, *The Western Design: An Account of Cromwell's Expedition to the Caribbean* (Kingston: Institute of Jamaica and Jamaican Historical Society, 1969), 10.

10. Ibid., 16, 19.

11. Taylor, *The Western Design*, 34, 36.

12. Ibid., 36: Taylor quotes Henry Whistler, "Journal of the West Indian Expedition (1654–1655)," reprinted in *Journal of the Institute of Jamaica* 2 (Kingston, 1899).

13. Wright, "The Spanish Naratives of Santo Domingo, The Notarial Account," *The Camden Miscellany* 13 (1924), 59: There is also the admission of a fourth prisoner: "he said their intention was to go to Jamaica."

14. H. P. Jacobs, "Jamaica Historical Review," *Jamaica Historical Society* 1, no. 1 (June 1945), 109–10.

15. Wright, " 'The English Conquest of Jamaica' by Julian Castilla (1656)," *The Camden Miscellany* 13 (1924), 522.

16. John Elijah Blunt, *The Jews of England* (London: Saunders and Benning, 1830), 70–71: "The Rabbi's extreme supporters embarrassed Cromwell when it was reported in the daily press that they had looked up his birth records to see if the *Lord Protector* was of the line of David and might himself be the Messiah!" When word of their investigation reached London, "Cromwell was suspected of being privy to their designs, and was exposed to raillery. At a meeting of the council the Jews were summoned . . . warmly upbraided and ordered to depart the country."

17. Evidence that Carvajal and Acosta were Jews comes from their Jewish descendants resident in the Caribbean.

18. Taylor, *The Western Design*, 61.

19. C. A. Firth, ed., *A Narrative by General Venables of His Expedition to the Island of Jamaica: with an Appendix of Papers Relating to the Expedition*, Royal

Historical Society (London, 1900). Venables's report to Cromwell. Richard Hill, Jamaica's foremost nineteenth-century historian, writes in *Lights and Shadows of Jamaican History: Eight Chapters in the History of Jamaica (1508–1680) illustrating the settlement of the Jews on the island* (1868), 35: "The family influence of Diego Columbus had rendered it very considerably Portuguese. Several Jewish families already here are progenitors of families still living and commenced the nucleus of Jewish influence so remarkable and so paramount in Jamaica at this day."

20. Taylor, *The Western Design*, 63: When Duarte de Acosta, who was held by the English as a hostage, sent his slave with a message to his brother Gaspar, the slave was garroted as a spy. Acosta, "incensed" at the murder of his slave, went over to the English. Venables noted: "A good deal of information was obtained from Acosta."

21. Wolf, "Crypto Jews Under the Commonwealth," 56: De Caceres's origins: born 1615 or 1623 in Amsterdam, died 1704 in England. He was the son of Moses de Casseres, one of the twelve founders of Neveh Shalom, and lived in Barbados from 1647 to 1654 and in Hamburg before he came to London. Maurice Woolf, "Foreign Trade of London Jews in the Sephardic Century," *Transactions of the Jewish Historical Society of England* 24 (1970–73), 47: his family was from Caceres, in Spain, near the Portuguese border, where many Jews lived before the expulsion, on the same latitude as Toledo and Lisbon.

22. Lucien Wolf, "American Elements in the Resettlement," *Transactions of the Jewish Historical Society of England* 3 (1896–98), 97–98, Appendix VII.

23. Thomas Carlyle, ed., *Oliver Cromwell's Letters and Speeches*, A Library of Universal Literature (New York: P. F. Collier and Son, 1800), Part 2, 428.

24. W. S. Samuel, "A List of Jews Endenization and Naturalization 1609–1799," *Transactions of the Jewish Historical Society of England* 2 (1968–69), 113.

25. Lucien Wolf, "Cromwell's Jewish Intelligencers," *Essays in Jewish History* (1934), 103: "sends first authentic warning of treaty . . . the text of which he conveys 'is kept very close' but he obtained a copy for 20 [pounds]." Source—Birch: Thurloe Papers, v. 645. March 56, Blake sailed from England to blockade Cádiz. When the galleons arrived, he captured six of the eight ships and two million pieces of eight, and the following year burned or sank the Spanish fleet in Tenerife in the Ca-

nary Islands. This ended all hope of sending an expedition to the West Indies in the fall to retake Jamaica.

26. Wolf, "Cromwell's Jewish Intelligencers," 112.

27. Wolf, "Crypto Jews Under the Commonwealth," 56.

28. *Interesting Tracts Relating to the Island of Jamaica which throw great light on the history of that island from its conquest down through the year 1702* (St. Jago de la Vega, 1702), 1–2: "A Proclamation of the Protector, *Relating To Jamaica:* we therefore, . . . [decree] that every planter or adventurer to that island shall be . . . free from paying any excise or custom for any . . . goods or necessaries which he or they shall transport to the island of Jamaica . . . for a space of ten years."

29. Anita Libman Lebeson, *Pilgrim People* (New York: Harper and Brothers, 1950), 48–49; Arnold Wiznitzer, *Jews in Colonial Brazil* (New York: Columbia University Press, 1960), 174–75.

30. Fraser, *Cromwell,* 566.

31. Ibid., 561; Bernard Martin, *A History of Judaism,* vol. 2 (New York: Basic Books, 1974), 163.

32. Lucien Wolf, *Menasseh Ben Israel's Mission to Oliver Cromwell* (London: Macmillan, 1901), 78–79: Text of Menasseh's address to Cromwell. Along with fulfilling the Messianic requisite, Menasseh noted: "Profit is the most powerful motive all the world prefers before all things," and stressed the wealth their return would create. There is no record of what they discussed when they met, but it is easy to imagine a lively volley of opinions on Scripture, prophecy, and trade. Menasseh, in addressing him, assumed "a most submissive and obsequious posture imaginable," but was quick to remind the Protector of the fate of leaders who treated Jews harshly: "No monarch has ever brought suffering to Jews without eventually being heavily punished by God."

33. D'Blossiers Tovey, *Anglia Judaica: A History of the Jews in England* (1738); retold by Elizabeth Pearl (London: Weidenfeld and Nicolson, 1990), 143–44.

34. Wolf, "Crypto Jews Under the Commonwealth," 64. London Jews petition Cromwell: "to shelter himself from those tyrannical proceedings and enjoy those benefits and kindness which this commonwealth afforded to afflicted strangers as yr Highness hath bin pleased to show yourself on behalf of the Jews."

35. Ibid., 65.

36. Ibid., 66.

37. Gilbert Burnet, Osmund Airy, ed., *A History of My Own Time*, vol. 1 (London: Company of Booksellers, 1725), 76.

38. Carlyle, ed., *Oliver Cromwell's Letters*, vol. 22, 427–30.

39. Thomas Birch, ed., *A Collection of State Papers of John Thurloe, Esq. Secretary, First to the Council of State to the Two Protectors Oliver and Richard Cromwell* (London, 1742), vol. 4, 543–44: Sabada's journal entry dated February 1, 1656.

40. *State Papers of Thurloe* #4, 602.

41. Wolf, "Crypto-Jews Under the Commonwealth," 56.

42. Wolf, "American Elements in the Resettlement," 96–97, Appendix VII, Invasion of Chile letter: Simon de Caceres's scheme for the conquest of Chile. Carlyle, *Cromwell's Letters and Speeches*, vol. 3, 131; Wolf, "Cromwell's Jewish Intelligencers," 108–9.

43. Cecil Roth, *History of the Jews in England* (London: Clarendon Press, 1964), 56.

44. Woolf, "Foreign Trade of London Jews," 47. Samuel Tolkowsky, *They Took to the Sea* (London: Thomas Yoseloff, 1964), 245: In April 1661, the king of Denmark endorsed the Caceres brothers' request to Charles II to live and trade in Barbados and Suriname.

45. Jonathan I. Israel, *Diasporas Within a Diaspora, 1540–1740*, Brill Series in Jewish Studies (Boston: E. J. Brill, 2002), 298–99, quoting Simon De Vries, *Historie van Barbaryen*: From 1626, when the port city of Salé, Morocco, just north of Rabat, formed "a self-governing pirate republic," the leaders and financial backers of the corsairs were "a small resident community of Portuguese Jews from Amsterdam [who] divided between them the captured booty taken from Christians." The States General, in a dispatch to Morocco's sultan, identified two familiar names, Moses Cohen Henriques and Aaron Querido, as "prominent" traders who supplied arms and munitions to Salé. Other familiar figures were the sons of the Palache brothers, members of the Bueno Mesquita family, and Moses's cousin, Benjamin Cohen Henriques, described in 1634 as Salé's "pre-eminent resident Dutch Jewish merchant." Peter Lamborn Wilson, *Pirate Utopias: Moorish Corsairs and European Renegadoes* (New York: Autonomedia, 2003), 73.

46. Richard Hill, *Lights and Shadows of Jamaica History* (Kingston, Jamaica: Ford & Gall, 1859), 37: "The Jewish families laid the foundation of the

trade and traffic of Jamaica as soon as mercantile business became organized with the Freebooters. With the Jewish settlers, properly opens the connexion of the colony with the Buccaneers."

Chapter Nine: The Golden Dream of Charles II

1. Benjamin Keen, ed. and trans., *The Life of Admiral Christopher Columbus by His Son Ferdinand* (New Brunswick, N.J.: Rutgers University Press, 1992), li: As Columbus wrote in his Book of Prophecies: "O, most excellent gold! Who has gold gets what he wants, imposes his will on the world, and helps souls to paradise."

2. Isaac S. and Suzanne A. Emmanuel, *History of the Jews of the Netherlands Antilles* (Cincinnati: American Jewish Archives, 1970), 40–43.

3. Samuel Oppenheim, "An Early Jewish Colony in Western Guiana and Its Relation to the Jews of Suriname, Cayenne and Tobago," *Publications of the American Jewish Historical Society* 16 (1907), 108–9.

4. Emmanuel, *History of the Jews of the Netherlands Antilles*, 44: In 1659, David Cohen Nassi, who contracted with the Company to found a Jewish colony in Cayenne, bought "52 negro slaves from Abraham Cohen do Brazil who had paid the Company 2995.50 florins cash for them and he would reimburse Cohen within three years." Zvi Loker, *Jews in the Caribbean: Evidence on the History of the Jews in the Caribbean Zone in Colonial Times* (Jerusalem: Misgav Yerushalayim, Institute for Research on the Sephardi and Oriental Jewish Heritage, 1991), 59–60: In August 1659, Abraham Cohen and A. Luis, merchants in Amsterdam, ship "goods and passengers" to Cayenne with the agreement of the West India Company; in November 1659, Abraham Cohen and A. Luis, acting under Power of Attorney of the New Cayenne Company, send the ship *Abrahmas Offerhande* "laden with wares" to Cayenne. March, 3 1660: "Abraham Cohen chartered *the Hamburch* to ship cargo and several Jews to Curacao and Cayene"; May 1660: "A. Cohen to ship to A. Luis ⅙ part of his property from the island 'Ayami' on the river in the wasteland of the Wild Coast."

5. Loker, *Jews in the Caribbean*, 107.

6. Emmanuel, *History of the Jews of the Netherlands Antilles*, 43.

7. Brian Masters, *The Mistresses of Charles II* (London: Blond and Briggs, 1979), 45.

8. Jean Plaidy, *The Wandering Prince* (New York: Fawcett, 1971), 164–65.

9. Quoted in Antonia Fraser, *Royal Charles* (New York: Alfred A. Knopf, 1979), 139, 173.

10. See http://www.contemplator.com/england/phoenix.html.

11. Fraser, *Royal Charles*, 139.

12. Masters, *The Mistresses of Charles II*, 45.

13. Ibid., 47.

14. A. G. Course, *A Seventeenth-Century Mariner* (London: Frederick Muller Ltd., 1965), 24–26.

15. Cecil Roth, *History of the Jews in England* (London: Clarendon Press, 1964), 167.

16. Lucien Wolf, "The Jewry of the Restoration," *Transactions of the Jewish Historical Society of England* 5 (1896–98), 13.

17. Lucien Wolf, "Status of the Jews in England After the Resettlement," *Transactions of the Jewish Historical Society of England* 4 (1899–1901), 181–82.

18. Ibid., 182.

19. Edgar R. Samuel, "David Gabay's 1660 Letter from London," *Transactions of the Jewish Historical Society of England* 25 (1973–75), 38–42.

20. Antonia Fraser, *Royal Charles*, 195: Fraser quotes an entry in *Calendar of State Papers, Domestic Series, Charles II*, no. 140, November 30, 1660.

21. Roth, *History of the Jews in England*, 160–61.

22. Wolf, "The Jewry of the Restoration," 15: María Fernandez de Carvajal, née Rodrigues, was maternal aunt of Antonio Rodrigues Lindo (brother of Lorenzo), who was arrested in Lisbon for Judaizing when he was twenty-three in 1660. Of María, a tough gal—"when the community was threatened in 1660, she called a meeting of her co-religionists at her house in Leadenhall St, that petitioned Charles II for 'his Majesty's protection to continue and reside in his dominions.' "

23. Wolf, "The Jewry of the Restoration," 15–16: While Charles hadn't yet formally sanctioned their presence, he had reason to. While most Jews sided with the Protector, others in Amsterdam and London, led by the da Costa family, were sympathetic to his cause. Reportedly, they advanced Charles one million guiders (about $600,000). Thus, while Cromwell had his Jewish intelligencers, other Jews supported the exiled king.

24. *Calendar of State Papers, Colonial Series, America and West Indies, 1661–1668* (National Archives, Kew, Surrey, England), 7/24/1661 #139: In April

1661, Charles approved their petition to live and trade in Barbados and Suriname, endorsed by the king of Denmark.

25. Within two years after his restoration, the number of London Jews holding bank accounts increased from thirty-five to ninety-two.

26. Albert M. Hyamson, *The Sephardim of England: A History of the Spanish and Portuguese Jewish Community, 1492–1951* (London: Methuen, 1951), 19.

27. Yosef Kaplan, *Jews and Conversos: Studies in Society and the Inquisition* (Jerusalem: Magnes Press, 1981), 214, 221.

28. *Calender of State Papers, Colonial America and West Indies, 1661–1668*, no. 216, 69.

29. Charles II's contract with Abraham Israel de Piso and Abraham Cohen, Egerton MSS., folios 152b–158b, British Museum.

30. Domestic Entry Book, Charles II, vol. 14, 57, National Archives, Kew, Surrey, England.

31. Samuel, "Sir William Davidson, Royalist," 46.

32. Nigel Cawthorne, *Sex Lives of the Kings and Queens of England* (Chicago: Trafalgar Square, 1997), 72.

33. Samuel, "Sir William Davidson, Royalist," 46.

34. Herbert Friedenwald, "Material for the History of the Jews in the British West Indies," *Publications of the American Jewish Historical Society* 5 (1897), 69, transcribes the letter as "the gold finding Jew left . . . here *ore* and directions to find the gold." Samuel transcribes the same passage as "*care* and directions . . ."

35. Nuala Zahedieh, "The Capture of the Blue Dove, 1664: Policy, Profits and Protection in Early English Jamaica," in R. McDonald, ed., *West Indies Accounts: Essays on the History of the British Caribbean and the Atlantic Economy* (Kingston: University of the West Indies Press, 1996), 29–47.

Chapter Ten: Buccaneer Island

1. S. A. G. Taylor, *The Western Design: An Account of Cromwell's Expedition to the Caribbean* (Kingston: Institute of Jamaica and Jamaican Historical Society, 1969), 111–12.

2. C. H. Haring, *The Buccaneers in the West Indies in the XVII Century* (Hamden, Conn.: Archon Books, 1966; reprint of 1910 edition), 92; Dudley Pope, *The Buccaneer King: The Biography of the Notorious Sir Henry Morgan, 1635–1688* (New York: Dodd, Mead, 1978), 74.

3. Taylor, *The Western Design*, 113.

4. Ibid., 118.

5. Michael Pawson and David Buisseret, *Port Royal, Jamaica* (Oxford, U.K.: Clarendon Press, 1975), 62.

6. S. A. G. Taylor, ed., "Edward D'Oyley's Journal," part 2, transcribed by F. J. Osbourne, *Jamaican Historical Review*, vol. XI, 1978, 69: In September 1657, D'Oyley wrote the Committee of Officers and Merchants: "I am sending to Hispaniola for about 250 buccaneers, vizt. French and English that kill cattle who would come to us if they might have that liberty which I intend to give them."

7. Taylor, *The Western Design*, 133.

8. Ibid., 141–42: Privateers were empowered to attack Spanish ships. By attacking Spanish settlements rather than Spanish ships, they did not have to fork over some of the loot to the licensing authorities.

9. Pawson and Buisseret, *Port Royal, Jamaica*, 80.

10. Ibid., 131.

11. Pope, *The Buccaneer King*, 77.

12. Taylor, *The Western Design*, 205; Pope, *The Buccaneer King*, 80.

13. Pawson and Buisseret, *Port Royal, Jamaica*, 220.

14. Haring, *The Buccaneers in the West Indies*, 109.

15. Ibid., 110.

16. Pawson and Buisseret, *Port Royal, Jamaica*, 97.

17. Ibid., 99.

18. Ibid., 83.

19. *Calendar of State Papers, Colonial Series, America & West Indies, 1901*, 593: January 28, 1692, the president of the Council of Jamaica to the Lords of Trade and Plantations: "The Jews eat us and our children out of all trade, the reasons for naturalizing them not having been observed; for there has been no regard had to their settling and planting as the law directed . . . they have made Port Royal their Goshen and will do nothing but trade . . . This is a great and growing evil."

20. Pope, *The Buccaneer King*, 86.

21. Salvador de Madariaga, *The Rise of the Spanish American Empire* (New York: Free Press, 1965), 162.

22. Pawson and Buisseret, *Port Royal, Jamaica*, 119.

23. H. R. Allen, *Buccaneer: Admiral Sir Henry Morgan* (London: Arthur Barker Ltd., 1976), 23.

24. Quoted in Clinton Black, *Port Royal* (Kingston: Bolivar Press, 1970), 21.

25. Alexander Winston, *Pirates and Privateers* (London: Arrow Books, 1972), 30; a reprint of *No Purchase, No Pay* (London: Eyre & Spottiswoode Ltd., 1970), one of the best books on buccaneers.

26. Philip Lindsay, *The Great Buccaneer* (London: Peter Neville Ltd., 1950), 103.

27. Pope, *The Buccaneer King*, 163.

28. Pawson and Buisseret, *Port Royal, Jamaica*, 119.

29. John Esquemelin, *The Buccaneers of America. A true account of the most remarkable assaults committed of the late years upon the coasts of the West Indies by the Buccaneers of Jamaica and Tortuga by John Esquemelin One of the Buccaneers who was present at those tragedies* (New York: Dover Publications, 1967), 65–69.

30. Stephen Alexander Fortune, *Merchants and Jews: The Struggle for British West Indian Commerce, 1650–1750* (Gainesville: University of Florida Press, 1984), 35.

31. Zvi Loker, *Jews in the Caribbean: Evidence on the History of the Jews in the Caribbean Zone in Colonial Times* (Jerusalem: Misgav Yerushalayim, Institute for Research on the Sephardi and Oriental Jewish Heritage, 1991), 164–67; best one-stop source of period documents.

32. Egerton MSS., folios 152b–185b, British Museum.

33. *Calendar of State Papers, Colonial Series, America & West Indies*, 1669–1674, 7, no. 968, 15-11-1672. Petition of Rabba Couty to the King; vol. 9, no. 306, 22-21-1672: The King to Sir Thomas Lynch re: Rabba Couty.

34. Loker, *Jews in the Caribbean*, 181.

35. Ibid., 177–82; Richard Hill, *Lights and Shadows of Jamaica History* (Kingston, Jamaica: Ford & Gall, 1859), 120–21.

36. Hill, *Lights and Shadows*, 125, cites: Appendix to the Journals of the Assembly, 22 Charles II. A. 1670.

37. Pope, *The Buccaneer King*, 23; Winston, *Pirates and Privateers*, 37.

38. Allen, *Buccaneer: Admiral Sir Henry Morgan*, 131.

39. Ibid., 75; Pope, *The Buccaneer King*, 106, 155.

40. Allen, *Buccaneer: Admiral Sir Henry Morgan*, 75.

41. Carl and Roberta Bridenbaugh, *No Peace Beyond the Line: The English in the Caribbean, 1624–1690* (New York: Oxford University Press, 1972), 170.

42. Lindsay, *The Great Buccaneer*, 103–5.

43. Ibid., 106.

44. Ibid., 106–7.

45. Ibid., 151.

46. Ibid., 108.

47. Pope, *The Buccaneer King*, 215.

48. Lindsay, *The Great Buccaneer*, 112.

49. Winston, *Pirates and Privateers*, 88.

50. Ibid., 87.

51. Lindsay, *The Great Buccaneer*, 177.

52. Pope, *The Buccaneer King*, 257.

53. *Calendar of State Papers, Colonial Series, America & West Indies*, 1669–1674, 27, no. 697, 17-14-1671.

54. Nuala Zahedieh, "The Merchants of Port Royal, Jamaica, and the Spanish Contraband Trade, 1655–1692," *William and Mary Quarterly*, 3rd ser., 43, no. 3 (1986), 580.

55. Israel, *Diasporas Within a Diaspora*, 443: "A bitter quarrel erupted in the mid 1670's pitted Barbary Jews residing in Tangiers against Abraham Cohen, who they complained, 'did continually affront, molest and disquiet them that they could not attend to their callings.' "

56. Zahedieh, "The Merchants of Port Royal," 575.

57. Ibid., 581–82.

58. *Calendar of State Papers*, 1669–1672, 28, no. 63, 11-6-1672, Petition of the Merchants of Port Royal to Sir Thos. Lynch, Governor of Jamaica. Full transcript in Hill, *Lights and Shadows*, 124–25.

59. *Calendar of State Papers, Colonial Series, America & West Indies*, 1669–1672, no. 999, 453.

60. Fortune, *Merchants and Jews*, 26–27; Gedalia Yogev, *Diamonds and Coral: Anglo-Dutch Jews and 18th Century Trade* (Leicester, U.K.: Leicester University Press, 1978), 28–60: Statistics show Jamaica's Jews were of major financial value to England.

61. Winston, *Pirates and Privateers*, 89.

62. Pope, *The Buccaneer King*, 263.

63. Ibid., 262.

64. Ibid.

65. Ibid., 268.

66. *Calendar of State Papers*, 1668–1674, no. 503, 552: Council of Jamaica petitioned the Royal African Company "demanding more slaves." The

Company replied, "On January, 1674 . . . seven ships had been sent to Jamaica with 2320 negroes and in 1676 four more ships with 1660 negroes and 1540 sent in November 1676."

67. Cohen Abraham to Moses Cohen Henriques, signed May 5, 1675, Spanish Town Record Office, Liber 6, 1674, no. 232.

68. Spanish Town Record Office, Liber 6, no. 275, July 1675, Sept. 8, 1675 sells land to Mathew Mattson of Port Royal, witnessed by Humphrey Knollis and Thomas Helyar.

69. Moses Cohen naturalization, Spanish Town Record Office, Liber 13, 1681, no. 220.

70. Henry Barnham, *An account of the Island of Jamaica, from the time of the Spaniards first discovery to the year 1722* (London), British Library, Sloane Ms 3918, 6. When Morgan was in England, the then nineteen-year-old Christopher Albemarle was the buccaneer's sidekick. Half Morgan's age, he hero-worshipped his elder, being himself a wild youth given to drink, frequenting brothels, and enjoying sordid escapades that owing to his aristocratic status were excused, even admired.

71. Beeston sold the first land to Daniel Naharr, May 17, 1693 (Liber 24 of deeds folio 46) and subsequently Jews bought sixteen of the 270 lots of land sold in 1693–1702.

72. Fortune, *Merchants and Jews*, 65.

73. The following names are from Leon Huhner, "Jews Interested in Privateering in America during the 18th century," *Publication of the American Jewish Historical Society* 23 (1915), 163–77: Isaac Hart: In 1758, during the French and Indian War, one of Newport's foremost citizens and wealthiest merchants, Isaac Hart, owned and fitted out two ships—the *General Webb* and the *Lord Howe*—that saw action. *Napthali Hart*: Also of Newport, he owned and equipped the *Dolphin* and the *Diamond*, which sailed for the British in the American Revolution.

Facing the world's finest navy, Congress in March 23, 1776, commissioned privateers "to capture all ships and cargoes belonging to Great Britain taken on the high seas." They include four of the founders of Mikve Israel in Philadelphia: Benjamin Sexias, the brother of the New York rabbi Gershon M. Seixas, co-owner with Isaac Moses of the *Fox*, a brig with eight guns. Moses also owned the *Marbois*, a brig of sixteen guns and a crew of eighty-five. Abe Sasportas owned *Two Rachels*, a brigantine of eight guns. Michael Gratz was a partner with

Carter Braxton, a signer of the Declaration of Independence, but no names of their vessels are known. Mendes fils Cadet of Portsmouth, New Hampshire, master of the *Wilks*, a sloop of ten guns and a crew of sixty, co-owned with Gideon Samson of Exeter. Moses M. Hays, a leading citizen of Boston and uncle of Judah Touro, owned *Iris*, a brig of eight guns. Robert Morris, the financier of the Revolution, and Moses Levy, one of the three buyers of land for the Newport synagogue, jointly owned *Havannah*, a schooner of six guns. Morris also owned *Black Prince*, a brig of twelve guns, with Isaac Moses of Philadelphia.

74. Bertram Wallace Korn, *The Early Jews of New Orleans* (Waltham, Mass.: American Jewish Historical Society, 1969), quoting from *The Journal of Jean Lafitte* (New York, 1958), 98–99.

Epilogue: Searching for the Lost Mine of Columbus

1. *Calendar of State Papers, Colonial Series, America & West Indies*, 1661–1668, nos. 948, 949 (March 1, 1664).

2. Jacob Andrade, *A Record of the Jews in Jamaica* (Kingston: Jamaica Times, 1941), 139: The same date—March 25, 1670—Cohen bought valley land, Solomon de Léon purchased nine hundred acres in the same area.

3. Frank Cundall and Joseph Pietersz, *Jamaica Under the Spaniards*, abstracted from the Archives of Seville (Kingston: Institute of Jamaica, 1919), 49.

INDEX

Bordeaux, France, 72, 170
Braudel, Fernand, 5
Brazil, 7–9, 33–34, 38, 48, 104, 112–17, 120,
    121–22, 125, 127–48, 155, 157, 164,
    179, 180, 181, 184, 194, 207, 209, 224,
    255, 258, 259, 286n, 288n, 289n, 296n,
    302n, 304n
brazilwood, 37–38, 114, 133, 146, 216
Brethren of the Coast, 10, 202, 203–6
broker licenses, 135–36
Brotherhood of the Jews of Holland, 118–19,
    125, 179
buccaneers, 204–6, 222–33, 235, 237–53,
    255, 308n, 311n
Bueno Henriques, Abraham, 146
Bueno Henriques, Daniel, 302n
Bueno Mesquita, Abraham, 176
Bueno Mesquita, Benjamin, 158, 176, 178,
    180, 215, 217–18, 219, 307n
Bueno Mesquita, Joseph, 176, 217–18, 233
Buisseret, David, 228
Burnett, Bishop, 195, 199

Cabalists, 16, 137, 196–97
Cabildo, 162–63, 172–73, 175, 176, 177,
    180, 192
Cabral, Pedro Alvares, 30, 32–35, 36, 114
Caceres, Simon de, 185–86, 193, 196, 199,
    201–3, 214, 222, 305n, 307n
Cádiz, Spain, 55, 171, 179, 305n–6n
caiguaes (Portuguese servants), 26–27
Calado, Manuel, 129
Calicut, India, 31–32, 34–35, 279n
California, 29, 39–40, 149
Calvinism, 80, 81, 82–83, 84, 97–98, 129,
    131, 132, 134, 138, 141, 143–44, 158,
    176, 180, 303n
Campeche, Mexico, 225, 232
Canary Islands, 115, 185, 196, 203, 305n–6n
Cape Horn, 120, 201
Cape St. Anthony, 177
Cape Verde, 30, 33, 35, 36
capitalism, 5, 37–38, 40, 47, 53, 77, 83,
    135–36, 151, 152, 245–46, 275n, 298n,
    300n
Caribbean Sea, 10, 55, 73, 155, 158, 163–64,
    170, 183, 184, 189, 222, 238, 252, 253,
    254, 255, 292n, 296n
Carlisle, Earl of, 251
Cartagena, Spain, 50, 118, 175, 176, 188,
    193, 200, 209, 228, 239, 292n
Carvajal, Antonio, 184, 185–86, 189,
    190–93, 194, 195, 196, 198, 199, 201,
    202, 203, 209, 213, 227–28, 304n
Carvajal, María, 213, 309n
Carvalho, Sebastian, 142

Castilla, Julian de, 303n–4n
Catholic Church, 16–17, 48, 54, 64–65, 66,
    72, 82, 93–94, 96, 103, 105–6, 121,
    129, 131, 132, 159, 160, 161, 162–63,
    169, 211
cattle, 41–42, 52, 203–5, 311n
Cervantes, Miguel de, 14
Chamberlain, John, 283n
Chanoch, Moshe ben, 281n
Charles I, King of England, 165, 167–68,
    180, 183, 193, 195–96, 197
Charles II, King of England, 171, 210–16,
    218, 222, 224, 225, 226, 228, 233,
    237–51, 261, 307n, 309n, 310n
Charles V, King of Spain, 45, 48, 49–59,
    60, 66–73, 115, 169, 277n, 278n, 279n,
    280n, 298n
Chile, 56, 201, 225
Clarendon, Lord, 171–72, 261, 262–63, 272n,
    299n
Cobos, Francisco, 57
Cochin, India, 35, 37
Coelho, Duarte, 115, 117, 290n
Cohen Henriques, Abraham, 95, 111, 130–
    31, 133, 140, 142, 145, 146, 147, 148,
    155, 157–58, 178, 179, 180, 181–83,
    194, 196, 207–9, 215, 217–18, 219,
    227, 233–36, 241, 244, 249–50, 251,
    254, 256, 257–64, 289n, 302n, 308n,
    313n
Cohen Henriques, Benjamin, 307n
Cohen Henriques, Daniel, 182
Cohen Henriques, Esther, 231, 259
Cohen Henriques, Jacob, 157–58, 180, 208,
    217–18, 231, 302n–3n
Cohen Henriques, Moses, 94–95, 111, 122,
    123–28, 130, 138–39, 140, 146, 148,
    155, 158, 163–64, 194, 196, 231, 244,
    250, 251, 254, 256, 258–60, 300n, 307n,
    315n
Coimbra, Portugal, 94, 138–39
Colombia, 10, 52, 174, 176–77, 215, 224,
    292n
Colón, Bartholomew, 14, 20–21, 22, 24
Colón, Diego, 24, 25, 66, 305n
Colón, Fernando, 18, 22, 23, 24, 271n
Colón, Luis, 66, 280n, 296n–97n
Colón, María de Toledo, 66, 73, 280n
Colón, Nuño, 162, 163
Colonial Affairs Committee, 174, 175, 189
Columbus, Christopher, vii–viii, xi, 1,
    3, 9, 13–36, 46, 49, 51, 66–67, 115,
    118, 158–73, 177, 180, 182–83, 204,
    215–19, 233–35, 241, 250, 252, 256,
    257–64, 270n, 271n, 272n, 274n, 280n,
    296n–97n, 298n, 300n, 303n

Gondomar, Count, 88–89, 90, 165–67, 298n–99n
Granada, 14, 58
Grand Inquisitor, 68, 73, 94, 103–4, 149, 160, 176–77, 185, 300n–301n
Grand Western Design, 176, 182, 184, 189–90, 194–95, 203
Great Earthquake (1692), 252, 259
Great Gift (ship), 217–18
Great Pedro Bay, 200
Greenhalgh, John, 214
Grotius, Hugo, 287n
Guadaloupe, 152, 296n
Guinea, 48, 104
Gulf of Guinea, 33, 116
Gustav Adolphus, King of Sweden, 172
Gutiérrez Flores de la Caballeria, Marina, 45

Ha-Kohen, R. Josef, 279n
Havana, Cuba, 8, 47, 123, 127, 139, 163, 188, 189, 228
Hawkins, John, 164–65
Hebrew language, 77, 95
Henriques, Ainsley, 258, 259, 262
Henry II, King of France, 72
Henry IV, King of France, 80, 103
Henry VII, King of England, 6
Henry VIII, King of England, 191, 279n
hereditary rule, 14, 16, 17, 19, 24, 66
Hermyn, Don, 168, 169, 170–71, 262–63, 299n
Heyn, Piet, 119, 121, 122, 123, 124–26, 127, 258
hidalgos, 25–26, 43, 67–68, 159, 160, 204–5
Hispaniola, 20, 21, 22, 23, 24, 50, 184, 188, 190, 191, 192, 201, 202, 203–4, 230, 236, 275n, 311n
Hobbes, Thomas, 217
Hope of Israel, The (Israel), 196–97
Huero, Chief, 22, 23, 24, 25–26
Hungary, 48, 57

Incas, 50, 52–53, 56–57
India, 31–32, 34–35, 37, 38, 70, 104
Indians (Native Americans), viii, 18, 20, 21, 22–23, 24, 25–26, 49, 51, 65, 131, 138, 142, 149, 164, 165, 191, 203–4, 262, 272n, 280n, 303n
Inquisition, viii, ix–x, 3–5, 8–9, 11, 15, 16, 22, 27, 41–42, 45, 47–48, 51, 53, 54, 55–56, 63, 66, 68, 73, 79–80, 81, 82–83, 87, 89, 93–95, 96, 99, 103–4, 110, 113, 114, 118–19, 122, 127, 134, 138–39, 146, 148–55, 157, 159, 160, 163, 169, 170, 172, 176–77, 180, 185, 199, 202,

213, 215, 235, 253–54, 275n–76n, 281n, 288n, 292n, 300n–302n
interest rates, 135, 169
Isabella I, Queen of Castile and Aragon, 3, 13–15, 18–20, 24, 274n
Isaiah, book of, 132
Islam, 58, 75–76, 87
Island Record Office, 219
Israel, 38, 137, 143–44
Israel, Abraham, 139, 158, 176, 178, 182–83, 208, 215–18, 261, 301n–2n
Israel, Isaac, 158, 176, 180, 208, 215, 216, 217–18, 231, 302n–3n
Israel, Joseph ben, 94–95
Israel, Menasseh ben, 95–96, 102, 196–97, 255–56, 306n
Italy, 53, 58, 70, 170, 302n

Jackson, William, vii, 173–76, 184, 186, 189, 200
Jamaica, vii–viii, xi, 4–5, 6, 9–11, 13–27, 39, 48–57, 64–73, 115, 118, 140, 157–94, 199–206, 211, 215–19, 221–53, 255, 256, 257–64, 272n, 296n–97n, 303n–4n, 306n, 307n–8n, 311n
Jamaica Archives, 260
James I, King of England, 88, 165–66, 171, 195, 298n–99n
Jerusalem, 58, 132
jewels, 32, 54, 214
Jewish Historical Society of England (JHSE), 260
Jews:
    arrests of, 8, 113, 151–55, 178–79, 194
    Ashkenazi, 137, 138
    assimilation of, 100–102
    autos-da-fé for, 3, 6, 80, 93–94, 152, 153–55, 300n–301n
    baptisms of, 3, 4, 32, 39, 41, 55, 68, 146, 176, 275n–76n, 289n–90n
    bar mitzvahs of, 95, 125
    blood ancestry of, 26, 55–56, 73, 275n, 278n
    burned at the stake, 8, 15, 29–30, 41, 45, 93–94, 152, 153–55
    cemeteries of, 71, 91, 95n, 102, 103, 259
    children of, 94, 96, 116–17, 176, 275n, 289n–90n
    as "chosen people," 101–2, 143–44, 195–96, 255–56, 306n
    chronology of, 266–69
    circumcision of, 94–95, 137, 185, 285n, 288n, 290n, 295n
    conservative, 153
    conspiracies attributed to, 8, 138–39, 148–55

as conversos, viii–ix, 1, 2–4, 9, 15, 17–18, 22–27, 37, 39–40, 45–50, 54, 55–56, 63–68, 72–73, 78–83, 88, 93–96, 99–100, 105–6, 113–19, 129, 131, 140, 145–46, 150, 159–60, 169, 170–71, 176–80, 184, 186 196–97, 202–3, 207–8, 215, 224, 228, 254–56, 273n, 274n, 277n, 278n, 280n, 289n–90n, 300n, 302n

Diaspora of, ix, x, 3–4, 5, 8–9, 14–18, 22–27, 30, 58, 77, 98, 101, 107, 132–33, 148, 196, 244, 255

education of, 77, 95–96

as Esperandos (Hopeful Ones), viii–ix

expulsions of, 1, 3, 8–9, 16, 46–48, 93–122, 155, 157–58, 173, 175, 176–80, 185, 190, 203, 212, 233, 234, 241, 255, 261, 275n, 276n

as heretics, ix, 3–4, 6, 7, 8, 9, 41–42, 54, 55, 56, 72, 88, 145–46, 149, 152, 159, 168, 176–80, 198, 300n

intelligence networks of, 6–7, 79–80, 90–91, 118–19, 123–28, 153–55, 184, 191–92, 194, 195, 283n, 291n, 301n–2n, 309n

Jewish excommunications of, 105–11, 137, 294n–95n

as "Judaizers," x, 15, 29–30, 44, 67–68, 80, 81, 82, 93–94, 103–4, 113, 118, 138–39, 146, 152, 153, 160, 176–77, 275n–76n, 290n, 296n, 300n–301n, 309n

laws of, 95n, 96–97, 103–11, 137–38, 151, 198, 287n, 290n

leadership of, ix–x, 86, 105–11, 153, 194, 210–18, see also specific leaders

marriages of, 41–46, 96, 101, 284n–85n

as merchants, ix–x, 2, 4–7, 11, 37–38, 40, 47, 55, 58, 60, 73, 76–77, 78, 83, 97–102, 134, 148, 150, 214, 218, 224, 226–28, 233, 235, 243–47, 252–56, 274n, 275n, 285n, 287n, 292n, 311n

as moneylenders, 53, 63–64, 75, 77, 118, 134, 169, 178, 211, 213

names of, 4, 94–95, 284n

as navigators, 16–17, 30–37, 55, 114, 186, 189, 224

as New Christians, viii, 2–3, 15, 32, 39–40, 42, 47, 55–56, 63–64, 72–73, 81, 113, 114, 131, 147, 151, 277n, 278n, 281n, 284n, 285n, 290n, 300n

Orthodox, 96–97, 105–11, 153, 284n–85n, 294n–95n

persecution of, viii–x, 1–5, 8–11, 15, 16, 22, 27, 29–30, 41–42, 45, 46–48, 79–83, 89, 91, 93–94, 143–55, 176–80, 300n–301n

as pirates, viii, x, 5–6, 8, 10, 54, 58, 59–60, 75–92, 111, 122, 128, 130, 139, 158, 161, 174–75, 202, 203–6, 209–10, 219, 231–33, 244–45, 253, 254–56, 258, 259, 283n, 307n

population of, 98, 133, 134, 190, 227–28, 233, 243, 246, 300n

as "Portugals," vii–viii, 3, 9, 24, 27, 50–51, 55, 57, 66, 67–68, 72–73, 101, 121, 134, 146, 151, 155, 159, 160–63, 167, 170–74, 177, 185, 191, 197, 202–3, 207, 224–28, 243, 272n, 275n, 277n, 299n, 300n, 305n

reformed, 153

religious observances of, x, 4, 8, 37, 41–42, 64–65, 67–68, 69, 81–83, 86, 87, 95–97, 103–11, 125, 137–38, 151, 198, 210–11, 214, 275n–76n, 284n–85n, 287n–88n, 290n, 294n–95n

religious toleration for, 81–83, 97–102, 105–11, 120, 131–32, 143–46, 177–80, 183–84, 210–14, 255–56, 288n, 302n–3n

Sephardic, x–xi, 1, 5, 7, 46, 58, 72–73, 81, 98, 100, 137, 138, 140, 203, 227, 228, 245, 253, 255, 257, 276n, 286n, 303n

settlements of, 57, 64–65, 81–83, 98–99, 128–55, 157, 177–80, 181, 184–86, 206, 208–10, 226–28, 254–56, see also specific settlements

as shareholders, 135–36, 179–80, 245–46

as ship owners, 5, 9, 10, 38, 95, 99–100, 135–36, 209–10, 224, 314n–15n

as smugglers, 160–61, 162, 165 169–70, 228–29, 295n

as soldiers, 113–22, 142–43, 147, 274n

synagogues of, 8, 10, 46–47, 76, 86, 95–97, 102, 104, 105–11, 132, 137–38, 141, 148, 178, 184, 199, 208, 211–12, 214, 228, 253, 256, 259, 272n, 283n, 284n, 288n, 294n–95n, 300n, 303n, 305n

wealth of, x, 4–5, 8, 22, 63–64, 73, 76–77, 81, 95–102, 114, 130, 135–36, 139–40, 148, 149, 152, 177–78, 210–14, 226–27, 243–47, 250, 255–56, 300n

women as, viii, 8, 26, 37, 41–46, 53, 56, 57, 59, 94, 100, 137, 138

Jews and the Slave Trade (Faber), 136

João, Mestre, 33–34

John, King of England, 185

John IV, King of Portugal, 63, 64, 68, 94, 114–16, 140, 145–46

Knights of Malta, 61, 70

kosher diet, 87, 108

Nuestra Señora de Atocha (ship), 163
Nueva Sevilla del Oro, Jamaica, 25–27, 49, 125–26

Ojeda, Alonso de, 35
Old Christians, 2–3, 8, 43, 46, 73, 97, 99, 152, 275*n*, 285*n*
Old Testament, 106, 107–8, 143–44, 195–96
Olivares, Count-Duke, 168–69, 170, 171, 300*n*–301*n*
Ordaz, Diego, 41, 42, 43
Orinoco River, 33, 165–66
Osorio, Bento, 119, 126, 179
Ottoman Empire, 53–54, 58, 69, 70, 72, 79
Ovando, Governor, 19, 21, 272*n*

Paine, Nicolas, 184
Palache, Jacob, 97
Palache, Joseph, 6, 77, 78, 79–80, 83–84, 87, 91, 282*n*, 307*n*
Palache, Malica, 86
Palache, Moses, 85, 282*n*, 283*n*
Palache, Rebekah, 111, 207, 244, 289*n*
Palache, Samuel, x, 6, 75–92, 96, 97, 98, 99, 102, 103, 104, 105, 110, 111, 118, 122, 125, 127, 155, 165, 186, 194, 201, 207, 209, 254, 281*n*, 282*n*, 283*n*, 307*n*
Panama, 10, 18, 21, 161, 239–42, 292*n*
Panama City, 239–42
papacy, 30, 59, 63, 64, 154–55, 191, 210
Paparrobalos, Antonio Dias, 128
Parnassim, 143, 177–78, 179, 181–82, 208, 295*n*
Passover, 82, 198
Patenta Onrossa (Honorable Charter), 144, 145–46, 179, 209, 295*n*
Penn, William, 186–88, 192, 193
Pepys, Samuel, 247
Pereira, Samuel, 100, 133–34
Pérez, Manuel Batista, 150–51, 153
Pernambuco province, Brazil, 127–29, 135
Peru, ix–x, 4, 8, 9, 10, 48, 52–53, 120, 140, 148–55, 164, 166, 185, 224, 240, 292*n*
Philip II, King of Spain, 55, 71, 73, 283*n*, 297*n*, 298*n*
Philip III, King of Spain, 78–79, 84, 87, 90, 113, 155, 163, 297*n*
Philip IV, King of Spain, 7, 118, 120, 160–62, 163, 168–69, 171, 179, 189, 223, 225, 237, 238, 240, 262, 292*n*
pigs, 41–42, 52, 204
Pimental, Manuel, 102–3, 287*n*
pimento, 140, 216, 218, 233
pirates, viii, x, 5–6, 8, 10, 54, 58, 59–60, 75–92, 111, 122, 128, 130, 139, 158, 161, 174–75, 202, 203–6, 209–10, 219,

231–33, 244–45, 253, 254–56, 258, 259, 283*n*, 307*n*, *see also* buccaneers; corsairs; privateers
Pizarro, Francisco, 52
Pizarro, Hernando, 52–53, 56–57
polygamy, 96–97
Ponce de León, Francisca, 44–45
Ponce de León, Juan, 44, 166
Ponce de León, Juan González, 44–45
Poras, Diego, 20–21, 272*n*, 273*n*
Poras, Francisco, 20–21, 25, 272*n*, 273*n*
Portobelo, Panama, 238, 292*n*
porto torture, 153–54
Port Royal, Jamaica, 4–5, 10, 193, 217–19, 224–33, 235, 243–45, 249–50, 251, 252, 255, 259, 311*n*
Portugal, vii, viii, 1, 7, 11, 30, 31, 32, 35–40, 50–51, 56, 63, 64, 65, 68, 70, 73, 78, 81, 93–95, 97, 99, 101, 112–17, 127–29, 130, 138–55, 173, 194, 196, 207, 226, 274*n*, 275*n*, 280*n*, 284*n*, 285*n*, 286*n*, 290*n*, 296*n*
Potosí, Bolivia, 4, 112–13, 139, 149, 240, 292*n*
Preveza, battle of, 68
privateers, 8, 54–55, 80, 87–89, 130, 137, 163–65, 173–74, 203, 206, 209–10, 237–43, 247, 251, 253, 314*n*–15*n*
Prophet Samuel (ship), 202
prostitutes, 100, 101, 223, 229–31
Protestantism, 48, 54, 72, 171, 172, 181, 183–84, 195–96, 210, 221, 247–48, *see also* Calvinism
Puerto Rico, 44, 50, 51, 162, 176, 184
Puritans, 172, 181, 183–84, 195–96, 210, 221

Querido, Aaron, 307*n*
Querido, Diego Diaz, 103–5, 118

rabbis, x, 11, 75–92, 96–97, 105–11, 122, 137, 145, 155, 181, 182, 212, 254, 281*n*, 295*n*, 304*n*
Raleigh, Walter, 164–66, 298*n*–99*n*
Ramirez, Governor, 190, 191, 192
Recife, Brazil, 8–9, 127, 128–30, 133, 137–38, 143, 144–48, 149, 157, 176, 177–78, 194, 245–46, 259, 289*n*, 302*n*
Reformation, 48, 72
Rembrandt, x, 97, 102
Robles, Antonio, 196–97
Robles trial (1656), 197–98, 201–2
Rocamora, Vincente de, 299*n*
Rodrigues Cabrilho, João, 39–40
Rodrigues Lindo, Antonio, 309*n*
Roman Empire, 1, 58, 196